Professional Administrators
for America's Schools

THIRTY-EIGHTH YEARBOOK, 1960

American Association of School Administrators

contents

Copyright 1960

American Association of
School Administrators

A department of the
National Education Association
of the United States

Price $5.00

Library of Congress
Catalog Card No.: A 60—8600

Yearbook Commission_____1960

Hollis A. Moore, Jr.
Executive Secretary, Committee for the Advancement of School Administration, AASA, Washington, D. C., **Chairman**

Melvin W. Barnes
Superintendent of Schools, Oklahoma City, Oklahoma

Elmer Ellis
President, University of Missouri, Columbia, Missouri

John I. Goodlad
Director, Center for Teacher Education, University of Chicago, Chicago, Illinois

Daniel E. Griffiths
Associate Professor of Education, Teachers College, Columbia University, New York, New York

Warren G. Hill
Commissioner of Education, Augusta, Maine

Kenneth E. McIntyre
Professor of Educational Administration, University of Texas, Austin, Texas

S. P. Marland, Jr.
Superintendent of Schools, Winnetka, Illinois

Paul J. Misner
Superintendent of Schools, Glencoe, Illinois

Lawrence E. Toddhunter
Assistant Superintendent of Schools, Fresno, California

foreword

One of the prerogatives of the president of the American Association of School Administrators is to suggest a topic for a yearbook and to appoint a commission to write it. This is a prerogative which I embraced with some fervor.

In December of 1948, along with other administrators from midwestern states, I attended a conference to spell out critical areas that might convince the W. K. Kellogg Foundation that they should finance a "Cooperative Project on the Superintendency of Schools."

The eventual sponsorship of this study by the Kellogg Foundation was heralded to be potentially as important to school administration as the Flexner studies of earlier days had been to medicine.

The monumental work that has been accomplished in the last 10 years under the direction of the committees of the AASA and with the financial aid of the Kellogg Foundation could be, in my opinion, the initial gambit to bring the stature of the superintendency to its rightful height in American life.

The need to spell out the proposals into action programs was an obligation of our organization to the Kellogg Foundation. This is why I, as a participant in the preliminary exploration and later as one who was engaged in the development of the project, felt it was a personal responsibility to select as the topic of this yearbook: PROFESSIONAL ADMINISTRATORS FOR AMERICA'S SCHOOLS.

Because of the critical importance of the project, a Commission of the distinction of this one was appointed, and the Executive Secretary of the Committee for the Advancement of School Administration was asked to serve as chairman. His breadth of understanding of all of the facets of the work of the last 10 years has been brought into this great work.

The Executive Committee of the American Association of School Administrators believe with me that the use of the

v

material and recommendations included in PROFESSIONAL ADMIN-
ISTRATORS FOR AMERICA'S SCHOOLS can be the contribution to
American education that the AASA and the W. K. Kellogg
Foundation envisaged it would be if time, money, and ability were
dedicated to its development.

PHILIP J. HICKEY
Superintendent of Instruction,
St. Louis Public Schools
President, American Association
of School Administrators, 1957-58

introduction

"Do a wrap-up job on school administration during the 1950's and, at the same time, point the way for the profession in the next few years." This was the informal charge given to the Commission in the spring of 1958. Our assignment has been a tough one, but exciting. If the result stimulates dissent as well as concurrence, we are rewarded.

A few months after we started our task we learned that ours would be the last of the AASA yearbooks in the current series—a series which started in 1923. This tag, "last of the AASA yearbooks," has given added incentive to do the very best job possible. In many respects, however, our book resembles the beginning instead of the end of an era: there are some significant departures from past AASA yearbooks. For example, the book contains initial reports of research studies, two of which are of considerable magnitude.

This is not to type the book as a "research report" exclusively, or even primarily. Instead, we hope it will stand or fall on the strength of its recommendations for profession-wide policies and programs. In this 1960 Yearbook are proposals for making school administration the profession its leaders covet and often claim. We certainly are not deluded into thinking that the profession would, even if it could, place an immediate stamp of approval on all our suggestions. Rather, the proposals need to be debated, amended, tried out, changed, and changed again, and finally made a part of the dynamics of professional advancement.

In describing another unique characteristic of this yearbook we could start with the phrase: "Never before have so many people . . . " Almost 900 superintendents participated in the career pattern study which is reported in Chapter II. This was not a small token operation. The questionnaire itself was eight pages long, and the questions required thought and advance

vii

preparation to answer. In another study more than 300 super-intendents served as liaison between the Yearbook Commission and colleges and universities. The superintendents received from us the research instrument on preparation programs, took it to the college authorities, and followed up through the point of returning it — properly executed — to the Commission. Full details of this procedure are reported, with the results of the study, in Chapter III.

We acknowledge the help of many persons outside Commission membership in the completion of our assignment. Throughout the life of the Commission the counsel of Philip J. Hickey and Finis E. Engleman has been frequently sought and always generously given. These two men, both veteran school administrators, have reviewed our drafts carefully and thoroughly at just the right moment and with just the right combination of criticism and encouragement.

We had need of special help with particular sections of the book. No person, other than the members of the Commission itself, contributed as much to the book as did Kenneth St. Clair, a graduate student at the University of Texas. Mr. St. Clair attended one of our four Commission meetings and had much to do with the preparation of one of the chapters. Without his expert assistance we would have been left with a serious gap in the coverage of the topic assigned to us.

In addition we called upon H. Thomas James, associate professor, and Francis M. Trusty, research assistant, both of Stanford University, for special help with two chapters.

D. Richard Wynn, associate professor of education, Teachers College, Columbia University, and Mary Emerick, graduate student, performed valuable work in analyzing the returns from one of our studies.

Expert guidance in the research studies for Chapters II and III came from Sam M. Lambert, director, and Ray C. Maul, assistant director, NEA Research Division.

In the important function of editing we had competent help from Sidney Dorros, director, NEA Publications Division, ably assisted by Ann Marie McGovern. Art and layout work were done by James L. Walker and Thomas T. Gladden, from the same NEA division.

The Commission is indebted to Mrs. Margery G. Grubb and

Mrs. Margaret O. Gallagher for their help in manuscript preparation.

The plan of our yearbook falls most easily and simply into two parts—Today and Tomorrow. The Today section begins with a true-story description of a school board looking for a new superintendent of schools. In the process the board tries to evaluate potential candidates on the basis of their personal qualifications, their professional preparation, and their prior experience. The issues which come before a board in such a situation spotlight the topics which are important to a discussion of the profession of school administration.

Chapter I ends with questions, rather than with answers; but before we try to answer the questions about selection, preparation, and the continuing education of administrators, we offer an analysis of the current scene.

Chapter II describes in profile the American school superintendency—how superintendents are selected, their personal history and collegiate experiences, and their evaluation of current professional practices. Chapter III describes the present effort in colleges to prepare school administrators through course work, field activities, and other means. In-service education of school superintendents is described in Chapter IV—not only described but analyzed critically in terms of depth and of appropriateness of present offerings.

Chapter V stands as our transition chapter from where we are now to where we would like to be. More than that, it presents the reason why Tomorrow should be different from the present scene. If we have a case for change, Chapter V makes it for us in terms of the new and complex responsibilities of the school superintendency as it has developed in modern day America.

Chapters VI, VII, and VIII are the proposal chapters, and Chapters IX and X look at the problems which we face in implementing our proposals. The concluding chapter proposes a number of controls the profession must exercise in order to fulfill its stewardship pledge to the public.

We recognized from the start that our task was a big one. There are few references in the literature to which we could turn as we sought guidance on many of the essential issues. We know we are presenting proposals which some readers will feel go too far in prescribing specific action in areas where much is yet to be known; on the other hand, others will chide us for being too general as we admit a wide range of possibilities still left open. Frankly, we hope to draw criticism on both of these scores, because we would not like to err overwhelmingly in either direction.

During the preparation of the yearbook the members disagreed many times on important points, and on most of these we came eventually to consensus. On one important issue, however, we remained as united as we were constant—the position of America in these days and in the days to come will hinge quite largely on how successfully we educate our total citizenship. When we ask so much from our schools, we must guarantee that those schools have the benefit of superior wisdom and judgment from professional administrators.

THE COMMISSION

chapter 1

A Board Seeks
a Superintendent

Each year about 2000 school boards in the United States look for and select a new superintendent of schools. Within the limits of state license requirements and local policies, the selection is clearly up to the board. It is as important a decision as any a board can make. On this decision hinges the character of leadership of the school systems affected for years to come.

In choosing the schools' chief executive officer, the board usually looks at the collegiate record, sequence of jobs, and letters of recommendation for several candidates. It must somehow judge which candidate is a more competent administrator—broadly educated as well as thoroughly grounded in the intricacies of getting the job done through administrative devices. It must decide which candidate "would best fit into our community."

For better or worse, a new superintendent is chosen. During the difficult process of screening and final selection, however, many of the critical profession-wide problems come into sharp focus. Is the preparation in college appropriate for the job? Are today's most able people being attracted to the job of administering schools? Have pressures and conflicts inherent in the superintendency pushed many capable educators into positions other than educational administration? Can a superintendent be a good businessman and a thoughtful scholar at one and the same time?

Because such critical problems are reduced to specifics when a school board searches for evidence

1

about potential candidates for the job of superintendent of schools, the 1960 Yearbook Commission decided to use an actual case in an actual community to introduce its yearbook on professional administrators for America's schools.

Although the Commission was obliged to choose its case before the outcome was known, the historical facts have not been altered. A member of the Commission interviewed the board of the community chosen, reviewed credentials of prospective candidates, analyzed what qualities the board was apparently seeking in an administrator, and queried the board after its final selection had been announced. The situation reported here is not ideal—it is a slice of reality. It is presented by the Commission in the hope that the genuine experiences of one board of education will reveal some of the essential issues to be discussed later in this book.

THE COMMUNITY SETTING

The town is "Riverdale."[1] It is a community of about 25,000 people, more exurbia than suburbia. A large percentage of its adult male population commutes each day to the nearby city, largest in the state. As would be true of many similar towns in America, there is a major university nearby and several private and state colleges within easy driving distance, all of which offer some work in teacher education. Some of these institutions have programs especially designed to prepare men and women for positions of administrative responsibility in school systems.

The town has very little industry, and the tax rate on local property is high. Its expenditures per pupil are decidedly above average, and its citizens indicate in a number of ways their greater-than-average concern for quality education in the elementary and secondary schools of the community. The average education attainment level of Riverdale adults is above the national average.

The superintendent who resigned prior to the Commission's contact with Riverdale had been there about six years. During that time he had made an excellent record, as judged by members of the school board and most people in the community. During his tenure, he had completed requirements for his doc-

---

[1] The name is fictitious, but the town and the facts are real.

torate in educational administration at a nearby university. Undoubtedly he could have remained in the community as superintendent for many more years but preferred instead to accept a job in a nearby state which offered wider opportunity in a larger school system and a sizable increase in salary.

When the board was asked why the superintendent had been so well accepted in Riverdale, its explanation was: "He was an educator, not solely a businessman; he was a man with ideas. He brought in innovations in personnel administration and curriculum." Actions of the board in seeking a replacement for the resigning superintendent showed that the board hoped it would find a replacement who was "willing to experiment" in curriculum matters—especially in giving attention to highly gifted students. Procedures for investigating candidates,[2] therefore, included visits to classrooms in the school system where the candidate was currently employed.

Riverdale's school board was composed of five members. A housewife and former teacher was chairman of the board. Three of its members were in the professions; the fifth member was a business executive. The board appeared to be relatively free of friction, although differences of opinion naturally occurred on certain topics. All members of the board expressed a desire to have an administrator who would assume genuine leadership; none of the board members showed any signs of wanting to take over administrative responsibilities on his own. Most Riverdale board members said that the experience of being without a superintendent of schools for several months showed them the importance of a "strong leader" if the school system is to function efficiently.

THE SEARCH FOR GOOD CANDIDATES

None of the five members of the school board had before chosen a superintendent for Riverdale. When, in late July, their superintendent's resignation abruptly created for them the problem, they deliberated over the best course to follow. The board decided early to go outside the local district for a new superintendent.

---

[2] "Candidate" in this sense does not imply that the person was actively seeking the post. In some cases the initiative rested with the board, not with the prospective superintendent.

Letters to Placement Offices

The board turned first to the placement offices of four or five nearby colleges. The board requested from these placement offices the names of 25 placement contact persons in "leading universities across the country where school administrators are trained." A letter was then sent to the 25 institutions. Most replied, although some declined to recommend a candidate for the position. The letters which went to the placement offices gave a few details about the community and the particular qualifications which this board desired in a candidate. The following statement of qualifications accompanied the letters:

Statement of Qualifications
for Candidates for Superintendency of Schools
RIVERDALE

I. *Education*
  a. Minimum of master's degree. Earned doctor's degree preferred.
  b. Must be qualified for certification in this state.
II. *Experience*
  a. At least three years of experience as a superintendent or assistant superintendent in a school system of at least 100 teachers.
  b. Experience as a principal.
III. *Personal Information*
  a. Age: 38 to 55.
  b. Married man preferred.
IV. *Personal Qualities*
  a. Must have proven leadership and administrative ability.
  b. Must have an understanding of and interest in community projects.
  c. Must be especially skillful in working with school personnel, school board, and community organizations.
  d. Must be stimulated by the challenge of planning, launching, and evaluating fresh approaches to the solution of educational problems.
  e. Must be able to express and interpret effectively the philosophy, the programs, and the needs of the schools.

Placement offices in two or three nearby universities were given special encouragement to submit the dossiers of prospective candidates. One institution submitted papers for several candidates. All other institutions submitted fewer, the average number being two per institution.

Letters to Superintendents

Another approach which the board used was to ask members of the education faculty of a nearby university for the names of

12 to 15 communities which were noted for their excellent school systems. Letters went to the superintendent in each of these communities announcing that the position of superintendent was open and suggesting that "perhaps some member of your staff would be qualified for this position." This procedure was followed since Riverdale board members agreed that they would accept someone who had been associated with a top-quality school system in a secondary role in preference to the chief administrator of a district not distinguished for instructional achievements.

There were a few applications from schoolmen nearby who nominated themselves as soon as they had heard of the vacancy. Most of the board members took a dim view of this procedure, but one candidate brought to their attention in this way remained rather high on the list through the early stages of investigation.

Narrowing the Field

After the credentials were assembled, the next step was for each member of the board to review carefully all the papers on the 65 nominees (all men). The board used a system of ranking, and from it emerged a list of 18 names which were sufficiently attractive to warrant further investigation. Each of the 18 was contacted and asked if he would like to be considered an applicant for the position. Thirteen replied affirmatively. Some of them were then called in for interview, while others were initially contacted via a visit by board members (usually traveling in pairs) to the community where the candidate was employed.

There were some topics which the Riverdale school board thought so important that they were discussed with every candidate who was interviewed. Comparing the answers given by each candidate to these questions was helpful in establishing common denominators of appraisal. These items, which suggest some things about which a school administrator should be knowledgeable, were: ability grouping, acceleration of able students, special gifted child programs, merit salary schedules, means of lay group participation, re-employment of teachers, testing, guidance counseling, and the place of football in a school program.

A Disappointing Candidate

A candidate who was the first choice of several board members at one time during the selection process was a disappointment to them after more careful interview and investigation. The reason for such disappointment is worthy of note, since it points up an important consideration in the preparation of effective school administrators.

The prospective candidate (a high school principal) was one whose credentials were possibly more attractive than anyone's on the Riverdale school board list of prospects. His educational philosophy (as he stated it in writing) was superb. His record of achievements, both academic and professional, was notable. Until he was interviewed at length by the board and his school system was visited by board members, he was a very likely choice. During the board's visit to his school system, however, the candidate gave an appearance of aloofness to colleagues. He lacked warmth, and he gave quick and confident answers to all the questions which were raised. One school board member called these "textbook answers," apparently meaning a kind of superficial use of knowledge about education.

A recheck of the letters of recommendation—a source by no means famous for its reliability—revealed many statements about his efficiency, his knowledge, his perception of the importance of education. Typical of letters of recommendation, they all recommended the man strongly; they were discriminating only in what they did *not* say. The board noted that his professors and his colleagues neglected to mention his warmth or ability to deal effectively with people or to attract their loyalties and enthusiasm. The omissions were noted in a recheck following the board's personal visit with the candidate. Boards which neglect to go to similar lengths to get the most accurate picture possible of the candidate can get a distorted picture of his ability from letters of appraisal. One explanation is that a graduate program where faculty contact with students is the lecturer-listener type tends to preclude accurate faculty judgment about a student's skill in human relationships in a job setting.

INFORMATION ON CANDIDATES

In an interview with a member of this Commission, board members admitted more interest in the experiences of a candidate in previous positions than in his college preparation.

Although all members of the board were college graduates, some of them were quite hazy as to just what constitutes a preparation program for a school administrator in a good college or university. They said: "We assume the profession takes care of that; if a man is a bona fide graduate and is licensed, we take for granted his graduate training is adequate." In addition, they expressed doubt that a candidate's "college record" was crucial information, anyway, when the gap of years was 15 or more between completion of most of his college work (except summer institutes and the like) and consideration for the job of superintendent.

Very few placement folders of candidates reviewed by the board gave details of actual course work completed. In most cases only the highest degree attained was recorded and the special areas of concentration and specialization given. There was practically no mention of undergraduate preparation, and few course grades were recorded. Test scores on any standardized batteries of examinations were even rarer than course grades. The placement files omitted evaluation of performance as an intern, trainee, or survey team member.

A closer look at the preparation of the 18 candidates who survived the first screening in Riverdale will perhaps give some indication of the typical preparation for school administration.

Undergraduate Preparation

About half (nine) of the men considered for the job at Riverdale had a four-year undergraduate course which omitted work in professional teacher education. Ten of the 18 held liberal arts (A.B. or B.S.) degrees—in most cases, from private liberal arts colleges. Frequently, the undergraduate major was not recorded. For those whose undergraduate specialization was noted, seven majored in history or history combined with French, political science, or economics. Three majored in education, two in science and math, two in engineering, and one in English. The major subjects of the rest were not noted. In addition to the 10 who graduated from liberal arts colleges, three graduated with a B.S. from teachers colleges, and five had baccalaureate degrees from colleges or universities which offered a minor in education at the undergraduate level.

Graduate Preparation

The story was a different one at the graduate level. Twelve of the 18 held doctor's degrees; six, the master's degree. All 18 candidates majored in educational administration at either the master's or doctoral level. It was impossible to tell what amount of the graduate work taken was in courses labeled "school administration." For the most part, however, it appeared to be a heavy concentration, particularly beyond the master's degree. Six of the 18 candidates had served as research assistants or part-time lecturers in the university where the doctorate was taken. Only one of the 18 (one of the youngest under consideration) had served in an internship in one of the recently inaugurated school administration internship programs in a private university. The candidates were predominantly graduates of private universities for the highest degree held. Only four of the 18 were graduated from state universities.

Previous Experience

Although in the statement of qualifications the school board had indicated its preference for candidates who had served in previous superintendencies, six of the 18 were men without such experience. All of the 18 persons, however, had served at one time as teachers. Fourteen of the 18 had also served—or were currently serving—as principals or assistant principals of elementary or high schools. Some had moved directly from teaching positions to superintendencies. Only one person had served previously as an administrative assistant to a superintendent.

Three Sample Papers

Perhaps a close examination of the papers of three candidates will be more revealing than a glance at the statistics for the entire group. These three were chosen as samples since more complete information was available for them than for others. (Names, of course, are fictitious.)

Mr. Reed was 36 years old and had a wife and two children. He was graduated from a public high school and earned his A.B. degree from a well-known New England liberal arts college. He received his M.A. in the graduate school of arts and sciences at a private university and later his Ed.D. from the same university. Mr. Reed's undergraduate majors were history and government with a minor in economics. His M.A. degree was taken in the same general field, while his doctorate was in educational administration. He had a reading knowledge of Latin,

French, and German. He took the following courses as an undergraduate:

First year

Horace—Latin
Speech
Europe (from Rome to 1660)
Europe since 1660
Man and Culture
General Biology
Human Geography
Applied Hygiene
Gym Work

Third year

Elementary German
History and Philosophy of
  Education
Principles of Secondary
  Education
Principles and Problems of
  Economics
Europe since 1815
Geological Topics
Gym Work

Second year

Argumentation
Cicero
American History
American Government
General Psychology
Social Psychology
Physical Geology
Historical Geology
Gym Work

Fourth year

International Economics
Contemporary World Politics
Algebra
Trigonometry
Analytical Geometry
19th Century German Prose
Labor Problems
Latin American History
Differential Calculus
College Physics
Gym Work

He completed the following graduate courses:

History of Continental Europe
History of the Westward Movement
American Biography
Human Relations
Human Relations Research (Business Administration)
Educational Problems in the West
Curriculum of American Colleges
Principles of Student Personnel Work
Principles of Mental Hygiene
Secondary Schools; Origin and Administration
Educational Measurement (two courses)
Contemporary American Culture
Education and Society
Individual Research (in two courses)
Educational Administration: Improvement of Teaching/Learning
                               Situation
Educational Administration: Determination of Educational Policy
Educational Administration: Financial Support
Educational Administration: Two Additional Seminars
Party Government in the United States
Seminar in History
Social Structure of the United States
Research and Problems of the Social Structure

9

While an undergraduate Mr. Reed was a student assistant in geology and social science. After service in the U.S. Army in the latter part of World War II, he was a teacher of Latin, physics, and math. In addition, he supervised dormitories during the summer session in a private secondary school. Later, for two years, he taught United States history in a private secondary school. He was a research assistant in a laboratory of social relations at a nearby private university. During one summer session he served as an assistant to a professor of school administration. In 1952 he became assistant principal of a high school in a suburban community and two years later became principal of a junior/senior high school in a neighboring community. He held the latter position when the Riverdale board contacted him. He listed membership in Phi Beta Kappa and the National Education Association.

Mr. Johnson was 41 years old and had a wife and one child. A graduate of a public high school, he had a Bachelor of Science in Education degree from a small state university and a Master of Education from a private university. He had not completed his doctorate, but had attended summer sessions at two private universities other than the one at which he received his master's degree. His undergraduate majors were French and social studies; his minor was education. As an undergraduate he took the following courses:

First year	*Second year*
Military Science	Military Science
Physical Education	Physical Education
English Composition	Psychological Principles
French Grammar	of Education
Geology	French Grammar
History of Civilizations	Structural Geology
	Early American Literature

Third year	*Fourth year*
Social Principles of	Political Science
Secondary Education	Principles of Sociology
Principles and Problems	History of Education
of Teaching	French Syntax
17th and 18th Century	Teaching of
French Literature	Foreign Languages
French Composition	Democracy in Education
Beginning German	Philosophy of Education
Modern English Literature	Meteorology
Public Speaking	Problems of the Family

As a graduate student, he took the following courses:

Current Social Problems
Social Pathology
Educational Administration
Educational Policy
Principles of Teaching
Organization, Administration, and Curriculum of Secondary Schools
    (two courses)
Educational Policy
Educational Measurement
Guidance
Student Personnel Work
Supervision of Elementary Schools
Educational Programs for Children
Principles of Educational Administration
School Plant Administration
Problems of Staff Personnel
History of Education in Western Culture
Educational Administration as Social Policy
Human Relations in Educational Administration
Educational Administration and Adaptation
Advanced Educational Administration (two courses)
Seminar in Educational Administration (two courses)
Introduction to Group Development
School Finance
School Plant Planning
Administrators' Workshop
Childhood Education

Mr. Johnson began teaching in 1940 and for two years taught social studies and coached football and skiing in a high school. For four years he served in the U.S. Marines and upon his discharge first served as acting principal in a junior high school in the town where he had taught and later as social studies teacher and high school ski coach again. Following that he served for one year as coordinator of the adult evening school in the community. He then moved to a suburban community and for four years was principal of the elementary school. Since 1954 he had been superintendent of the same district.

Mr. Smith was 45 years old and had a wife and three children. He graduated from a public high school and had a baccalaureate degree from a state teachers college. His master's degree was from a private university which has a major interest in teacher education. He had some additional work at another private university but had not completed the work for his doctorate at

11

the time he was in touch with the Riverdale board. It would appear that he did not intend to acquire a doctor's degree; he would probably restrict his contacts with a college solely to summer short courses and workshop activities.

The school board did not have a transcript of Mr. Smith's undergraduate or graduate courses. They did, however, have a complete account of the professional jobs he had held. He served for a brief time as an elementary school teacher-principal, and after that served as superintendent in two small communities before moving to the position which he occupied at the time the Riverdale school board interviewed him—the superintendency of a suburban district several hundred miles from Riverdale. In addition to administrative experience, Mr. Smith taught in summer sessions at four colleges over a period of several years.

THE BOARD'S DECISION

The school board at Riverdale carefully considered Mr. Reed, Mr. Johnson, Mr. Smith, and 10 others. After interviews, visits by board members to the respective communities where the candidates were living, and further checking with placement offices, the board made its decision. The unanimous choice for superintendent of their school system: Mr. Smith.

An important question to ask in this yearbook on preparation programs for school administrators is "why"—what qualities about Mr. Smith attracted the school board and convinced them that he was prepared both by his studies and by his experience to be the superintendent in their school system?

What kind of a person was the Riverdale board looking for? As one of the board members put it, "We know as a board what we believe in as far as school program is concerned, and frankly we are looking for a like-minded guy." Another board member talked in seemingly paradoxical terms, "We want a person who has some fixed notions about education, but who is still open-minded enough to experiment." "We want a superintendent who is neither tainted with a Bestor brush nor given to bursts of radicalism," said another board member. All of the Riverdale board seemed convinced that the chief ingredient in a new superintendent was the ability to develop and carry through with new ideas. They were quite specific in wanting a superintendent who talked more about education and curriculum than about money and buildings.

Reasons for Choice

If this was the kind of person they wanted, what made the school board think Mr. Smith was the right one?[3] The written and oral comments about him which came from professors and placement offices were leads to further exploration. They hinted at his ability to inspire teachers to be experimentation-minded, his willingness to try out new ideas, his decisiveness, and a kind of imperviousness to minor, nagging pressures and complaints.

The Riverdale board was initially cynical about letters of recommendation. In most instances their experiences justified the position that little discernment is revealed in such letters. Yet, the letters of recommendation in Mr. Smith's folder were unusual ones—unusual in the sense that several of them praised him as an educational leader and talked about his enthusiasm, his sensitivity to new ideas, and his effectiveness in implementing experiments.

Board members were obviously impressed by the "candidate's page" in the personnel folder, where Mr. Smith wrote about specifics of the school programs with which he had been affiliated —such things as special attention to the gifted, improved ratio of counselors to pupils, the core program in the seventh and eighth grades. He illustrated with facts rather than with arguments how he had been forced to cope with rapid growth in his districts. This was important to the board members in Riverdale, because they had agreed to find someone who had administered a school system of comparable size and characteristics. They were interested also in finding evidence of teaching ability and a warm and enthusiastic personality which would rally the support of teachers and other administrators.

The Riverdale board used both the letters of appraisal and the interview with Mr. Smith as beginning points, not as final revelations of his ability. Visits to Mr. Smith's current location followed. The board "saw for itself" at first hand. It is inter-

---

[3] This Commission is obviously not sitting in judgment over the choice of Smith in preference to the other candidates. It is merely reporting the facts and using the facts and issues in back of them as focal points to introduce the essential topics of the yearbook.

esting to observe that some of the criteria (see page 4) originally set up by the Riverdale school board were not met by Mr. Smith. Furthermore, some qualifications which were ignored in Smith's case were satisfied by other candidates: (a) teaching experience at the secondary school level, (b) possession of a doctor's degree, and (c) undergraduate preparation in a liberal arts school rather than in a teachers college.

Flexibility of Criteria

The Riverdale board had, at the beginning of its search for a superintendent, fallen into a familiar trap: It had set up objective measures for something which was basically subjective. Boards often develop a stereotype of the administrator they want to employ; Riverdale's board, later, avoided getting stuck with the technicalities of criteria established. Rigid compliance with the criteria would have limited the choice; failure to establish some criteria would have left the board with no starting point. It became obvious to the board that even though Mr. Smith had attended a state teachers college, he had some of the broad cultural interests they had previously supposed they would be able to find only in liberal arts college graduates. Furthermore, the depth of administrative skill which the board thought could be developed only in a doctoral program had apparently been achieved by this person in two years of graduate study in the administrator preparation program of a well-known college of education—coupled with the experiences which he gained on the job. The board was satisfied, also, that an understanding of secondary school curriculum and of the process of curriculum making had been gained by Mr. Smith even though he had never taught or administered a junior or senior high school.

Board's Evaluation of Preparation Programs

After the selection of Mr. Smith was completed, the Riverdale school board was asked the question: "Now that you have talked with a number of school administrators and have sized them up as potential superintendents for this district, what evaluation do you have about graduates of our preparation programs?" Individual members of the board had these things to say:

We are told that because of our salary and the kind of community we have, our job attracted a group of candidates considerably above the average in preparation and experience. If this is true, the ranks of well-prepared school administrators are very thin, indeed.

We were shocked to see how poorly educated in the humanities and in the arts were some men who now hold significant administrative positions. Most administrators prefer to talk more about buildings and budgets than about curriculum and the learning process.

We were on our guard about a candidate as soon as he referred us only to his achievements in previous jobs if those achievements were in areas other than instruction.

We were painfully aware how many school administrators fail to be articulate either in speaking or in writing. There is a clear need for more preparation in the area of communications.

A lack of firmness of conviction and determination to stick by one's ideas and defend them against criticism was seen by members of the board as a failure on the part of many of the candidates during interview. "Some call it leadership," said one school board member, "but let's put it this way: Members of this board have a lot of ideas about the kind of school program we want, but we don't want any superintendent here who sees his chief role as being errand boy for us." Other board members said they had the feeling in talking with some candidates that they were trying to sense the right thing to say during the interview in order to get the job, regardless of how it might fit in with their own philosophy of education. Part of a man's preparation, according to the Riverdale board, should give him the personal security as well as the philosophical outlook which would establish a clear sense of direction.

MAJOR PROFESSIONAL ISSUES

The unfolding of the story of Riverdale's selection of a superintendent has given us perspective to view several important professional concerns. The Yearbook Commission argues for no general conclusions on the strength of this single case alone. Yet the example of a single community gives focus to some of the urgent issues which call for decisions.

The Guarantee of Quality Preparation

The Riverdale school board had no opportunity—nor, indeed, the disposition—to evaluate the quality of preparation of the people it was considering for the superintendency there. No board could. It is the *profession's* responsibility to make sure that training is of high quality. It would be impossible for each board to appraise with any breadth at all the early preparatory experiences of practicing school administrators. What controls, then, on the procedures of preparation and certification must the profession establish? How can such controls have meaning, firmness, and validity? How can the profession proceed to evaluate systematically and thoroughly the resources and the program requirements in preparation programs—preserving at the same time the encouragement for universities to experiment? Do we have a public obligation to guarantee, not only that high-quality programs are the only ones permitted to exist, but that the college-determined supply and the community-determined demand for school administrators are in reasonable numerical agreement?

Significant Information for Boards

The key word here is "significant." From the standpoint of employment information alone, a cogent argument can be made for a preparation program which involves the student in actual tryout of administrative responsibilities in as real a situation as possible—internships, surveys, traineeships. Employing boards need information which comes from observing students in such circumstances. Dossiers which were available to Riverdale's board did not include such descriptive data. Should colleges accept a greater responsibility for providing thorough, appropriate knowledge about potential school administrators? The issue here is not for *more* information from the colleges but for information of a *different* kind—descriptions of the actual performance of the person in an administrative situation. Does this mean also the profession must develop both predictive and diagnostic instruments for the evaluation of school administrators?

Agreement on Content

As the Riverdale school board carried on its search, a job description of the superintendency—at least in the mind of that board—emerged. They expected certain competencies and looked

16

for evidence of acquaintance with clearly defined concepts. The educational preparation of the several candidates was highly individualized at the undergraduate level—somewhat less so in graduate school. The professional curriculum in educational administration still appears to be largely self-selected, often a matter of virtually free elective on the part of the graduate student. Should the profession, instead, clearly outline the undergraduate prerequisites which should be expected of persons who enter professional training? Should the graduate professional curriculum, too, be clearly established? Is there need for general agreement on a core of administrative study, consistent as to theory, in our professional schools?

The Time Lag

The Riverdale school board was looking for a mature person, one with previous superintendency experience and one who had almost certainly completed most of his college preparatory work several years earlier. They expected at the same time that the man would show substantial knowledge about the latest innovations in pupil grouping, instructional methods, teaching aids, personnel policies, and other recent developments. Is this too much to ask? What are the obligations, both personal and institutional, for seeing that this is not an impossible expectation? If research evidence is emerging from collegiate or governmental sources which brings new light to such problems as those which were raised by the Riverdale board, how can practicing administrators—busy with their multitude of tasks every day—still keep abreast of the rapidly changing scene in education?

Personal Qualities

Skill in human relations, personal warmth, and ability to incite enthusiasm—these were qualities highly rated by the Riverdale school board. The behavior of the administrator was obviously not alone a matter of knowing about how a school should operate. Some verve for leadership was a matter of concern to the board as it tried to visualize each candidate in the role of Riverdale superintendent, working enthusiastically with Riverdale's school staff and with the adults and children in the community.

17

Concern for personal qualities of the administrator raises at least two important questions:

1. What additions to the curriculum can help create administrative behavior which is most desired?
2. Is the initial selection of the person as important a matter as is the program itself?

In addition, policing by the profession of educational administration as to minimum scholarship requirements, ethics, and quality of performance on the job may be required in the future.

* * *

The basic proposition of this book is that school administration must move toward high professional standards. Central to such a proposition are matters of professional curriculum, selection and screening policies, research and in-service education, graduate school resources, and professional controls on standards. These issues are discussed in detail in the chapters which follow.

chapter II

Profile of the American School Superintendent

Is it true that the superintendent is a tired coach who aspired to a less strenuous job? Is he an academic lightweight? Is he a country boy who made good in the city, or a city boy who stayed on? What kind of preparation does the superintendent have? Is he a graduate of a state normal school or teachers college? Has he studied only professional education?

This chapter is concerned with these questions, and with many others. Its purpose is to describe the career line of the American school superintendent. We begin at the beginning with the superintendent's birthplace, family, and school. We follow him through high school, college, and graduate school to his first job and each succeeding job to his present post. We probe into his feelings, his attitudes, his ideas, to see what he thinks of himself and how he reached his present perch on the professional ladder.

The method of gathering data was, of course, a questionnaire responded to by an adequate sample of school superintendents. This means that the study described here is one of self-reported self-perceptions of certain of the superintendents in this country. One should be constantly aware of this as he reads this chapter since another data-gathering device, such as interviews, might give other or different data. Be that as it may, the reader is warned!

One other point bears mention. The responses of the superintendents were collected and tabulated by the Research Division of the National Education Association. Transferred to sheets $8\frac{1}{2}''$ by $11''$ the tables which the Division compiled make a stack one-

and-a-half inches thick. Merely to reproduce the 123 tables would take more pages than have been allocated to this chapter. With this in mind, the chapter has been written in a narrative style with as few statistics, tables, and graphs as is humanly possible. The data have been reported in more detail in a research report to be published by the American Association of School Administrators and the Research Division of the NEA.*

WHO ARE OUR SUPERINTENDENTS?

The discussion of the career patterns of superintendents starts with a look at the sample from which the rest of the material in the chapter emanates. This is followed by a presentation of the vital statistics of the superintendents, where they come from, how many positions they have held, how many years they have held their present posts, and the like.

The Sample

The questionnaire was sent to superintendents of urban districts, that is, districts in communities so classified by the U.S. Census Bureau. In order to be labeled "urban," the municipality must have a population of 2500 or over. Also included are county school systems that have within them an urban center of 30,000 population or over and smaller county districts if over half the population is urban. The 3812 urban superintendents were grouped in six population strata, and questionnaires were sent to varying percentages of each stratum. For instance, 100 percent of the superintendents in the two largest population groups were sent questionnaires, 50 percent of the next largest, 25 percent for the next two groups (the population groups with the most superintendents), and 50 percent of the smallest population stratum.

Questionnaires were mailed to a total of 36 percent of all urban superintendents in the country on November 17, 1958; one follow-up was sent. Eight hundred fifty-nine questionnaires were returned in usable condition: this constitutes a 62.7 percent return. See Table 1. The highest return came from groups IV and V (small population groups), over three-fourths of the

---

* The report was being written at the time this yearbook went to press.

superintendents in these groups responding. The smallest return, slightly over one-third, was from the lowest population group. The sample appears to be entirely adequate for the purposes of this study.

1 DISTRIBUTION AND RETURN OF QUESTIONNAIRE ON CAREER PATTERNS OF SUPERINTENDENT

POPULATION GROUP	TOTAL NUMBER OF URBAN SUPERINTENDENTS	URBAN SUPERINTENDENTS WHO RECEIVED QUESTIONNAIRES		URBAN SUPERINTENDENTS WHO RETURNED QUESTIONNAIRES	
		NUMBER	PERCENT	NUMBER	PERCENT
1	2	3	4	5	6
I. 500,000 & over	26	26	100	18	69.2
II. 100,000-499,999	148	148	100	84	56.8
III. 30,000-99,999	547	274	50	161	58.8
IV. 10,000-29,999	1,376	344	25	271	78.8
V. 5,000-9,999	1,122	280	25	223	79.6
VI. 2,500-4,999	593	297	50	102	34.3
Totals	3,812	1,369	36%	859	62.7%

Age. The range in the age of urban superintendents was half a century: replies came from two superintendents who were 30 years old and one who was 80. The average and the median ages were 51; the age most frequently reported was 54.

Sex. All of the superintendents in the sample were men, which means that we missed the few women in the country who hold superintendencies.

Position in family. One of the notions of how one learns to be a leader is that the oldest child has many more opportunities to develop leadership abilities than do other children in the family. If this is so, the superintendents in this study should tend to come from families with more than one child, and secondly, they should tend to be first born in the family. In examining the returns it was found that only 6.5 percent of the superintendents could be classified as "only child." The median number of children per family was 4.6, with the range being from an only child to 10 or more.

There was a tendency for superintendents in communities of over a half million population to come from smaller families, but it should be noted that the superintendents came from families which were larger than the mean at the time they were children, 1908. At that time the average family size was 4.6, while the families in which the superintendents were born averaged 6.6.

In looking at the position of superintendents in their families we find that almost 30 percent were first born in families of more than one child, which is somewhat higher than the expected percentage, 22. It can be concluded that superintendents came from families larger than the average at the time they were born, and they do appear to be first children more than would be expected by chance.

Birthplace, Age, Mobility, and Salary

There are many questions concerning superintendents which have been the source of speculation for years. In this section we will explore such topics as the schools and communities in which the superintendents grew up, their first jobs, first superintendencies, number of superintendencies held, how many years in their present positions, and salaries.

School and community. The superintendents tended to come from small communities. In fact, 72 percent were graduated from high schools in communities of under 10,000 population. According to the U. S. Office of Education Biennial Survey of Education for 1928-30, some 52 percent of all high school graduates came from high schools in communities of 10,000 or less population. Since the superintendents exceeded the national figure by 38 percent, it is obvious that there is a strong tendency for superintendents to come from small communities. Why this is the case would make an interesting research study. Only 2 percent received diplomas from high schools in communities of over a half million population.

There was a slight tendency for men to hold superintendencies in communities of the same size as the ones in which they received their high school diplomas. To illustrate the variation, four men who received diplomas in communities of under a thousand population are now superintendents in cities of over a half million population, and one who received his diploma in a city of over a half million is superintendent in the smallest class of urban district in the study.

Age at first job in education. Two-thirds of all superintendents took their first educational position between the ages of 20 and 24. It was rare that a superintendent took his first position in the education field after the age of 30, but a substantial number, some 16 percent, began their professional careers before the age of 20. More recent practice is quite different. In 1954-55 only one-tenth of 1 percent of the first-year teachers were under the age of 20.[1]

Age at first administrative or supervisory position. Some 90 percent of all the superintendents took their first administrative or supervisory position before the age of 35, with the average age at first position of this kind being 28. Superintendents in the largest cities started in administration earlier than did others, the average age in the over-half-a-million cities being 25.6. There was a high negative correlation between age at which a man took his first administrative position and size of the community in which he is now superintendent; that is, the younger the man started, the larger the city in which he is now superintendent.

Age at first superintendency. The average age at the first superintendency was slightly over 36, but the range was from under 20 to over 55. There was a high positive correlation between a man's age at first superintendency and size of the community in which he presently holds his position; in other words, the larger city positions are held by those who received their first superintendency at older ages. This may indicate a tendency for the larger cities to promote from within and to take more mature individuals for top posts. This is further supported by a high positive correlation between size of community and years of nonsuperintendency administrative and supervisory experiences; that is, those holding superintendencies in larger communities have had more experience in nonsuperintendency administrative and supervisory positions. In fact, the average for cities of a half million or more population was 17 years of nonsuperintendency administrative and supervisory experience; and it decreased, as the size of city decreased, to seven years in the smallest urban districts.

Mobility of superintendents. The commonly-held opinion that school superintendents are a highly mobile group was not sub-

---

[1] National Education Association, Research Division. "First Year Teachers in 1954-55." *Research Bulletin* 34:8; February 1956.

stantiated by the study. In fact, 44 percent of the men studied had held only one superintendency.

Thirty-eight percent of all superintendents in the sample have held the same position for the past 10 years or more. This percentage is fairly constant among the population categories, varying from 33 percent for the largest and smallest groups to 40 percent for the 30,000 to 99,999 and the 5000 to 9999 population categories. On the other hand, only 9 percent have held three or more superintendencies in the past 10 years. It may be that it is this small number of superintendents who create the impression that the average tenure of a superintendent is three or four years. The "hoppers," that is, those who have held six or more positions constitute less than 3 percent of the total sample. Eighty-five percent of the superintendents have held three or fewer chief school administrator positions in their careers. The statistics which indicate that superintendents do not flit from job to job appear to be fairly consistent, since a comparison of the number of superintendencies held with years of experience shows a rather constant percentage holding one position regardless of the number of years of experience.

On the whole, superintendents do not move from state to state. It was found that 85 percent of all superintendents in the sample had held positions in only one state, while a mere 3 percent held positions in three or more states. It is pertinent to note, however, that these statistics do not hold for all sizes of school districts. Large-city superintendents are much more likely to move across state borders than are superintendents of small districts. Approximately 36 percent of the men in cities of over 100,000 population have served in two or more states, and this percentage decreases irregularly to 12 percent in the smallest urban districts.

The median length of time in present position was slightly under eight years. This figure ranges from a median of a little over six years for the largest cities to slightly over eight years for the 5000-9999 class. Nine percent of the superintendents have served 20 or more years in their present positions, while 35 percent have spent less than five years in the superintendencies they now hold. The arithmetic average of time in present position is nine years.

All of this seems to indicate that tenure as an urban school superintendent is much more stable than had been thought.

Salary. How much are school superintendents paid? As might well be expected, salaries and size of school district have a high positive correlation. The variation in salaries was great, with some superintendents receiving three-and-a-half times as much as others in the same size school district. The average salary for all superintendents was $11,900 and the median, $10,700. Other than the size relationship there did not appear to be further significant generalizations in the salary data collected. See Table 2.

2   **MEDIANS AND RANGES OF SALARIES OF SCHOOL SUPERINTENDENTS BY POPULATION OF SCHOOL DISTRICT**

POPULATION OF SCHOOL DISTRICT	MEDIAN	RANGE
1	2	3
500,000 and over	$25,300	$19,000 to $35,000+
100,000-499,999	18,100	11,500 to 28,000
30,000- 99,999	14,400	7,000 to 23,000
10,000- 29,999	11,000	6,000 to 22,000
5,000- 9,999	8,900	Less than 6,000 to 19,000
2,500- 4,999	8,100	Less than 6,000 to 11,500

HOW DO SUPERINTENDENTS PREPARE FOR THE POSITION?

If "getting educated" is as important as most Americans seem to think, or at least say they think, we should be concerned with the way in which school superintendents get their education. The outline for this section is: the undergraduate program, the graduate program, and an evaluation by the superintendents of their graduate programs. Along the way we shall discuss the cost of becoming a superintendent, the length of time spent in graduate study, the number of different institutions attended, and the major and minor subject areas studied.

In Undergraduate College

To those who hold the conventional stereotype of the school superintendent, this section should be a surprise, if not a shock.

The commonly held stereotype of the superintendent is that he is a graduate of a normal school or teachers college and has studied only professional education. This stereotype is not consistent with the evidence.

Degrees received. It appears that 98 percent of the urban superintendents in the country hold a bachelor's degree of some type. Seventeen superintendents reported they did not hold a degree. All of these men had 15 or more years of experience in education, and nine of the group had 35 or more years of experience. It is obvious that those without bachelor's degrees are those who started many years ago.

Some 84 percent held either a Bachelor of Arts, Bachelor of Philosophy, Bachelor of Literature, or Bachelor of Science degree. Only 15 percent had earned a bachelor's degree in education, with a variation in range from 11 percent in the largest cities to 19 percent in the smallest districts.

Number of colleges attended. Superintendents reported that they attended a variety of colleges, and some indicated that they had attended several. While 70 percent attended only one undergraduate institution (normally considered as par for the course), one superintendent admitted to having attended five; 16 matriculated at four institutions of higher learning; and a rather larger percentage, 22, attended two undergraduate schools.

Major and minor fields. The superintendents reported a wide variety of major fields of study, and here again the stereotype of a physical education or math-science background was discredited. The major fields of study in order of frequency were behavioral sciences (anthropology, sociology, economics, etc.)—18 percent, education—17 percent, physical and biological science—15 percent, history and political science—15 percent, mathematics—11 percent, and English—9 percent. Only 3 percent reported that they majored in health and physical education, and 2 percent in industrial and vocational arts.

The undergraduate minors of superintendents follow somewhat the same pattern as their major courses of study. The minors were physical and biological sciences—19 percent, English —slightly over 15 percent, the behavorial sciences—15 percent, education—14 percent, mathematics—just over 11 percent, and history and political science—11 percent. Miscellaneous minors, each taken by less than 5 percent of the superintendents, were foreign languages, physical and health education, business and commerce, geography, and industrial or vocational arts.

What did those who majored in education take for a minor? By far the most popular minor was the behavioral sciences, with slightly over 21 percent. This was followed by history and/or political science—14 percent, mathematics—11 percent, English —11 percent, and physical and biological science—9 percent. Those who minored in education reported a somewhat different pattern of majors with history and/or political science leading with 22 percent, followed by the physical and biological sciences at 19 percent, mathematics—12 percent, and English—4 percent.

In summary, less than a fifth of the superintendents majored in education and one-seventh of them minored in that field at the undergraduate level. Major subject fields were taken in the following order of frequency: the behavioral sciences, the physical and biological sciences, history and/or political science, mathematics, and English. The undergraduate background of American school superintendents is strong in the intellectual studies of the modern liberal arts. They have studied the subject matter of people, of the world in which they live, of its government and culture, and of its ways of communicating. This finding should put to rest speculation that superintendents have been exposed only to professional education and physical education.

Most superintendents, when in undergraduate school, majored in what is now considered fashionable, that is, the hard, tough subjects. It is also encouraging to note the sizable percentage who majored in the behavioral sciences which are now being acknowledged as excellent preparation for administration.

In Graduate School

It is in graduate school that one receives the preparation designed specifically for administration in the public schools. Considering the ferment in the past 10 years over the preparation of administrators, it is high time that we found out just what school superintendents did study. In addition, it is interesting to discover what they think about their courses and other graduate activities.

Extent of graduate work. Ninety-six percent of urban superintendents hold at least one advanced degree. Some three-fourths hold master's degrees as their highest degree earned, 15 percent hold the Doctor of Education degree, and 6 percent hold the Doctor of Philosophy degree. As one would expect, there are more doctorates in the larger systems than in the smaller. In fact, 41 percent of the superintendents in cities of over 30,000 population hold either a Doctor of Education or Doctor of Philosophy degree, with the Doctor of Education ahead by two to one. Even though there are more doctor's degrees in the larger cities, it should be noted that 95 percent of the superintendents in the smallest urban communities have advanced degrees, probably indicating more pre-service degrees than was common a few years ago.

Major and minor fields. Whereas the undergraduate major and minor fields of superintendents covered a wide variety of subjects, the major and minor fields of graduate study are largely restricted to educational administration or education. Sixty-two percent of the majors for the master's degree were in educational administration and/or supervision, and another 27 percent were in the general field of education. The highest percentage for an academic field was roughly 4 percent in history and/or political science. When looking at minors for the master's degree, the percentage falls off, of course, for educational administration and/or supervision and is 28 percent, with education (general) next with 19 percent. The behavioral sciences are the highest academic area with 20 percent, and history and/or political science next with 13 percent. Guidance and counseling is surprisingly low, with less than 1 percent of the superintendents reporting that they chose the guidance field as a major and 4 percent as a minor.

Practically all of the doctor's degree holders have majors in educational administration (79 percent) or education (18 percent). It is interesting to note that the six doctoral degrees not in educational administration or education are in social sciences —two, law—two, philosophy—one, and psychology—one. The pattern differs for minors with 55 percent minoring in educational administration and/or supervision and education. The behavioral sciences ranked next with 20 percent, followed by guidance and counseling, history and/or political science, and a miscellany of other subjects.

While the undergraduate majors and minors of superintendents were predominantly in broad academic fields, the advanced degrees are predominantly professional degrees. The

28

superintendents have built professional preparation on a firm foundation.

Length of graduate study. Graduate study in educational administration was reported to have started between the ages of 25 and 30 although in a few cases it was delayed until the age of 40 or later. The median age at the beginning of study was 28.5 years. Superintendents in cities of a half million or more tended to start study the earliest (27.5 years), and superintendents in the smallest communities started study at the latest age (almost 30 years).

It appears that superintendents are beginning graduate work at a somewhat earlier age now than was once the case. Superintendents with less than 15 years of experience had a median age at the start of training of 27 years, five months. This rose irregularly with experience, so that superintendents with 40 years or more experience reported a starting age of 29 years and eight months.

While superintendents in cities of over a half million population reported they started graduate work in administration at the earliest age, they report completing their work at the latest age. The median age of these superintendents at completion of study was 38 years, four months. The age at completion of study decreased irregularly with the size of the city until in the smallest cities the age at completion of graduate work was 34 years, one month. This is partially accounted for by the fact that there are proportionately more doctorates in the larger cities than in the smaller districts, where many of the superintendents have not completed doctoral programs. As in the case of age at beginning of training, the age at completion is lower for those recently entering the profession. Men with less than 15 years of experience completed their work at a median age of 31.5 years. This age increased irregularly with experience, so that those with 40 or more years reported completing their work at the age of 38. Superintendents are now starting their graduate work sooner and are completing it at an earlier age.

The median length of time that superintendents were in preparation for their positions was five years and seven months, but the range was from one year to 20 years or more. In fact, 11 percent reported that it took 15 years or more to complete their work. As has been indicated, superintendents in the largest cities spent the most time (nine years), and the time decreased regularly with size of community to a median of four years, two months.

The time it takes to complete graduate work appears to be decreasing. Those with under 15 years of experience had a median time of three years and 10 months, and time increased irregularly with experience, so that for those with 40 or more years it took six years and five months to complete their programs of preparation.

It appears that altogether too much time is being spent to complete the doctorate in educational administration. Most institutions have a seven-year limit on work they will accept for the doctorate, yet 32 percent report spending *more* than seven years en route. The major reason for this is, no doubt, the fact that most graduate work in administration is done on a part-time basis.

Number of institutions attended. It has been speculated that a great many superintendents take their graduate work "cafeteria style," that is, at several different colleges and universities. This speculation appears to have been true in the past, but it also appears that the practice is abating. The median number of institutions attended by those who have completed a program of graduate work is 2.3, but the range is from one to more than five. Superintendents are almost evenly split (40 percent to 35 percent) between those attending only one institution and those attending two. A quarter of all superintendents have attended three or more institutions. For those superintendents with under 15 years of experience, the median number of institutions attended is just under two. The number increases regularly by experience categories, so that those with 40 or more years have attended a median of 2.4 institutions. "Cafeteria" attendance appears to be on the wane.

Cost. What does it cost for a superintendent to complete a program of preparation? In obtaining figures on the cost of programs the superintendents were asked for net costs, among other costs, which meant that they were to subtract scholarships, fellowships, G.I. aid, and other nonloan subsidies. They were also asked not to include wages they could have earned had they not been in school. The median *net* cost of a doctorate was $4400; of a 60-hour program, $2400; and of a master's degree, $1500. The range for the doctorate was from no net cost to over $10,000; for the 60-hour program, from less than $500 to over $10,000; and for the master's, from no net cost to $8000. Since these are self-reported net costs they cannot be checked, and the fact that superintendents were asked to recall expenditures made a number of years ago causes the Commission to consider the estimates to be somewhat less than precise.

What financial aid did the superintendents receive as they did their graduate work? Over three-fourths of those who completed their work reported they received no aid at all. It is clear that only a few men have received substantial aid. Practically all of the aid was received by 19 percent of the respondents with 1.2 percent (nine superintendents) receiving $5000 or more. Lack of financial aid is a major obstacle to full-time graduate work in educational administration and is a problem which should receive high-priority attention.

Evaluation of Preparation Programs

Just what do superintendents think about their graduate preparation? Three questions were asked: "On the whole how would you evaluate your program of graduate studies as preparation for the superintendency?" "What was its major strength?" and "What was its major weakness?" The answers proved to be quite interesting, and since it was felt that evaluation was very important, several types of analyses were undertaken.

Over-all judgments. Superintendents were asked to rate the quality of preparation on a four-point scale: "excellent," "good," "fair," and "poor." Those superintendents who had earned a doctor's degree rated the quality of their preparation higher than those who had a master's degree or 60 hours beyond the bachelor's degree. None of the doctors rated their training "poor"; only 7 percent "fair"; and the remainder were evenly split between "good" and "excellent." The other two groups, master's degrees and 60 hours beyond the bachelor's, rated their preparation almost identically. Twenty-seven percent said "excellent," 62 percent "good," and 11 percent "fair." Of the 790 responding to the question, only three rated their preparation as "poor." See Figure I.

When evaluations of preparation programs were compared to the size of the school district of the superintendent, it was found that respondents from the three size groups over 30,000 in population rated their programs the same, 3.3 on the four-point scale

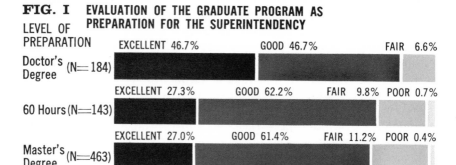

FIG. I EVALUATION OF THE GRADUATE PROGRAM AS
LEVEL OF PREPARATION FOR THE SUPERINTENDENCY

(poor—1, fair—2, good—3, excellent—4). The two smaller population groups were slightly lower than the largest-sized school districts in their evaluations.

When the evaluations of graduate programs were compared by groupings according to the total number of years of experience in education, there was little variation. The ratings were uniformly somewhat higher than "good" on the four-point scale which was employed.

A comparison was also made of the amount of money which it cost superintendents to finance their preparation and their ratings of the program. Here there is a direct, positive relationship between cost and perceived quality. Those who rated their preparation "excellent" had a median expenditure of $2300; those who rated their preparation "good," a median expenditure of $1950; and those who rated their preparation "fair," an expenditure of $1750.

In summary, it appears that superintendents are generally satisfied with the quality of their graduate preparation. Those who spend more money appear to be more satisfied, and those who have earned a doctorate also appear to be pleased to a greater extent than those with less than a doctorate. This conclusion is not surprising; it conforms to the natural connection most people make between "money expended" and "value received." It is to be expected that the men at the top of any professional group should be somewhat pleased with themselves and should believe that their preparation had something to do with their success. This finding is akin to the answers received by many when they query successful men in all walks of life as to the value of Latin in their preparation. These men invariably say that Latin contributed greatly to their success, and attribute to it almost magical powers. It would seem that attributing success in the superintendency to the melange of preparation programs to which they have submitted themselves is a finding in the same class as attributing the success of the Vice-President of the United States to his study of Latin.

Major strengths. Superintendents were asked to write, in response to an open-end question, major strengths of their program of preparation. Four-fifths of the respondents indicated one or more strengths. The listing of strengths includes virtually everything that is done in any program in the country. What is *not* on the list is more interesting than what is included. No one mentioned the internship or case studies as a strength, but this may be so because these two techniques are new and, as yet, have relatively limited use. The major strength reported was summarized as "faculty's ability, practical experience, and interest in students." This was reported by 27 percent of the respondents. It is interesting to note that the superintendents in the largest cities placed this first: almost 40 percent of them reported it as a strength. This strength was the one most frequently reported in all six population groups of school districts, but the percentage reporting it decreased from the largest to the smallest population area with the exception of one group. "Courses in administrational theory and practice-supervision, personnel, and school policy" followed with 18 percent reporting it, and no discernible pattern of responses among the population groupings. The next three strengths, all with more than 10 percent of the superintendents reporting, were "currency and flexibility of program, small classes, and field work"; "practicability of courses and methods"; and "courses in school finance." Among those strengths reported by fewer than 1 percent of the superintendents were courses in child accounting, administrative reporting, business office techniques, methods of teaching, secondary education, human relations, and elementary education.

When the reported strengths were compared with the level of the preparation program, i.e., doctorate, 60 hours beyond the bachelor's, and master's degree, the percentage of strengths reported was in the same order as the length of preparation. In other words, the more the preparation the more the strengths. The strengths reported are the same as above and are in the same

order of frequency with one exception: those with doctor's degrees reported "currency and flexibility of program, small classes, and field work" second rather than third.

Major weaknesses. The same procedure was followed to determine weaknesses as was used to determine strengths. Three-quarters of all respondents indicated one or more weaknesses in their graduate programs. As in the case of the strengths, the weaknesses ran the gamut of activities present in a graduate school. Twenty-one percent stated that the major weakness in their preparation was "too much theory; courses not practical." This response aroused the interest of the Commission because if the teaching of educational administration can be characterized by anything, it is the lack of theory, not its over-abundance. A sampling of 30 superintendents who had reported "too much theory" was taken and a letter sent to each. Each man was asked to write to the Commission and "explain what you meant by 'too theoretical.'" The Commission asked: "Did you mean that the courses were impractical? that you were unable to use what was taught? Can you tell me the name of the theory or theories which were taught to you? Would you please send me a short illustration of what you consider to be 'too theoretical'?"

Thirteen superintendents responded to the above letter. Their replies were very enlightening. The first point to become clear was that there was general misuse of the word "theory." Some superintendents acknowledged this and said they meant the opposite of "practical," thereby equating theoretical with impractical. Others apparently used theoretical to mean just plain "poor." Any course which was poor was "too theoretical," as they saw it. Probably the most general use of the term "theory" was as a synonym for "speculation," "supposition," and "ideal." These men said that graduate work in school administration was little related to reality, that it was concerned with what ought to be rather than what is.

Administrative theory is a set of assumptions from which can be derived principles which explain the nature of administration. The purpose of theory is to explain what "is," not to speculate as to what things "should" or "ought" to be.

Many of the superintendents speculated as to why teaching was "ought" oriented and guessed that the answer was that not enough professors had administrative experience.[2]   The superintendent who made the most vigorous statement to this effect ended his letter by stating that a reading of *Who Runs Our Schools?*[3] would give a picture of the rough and tumble of school administration.   The Commission cannot help but comment that *Who Runs Our Schools?* was written by a sociologist who has had no experience as a school administrator, nor does he have any training in the field.   It would seem that the "ought" orientation of some professors is a function of their immersion in the mythology of education rather than their lack of experience.   Many former superintendents who are now "professing" have no firmer grasp of reality because of their orientation toward "oughtness."   Even though they have a great deal of experience, they still teach what ought to be, not the realities of the situation.

The superintendent who recommended reading *Who Runs Our Schools?* however, was right in offering this as a more realistic picture of how things really are.   It is the Commission's considered judgment that the movement of the study of school administration towards the behavioral sciences is all to the good.   The field is moving from a base of folklore to a base of theory grounded in reality.

It should also be noted that not one superintendent in the special sampling named a theory which he had been taught.   Either the teaching did not "take," or no theory as such was taught. The Commission guesses that the latter was the case.

It would appear that superintendents are objecting to courses and books which are unrelated to the kinds of things which an administrator must do on the job, and schools of education should be warned that this is the case.

Other weaknesses reported by more than 10 percent of the respondents were faculty's ineffectiveness, such as poor scheduling

---

[2] See Cogger, Robert V. *College Teachers of School Administration.* Doctor's thesis. New Haven: Yale University, 1952. Based on a sampling of professors of school administration, Cogger reported the following job experiences:

    76% were at one time superintendents or assistant superintendents;
    66% were secondary principals or supervisors;
    40% were elementary principals or supervisors;
    25% were administrators in higher education;
    16% were on staffs of state departments of education;
    43% had experience in two of these fields.

[3] Gross, Neal C. *Who Runs Our Schools?* New York: John Wiley and Sons, 1958. 195 p.

and lack of experience; repetitious and unrelated courses; narrow scope of courses; lack of on-the-job training; lack of internship and other field experiences. Quite logically, the opposite of what were reported as strengths were reported as weaknesses. This is particularly true of student relations with the faculty. Where those relations were good, they were reported as strengths; where poor, they were reported as weaknesses. Apparently, superintendents saw the faculties as crucial to the success of their graduate preparation.

WHAT IS THE CAREER ROUTE?

There has been a considerable amount of speculation over what roads men take to the superintendency. How much of it has had solid basis in fact has never been known. The following questions are of interest: What is the career line of a typical superintendent? Is there only one career line that is typical or are there several? Do superintendents all have experience as principals? Do superintendents in the larger cities all have central office experience? Do superintendents start in very small districts and leap-frog their way up to progressively larger districts? Have the superintendents all been teachers? And, if so, what type?

Sequence of Educational Positions

There are only two types of educational positions which are generally held prior to becoming a superintendent. As might be expected, these are classroom teacher and building principal. Eighty-eight percent of the superintendents have been teachers at the elementary and/or secondary school level, and 83 percent have been building principals. There is an interesting comparison revealed in contrasting superintendents in the various population categories with these two variables. Only 65 percent of the superintendents in cities of over a half million have ever taught. This percentage increases as the size of city decreases until the highest percentage is reached in the 10,000-29,999 category and then it levels off at 89 percent for the two smallest categories.

On the other hand, the highest percentage of superintendents having been building principals is in the largest cities, 94 percent. This decreases regularly to 79 percent in the smallest cities. The only other job reported held by any substantial number of superintendents was a central office position. This is, of course, related to size of city. We find the percentage decreasing regularly from 71 for the largest to 5 for the smallest. The percentages by size of district indicate that the stereotype of how one becomes a superintendent is not quite true.

A variety of other educational positions were reported to have been held including college teacher, college official, state education department official, and county department official, but none of these positions was reported by more than 6 percent.

Five men reported that they had held no previous educational position of any kind.

Type of teaching position. Since most of the superintendents have taught, a look at what they taught should be informative. Twenty-two percent reported that they had at one time been elementary school teachers, and 75 percent said they had been secondary school teachers. Thirteen percent had some rural school teaching experience, and one of these is now the superintendent in a city of over half a million population.

The three subjects taught by the largest percentage of superintendents were social studies (30 percent), science (29 percent), and mathematics (28 percent). Twenty-three percent stated that they had been coaches, although only 8 percent were physical education teachers. English was taught by 13 percent. Other subjects such as speech, music, industrial arts, agriculture, and foreign languages were reported by small numbers of superintendents. Of the subjects tabulated, art was the one reported the least, there being four superintendents who were former art teachers.

Types of administrative positions held. The principalship was the most commonly held administrative position. Almost half of the superintendents were former high school principals, and 23 percent held elementary principalships at one time or another.

Sixteen percent of the superintendents reported they had been assistant, deputy, or associate superintendents. Some 12 percent reported they had been directors, supervisors, coordinators, or consultants. In the largest cities 71 percent reported they had held one of these positions, while 48 percent of the next largest size group and 32 percent of the 30,000-99,999 category did also.

Position held immediately prior to present superintendency.
What position was held by the superintendent immediately prior
to the position he now holds? Surprisingly enough, only 46 percent said they held a superintendency prior to their present position. The smallest proportion moving from a former superintendency to their present one was in the largest cities. Here,
fewer than a third moved from a chief executive's post. Over two-
thirds of those holding the chief administrator's job in the largest
cities moved from a position of assistant, deputy, or associate
superintendent. This was also true of more than one-third of
the superintendents in the 100,000 to 499,999 category.

Twenty-nine percent moved from a principalship (two-thirds
from high schools) to the superintendency. Five percent moved
to the superintendency from a teaching post, this move most common in the 5000 to 9999 population group. Four percent held
a variety of jobs such as college teacher, college administrator,
vice-principal, dean, counselor, or department head.

Population of district previously served. It is commonly believed that superintendents remain in a position only long enough
to get placed in a larger community. In order to test this notion
the population of the district in which each superintendent held
his last position prior to the present one was charted. See Table
3. (The bold-faced type in this table is the percentage of superintendents who moved from a position in a city of the same size
category. Other percentages are for those superintendents who
moved from cities of a different size category.) The results do
not justify the commonly held notion of the extreme upward
mobility of superintendents.

Superintendents do tend to move upward in terms of population of district rather than downward, but a substantial percentage move to communities of the same size category. Sixty-
three percent of the superintendents of 500,000 and over population came from cities of the same size category. This percentage
decreased to 36 percent in districts of 2500-4999, where 42 percent of the superintendencies were held by men moving up from
smaller districts and where 22 percent of the superintendents
previously held positions in larger communities. In cities of
10,000 population and above, however, the tendency to move from
a larger district to a smaller one was negligible.

3 POPULATION OF SCHOOL DISTRICTS IN WHICH RESPONDENTS HOLD SUPERINTENDENCY

Population Where Respondent Held Position Immediately Prior to Current Superintendency.	POPULATION WHERE RESPONDENT IS NOW SUPERINTENDENT					
	500,000 and over	100,000-499,999	30,000-99,999	10,000-29,999	5,000-9,999	2,500-4,999
1	2	3	4	5	6	7
500,000 and over	63%	1%	1%	—	—	—
100,000-499,999	31%	47%	6%	1%	1%	—
30,000- 99,999	—	33%	45%	4%	3%	2%
10,000- 29,999	6%	17%	32%	37%	11%	5%
5,000- 9,999	—	3%	6%	26%	37%	15%
2,500- 4,999	—	—	6%	21%	25%	36%
1,000- 2,499	—	—	3%	9%	18%	35%
500- 999	—	—	1%	1%	2%	6%
Below 500	—	—	—	—	2%	1%

The Common Patterns

There appear to be two major career patterns discernible in the responses. One of these patterns is to move up through "the ranks," and the other is to move from one superintendency in a smaller community to another in a larger community. The first of these two patterns appears to be most prevalent in the largest communities, while the second appears to be most common in smaller districts.

Of those superintendents in the cities with more than half a million in population, 56 percent reported they held an assistant, deputy, or associate superintendency in a district of the same population category as their present post. We assume this generally means the same city in which they now hold the superintendency. Another 13 percent reported holding a similar job in a city of from 100,000-499,999 population. No superintendent in a city of over 500,000 population moved to that position directly from a principalship. Twenty-nine percent of the superintendents in cities of from 100,000-499,999 population held a central office post immediately prior to their present superintendency as did 18 percent of those in cities of from 30,000-99,999 population. For smaller cities the percentages of those moving from central office to the superintendency were negligible.

The most common pattern reported by superintendents in cities of over 100,000 people was teacher—principal—central office administrator—superintendent. One-third of all of the superintendents in cities of this size reported having proceeded through all the steps of this sequence. Twenty-seven percent of the superintendents in cities of 30,000-99,999 population also reported they were the products of this sequence. For this size community this percentage was exceeded only by the group whose pattern was teacher — principal — superintendent. Thirty - seven percent came through this progression.

In the smaller communities the teacher—principal—superintendent pattern is much more common. The following are population groups and percentages of superintendents who followed this progression.

Population of School District	Percentages
10,000-29,999	58.1
5,000- 9,999	61.4
2,500- 4,999	60.0

HOW DO SUPERINTENDENTS GET THEIR JOBS?

Let us now look at matters commonly called "recruitment and selection." In this section we are concerned with how the superintendent got started, how he was placed in the positions he has held, why he thinks boards of education chose him, what he thinks about certification, and finally some self-perceptions of how Mr. Superintendent enjoys his job.

Beginning Interest in Administration

In obtaining data on the question of why the respondent became interested in educational administration, an open-end check list was used. The superintendent could check as many items as he desired on a nine-item list and then could write in whatever else he felt moved to write.

The most frequently mentioned reason for entering administration was that it offered higher salaries. There is little doubt that higher salaries was a potent incentive since it was reported by *80 percent* of the superintendents. Superintendents in the smaller communities reported "higher salaries" even more frequently than did those from larger districts. The second most frequently mentioned reason was that administration offered a better opportunity for service (67 percent). It may be that this reason was checked to salve consciences since its frequency followed the first-ranked rather closely. "Enjoy being a leader" was mentioned next with 54 percent. The fourth most frequently mentioned reason was "received encouragement from other administrators." The interesting thing about this one is that while it was mentioned by 54 percent of all the respondents, it was reported by 81 percent of the superintendents in cities of over a half million population. The frequency of this factor declined in proportion to the population group and was reported by only 42 percent of the men in the smallest districts.

The other reasons for entering administration, in order of frequency of mention, were as follows: received encouragement from board of education, received encouragement from college teachers, had administrative experience in other fields, did not enjoy a subordinate role in education, and shortage of administrative personnel in region.

Learning About Open Positions

The superintendents in the study were asked to indicate the three most valuable sources of information about openings in school administration on a check list and to rank these in order of importance. The rankings were then weighted and there appeared to be two sources of job information which far surpassed all others. The most valuable source was college placement agencies and the second most valuable, "informal information passed on by fellow administrators." The third most valuable source, which had less than half the weighted value of the second source, was letters and announcements from boards of education. The remaining sources in order of their mention were salesmen, college professors, commercial placement agencies, and state education department placement agencies.

Superintendents in cities of over half a million reported a different evaluation of sources of information concerning new positions. They ranked "letters and announcements from school boards which have a vacancy" highest, followed by college placement agencies.

Fewer superintendents responded to this question than to any other question. The over-all response was from three-fourths of the sample; however, only one-third of the superintendents in the largest cities reported their most valuable sources of information for new positions.

Number of positions applied for. It has been assumed by many that superintendents have many irons in the fire and constantly apply for other jobs. According to the response this is not so. Almost three-fourths of the men reported that they had not applied for a single post in the past five years. The number not applying was highest in the population group from 100,000 to 500,000, where it was 95 percent. It was lowest (58 percent) in the smallest communities. Six men reported that they had applied (unsuccessfully) for nine or more positions in the past five years. The practice of indiscriminately applying for superintendencies does not appear to be widespread.

Reasons for Appointment

Why did boards of education select the respondents for posts as superintendents? Each superintendent was asked to give three reasons on an open-ended question as to why he thought boards of education had selected him over other candidates for the positions he has held. One reason was reported far more often than any other. Seventy-nine percent wrote that they were selected because of their "record of past experience, reputation, and/or ability." The next most frequently reported reason was listed by only 41 percent—it was "educational background and training." Superintendents see themselves being appointed because of superior ability, reputation, experience, and training. Other reasons reported by from 25 to 12 percent of respondents were: recommendations—college, university, and other; personality traits, e.g., leadership, energy, enthusiasm, recognition of own limitations; community understanding, public relations ability; character traits, e.g., integrity, maturity, judgment, stability, industry; philosophy or program of education; understanding of children and youth.

It is interesting to note that while we are constantly told that the superintendency exists only as a service to the instructional program and that an understanding of children is of prime importance, this was given as the reason for appointment by only

12 percent of the men. As a reason it was reported only enough times to warrant a rank of seventh on a list of 11. The board of education in Riverdale (Chapter I) found much the same thing true of the candidates they interviewed.

Reasons given by fewer than 10 percent were impression made at interview or in methods of application; knowledge of some specific phase of school administration; physical characteristics, e.g., age, health, appearance, et cetera; and willingness to accept salary. The last reason was given by 5 percent of the respondents and was not restricted to the smaller communities.

These self-perceived reasons for appointment to the superintendency make a very revealing list. It appears that the men reported with candor and recognized the realities of life.

Most Important Qualifications

There have been several studies of the qualifications necessary for success in the superintendency. In fact, it is a favorite topic for doctoral researchers, and one can find lists of every sort of qualification imaginable if he will but look. In this study the superintendents were asked to evaluate each of 10 often stated qualifications on a scale ranging from "A"—Essential, to "B"—Important, to "C"—Of some small importance, to "D"—Unimportant. They were also asked to use the same scale in evaluating a list of topics of advanced study. The contribution of this study lies in the national sample (which is rare in studies of superintendents) and in the careful statistical treatment of the responses. Again, it should be pointed out that we are here considering self-reported, self-perceptions of these qualifications and one should not assume that there is any empirical evidence to justify their rankings.

Qualifications by population. A list of 10 qualifications was submitted to each superintendent and the rankings were compared in two ways: one by the population of the school district and the other by level of preparation. In computing rankings the following weights were used: Essential—4; Important—3; Of some small importance—2; and Unimportant—1. The range of rankings was from a high of 3.84 to a low of 2.53. The way in which the superintendents ranked the qualifications is extremely interesting and should alarm those who are responsible for the training and certification of school superintendents. That which is held as essential to the superintendency by certification agencies (teaching experience) is ranked very low by the superintendents, while other qualifications rarely developed in training programs and never asked for in certification have top billing.

When comparing the rankings of qualifications by the size of school district administered, we find one qualification ranked far ahead of the others.[4] In fact, *every* superintendent in cities of over half a million population placed this qualification first, and practically all of the superintendents in districts of other sizes did likewise. The top qualification as perceived by superintendents was the "ability to see the whole picture—each problem in its broader context." This skill is called *conceptual* in the literature. It has been indicated by several researchers to be an essential skill to successful administration and was here reported by American superintendents to be of most importance.

An "unusual understanding of people" was ranked second and an "unusual ability to live with a high-pressure job" ranked third, followed by secondary school administrative experience. Secondary teaching experience and "ability to handle the many technical aspects of the job" tied for fifth place. "High intelligence" was ranked seventh, with elementary school teaching experience eighth, and elementary school administrative experience ninth. Central office administrative experience was ranked tenth and lowest on the list although it is difficult to understand how this experience could help but contribute to conceptual skill. See Table 4.

Although there were few variations by population groups, "high intelligence" made a most intriguing showing. This qualification was ranked fourth by the superintendents in the largest cities but was ranked successively lower until the superintendents in the smallest communities ranked it ninth! "Ability to handle the many technical aspects of the job" also revealed an interesting pattern. The superintendents in the smallest communities ranked this qualification rather high (tied for third), but it was ranked successively lower by each population group, with one minor exception, until those in the largest cities ranked it seventh. A clear-cut difference occurred in ranking "central office administrative experience." Superintendents in cities of

---

[4] Item and group effect are both significant beyond the 1 percent level of confidence so that differences reported are not due to chance variations.

over half a million ranked this sixth, but all others ranked it tenth—no doubt because the majority lack sizable central office staffs. Teaching experience was also ranked differently by population groups. Elementary school teaching experience was ranked lowest in importance by superintendents in the largest cities, but it was ranked progressively higher as size of school system decreased until it was ranked seventh in the smallest districts. Secondary school teaching was considered somewhat more important, being ranked ninth by those in the largest cities and increasing irregularly to fifth by those in the smallest districts.

4 IMPORTANCE OF CERTAIN QUALIFICATIONS FOR THE SUPERINTENDENCY

RANK	QUALIFICATION	WEIGHT
1	2	3
1	Ability to see the whole picture—each problem in its broader context	3.84
2	Unusual understanding of people	3.69
3	Unusual ability to live with high-pressure job	3.51
4	Secondary school administrative experience	3.21
5.5	Secondary school teaching experience	3.17
5.5	Ability to handle the many technical aspects of the job	3.17
7	High intelligence	3.07
8	Elementary school teaching experience	3.00
9	Elementary school administrative experience	2.92
10	Central office administrative experience	2.53

Qualifications by preparation level. A superintendent's perception of the importance of the various qualifications does not vary much according to his level of preparation, provided he has at least a master's degree. Superintendents were categorized as to whether they had earned a doctor's degree, 60 hours beyond the bachelor's, a master's degree, or a bachelor's degree. The opinions of those with a bachelor's degree differed in several respects from those of their fellow superintendents with higher degrees. They regarded elementary school teaching and administrative experience as much more important than did those with

45

more preparation. (Each was ranked 4.5 by bachelor's degree holders as against eighth by other superintendents for teaching and ninth for administrative experience.) On the other hand, the bachelor's degree holders considered secondary teaching and administrative experience to be less important than did those with more preparation. The only other difference of any consequence was on the item "high intelligence," which was ranked fourth by those with doctor's degrees, while those with less preparation ranked it eighth.

Most Important Fields of Study

What fields of study do superintendents feel to be most important? In order to get an estimate of their perceptions, a list of 20 fields of study was prepared. Standard terms such as "school finance," "group dynamics," and the like were used, and an opportunity was offered for write-ins. While the terminology used is standard, it is standard in a peculiar way. Everyone uses the general terms, but uses them to cover different specifics. So we cannot be certain as to what actual content superintendents feel to be most important. The rankings were calculated by the same procedure used to obtain data on qualifications for the superintendency.

Fields of study by population. There was surprising consistency in the rankings by the six population groups. Two of the 20 items were ranked exactly the same by each group, and the largest variation in ranking of any one item was five-and-a-half places (which occurred only once). The five most important fields of study were school finance, curriculum, public relations, human relations, and school business management. It can be seen that of the first five only one deals with what is commonly considered an "educational topic," that is, a topic directly related to the instruction of children. The next five most important fields were personnel administration, administrative theory and practice, school plant planning, philosophy of education, and teaching methods. Since the topics ranked ninth and tenth are commonly considered "educational," we find a total of three items, within the first 10, which are directly related to education. Items ranked 11th to 15th were psychology, research, group dynamics, economics, and sociology. The five fields to which superintendents attached least importance were history of education, political science, mathematics, adult education, and physical science. See Table 5.

Fields of study by preparation level. There was remarkably little variation in the rankings of fields of study by preparation levels. Only one field, human relations, had a variation of five places, and this occurred between the group holding the doctor's degree and those with 60 hours beyond the bachelor's.

5 IMPORTANCE OF FIELDS OF STUDY TO THE SUPERINTENDENCY

RANK	FIELD	WEIGHT
1	2	3
1	School Finance	3.74
2	Curriculum	3.67
3	Public Relations	3.65
4	Human Relations	3.55
5	School Business Management	3.54
6	Personnel Administration	3.51
7	Administrative Theory and Practice	3.39
8	School Plant Planning	3.38
9	Philosophy of Education	3.27
10	Teaching Methods	3.25
11	Psychology	3.14
12	Research	3.00
13	Group Dynamics	2.89
14	Economics	2.62
15	Sociology	2.61
16	History of Education	2.52
17	Political Science	2.42
18	Mathematics	2.30
19	Adult Education	2.24
20	Physical Science	2.14

Certification

How many superintendents hold a certificate in administration? What kind of certificates do they hold? How long did it take to get certified? What do they think about certification? These were the questions to which we sought answers.

47

Number certified. Almost 93 percent of the superintendents responding to the questionnaire held certificates in administration. The superintendents in the smaller districts (under 100,000) held certificates to a greater extent than did those in the larger, and the percentage dropped to 78 in the largest cities.

Of those holding certificates practically all (only three exceptions) held a certificate for general administration. A wide range of additional certificates were also held; however, no single certificate was held by more than 14 percent of the superintendents. The conclusion as regards certification is quite obvious. Superintendents generally hold a certificate and it is the one appropriate for the superintendency. They do not appear to "collect" other types of administrative certificates.

Certification and job placement. Of those superintendents holding certificates, how many were appointed before being certified and how many were certified first? Fifty-nine percent of the superintendents held an administrative certificate prior to obtaining their first position. Of this number slightly more than half waited less than a year before gaining their first appointment. Slightly over 80 percent gained their first administrative post within two years of obtaining their certificate. For the remainder, time dragged on, so that eight men reported that 11 or more years elapsed between gaining their certificate and their first administrative position.

Looking at the other side of the coin, the men who took an administrative position and then got their certificate, time lags of considerable duration were noted. Some 41 percent of the superintendents took a position prior to certification. Slightly over a quarter of these had their certificate within a year, while the remainder, at a decreasing rate, took times up to and in excess of 14 years to obtain the certificate. In fact, 25 men reported taking 14 or more years.

Opinion of certification. The opinion of superintendents as regards certification was obtained from a seven-item check list on which they could check as often as they liked. Only half of the superintendents believed that their state's certification requirements were satisfactory as they stood. Thirty-one percent felt that more training should be required for certification. Only two men said that there should be less training. The number favoring more training was remarkably large considering the nature of the sample. Another large percentage, some 21, said the training should be of a different type. Sixteen percent also felt that more teaching experience should be required than is currently the case. This rating should be considered in contrast to the low rating given to the value of teaching experience for the superintendency. With only half the group satisfied with current certification requirements, there would seem to be cause for considering revision of state standards.

Self-Evaluation

Do superintendents consider themselves well prepared for their jobs? How do superintendents keep informed on the latest developments in educational administration? How many are planning to continue study in administration? There has been considerable interest of late in the in-service development of school administrators. The Cooperative Program in Educational Administration has fostered programs in all of its centers, and the AASA through its many activities has focused on this problem. So, too, have the many state and local associations and the area school study councils.

How well prepared? When the aggregate answer to the question, "Do you consider your present level of professional preparation adequate for your present position?" is examined, it gives one reason for serious thought. Slightly under three-fourths of the men reported they thought themselves adequately prepared for their present posts. The answers fluctuated to some extent depending upon the size of the school district, with those in the largest districts believing themselves best prepared and those in the 10,000 to 30,000 population class giving the lowest percentage of "yes" answers (66 percent).

When those who thought they were not adequately prepared were queried, they checked a variety of reasons for not undertaking further study. "Can't get time off" was the reason most frequently cited. The frequency of this answer corresponded directly, with one exception, to the size of school district, with 100 percent of the respondents in the largest districts giving this reason, decreasing to 46 percent of those in the smaller districts, with the over-all percentage standing at 64. "Feel I am too old" was the next most frequent response with 30 percent and "can't afford the cost" next with 24 percent. Some 14 percent were currently planning to take work while 7 percent said, "Although my present preparation is inadequate, it wouldn't be improved by further study."

Learning about new developments. The superintendents were asked to list two or three of the most valuable sources of information concerning new developments in school administration. Two major sources were reported with frequencies which far exceeded all others. "Professional reading: periodicals, textbooks, and research" was rated tops by 90 percent, followed by "professional meetings and workshops (other than state department, colleges and universities, or AASA)" at 78 percent.

No other factors came close to the frequency of mention of reading and meetings and workshops as sources of information about new developments. Activities sponsored by colleges and universities were credited as valuable resources by 23 percent, followed by membership in professional organizations, which was mentioned by 18 percent. The AASA, the Committee for the Advancement of School Administration (CASA), or state administrator associations were mentioned by 16 percent. State education department activities were noted by only 8 percent of the superintendents, although 11 percent of those in the smallest districts mentioned these activities. Three men rated school board meetings as their most valuable source of information about new developments in school administration.

When asked if their school districts had an outstanding program of in-service training for administrators, only 21 percent answered "Yes." It is doubtful whether undue modesty can explain away this low frequency of affirmative answers. As would be expected, outstanding programs were reported with greater frequency in the larger districts.

Would They Do It Again?

Whenever superintendents gather there is much talk about the rigors of their life. Some love to say they work in "ulcer mills," that if they had it to do over again they would choose some calmer, less precarious mode of living. Is this really the way superintendents feel about their work? Several questions were asked bearing on this point.

Superintendents were first asked, "If you had it to do all over again, would you choose educational administration?" They were asked to check a five-point scale and did so as follows:

"Certainly would"—54 percent; "Probably would"—33 percent; "Uncertain"—6 percent; "Probably would not"—5 percent; and "Certainly would not"—1 percent. See Figure II.

This certainly does not seem like a job that men are running away from! Further, it is clear that the larger the district the more enthusiastic the superintendent is about choosing administration as a life career. The percentage checking "Certainly would" rises from 49 for the smallest district to 67 for the largest. It should also be noted that no superintendent in the over half a million population districts checked either of the "would not" categories.

FIG. II   WOULD SUPERINTENDENTS CHOOSE EDUCATIONAL ADMINISTRATION AGAIN?

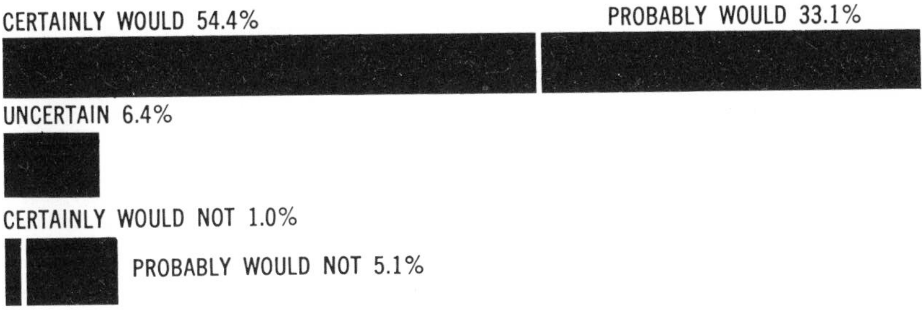

CERTAINLY WOULD 54.4%   PROBABLY WOULD 33.1%

UNCERTAIN 6.4%

CERTAINLY WOULD NOT 1.0%

PROBABLY WOULD NOT 5.1%

When men were asked if they had ever held an educational position which they enjoyed more than the superintendency, slightly over a third answered, "Yes." The percentage of "yes" responses was somewhat greater in the smaller districts than in the larger. The position most frequently mentioned as more enjoyable by the one-third was classroom teaching, which was listed by 54 percent of the group. Here again, the larger frequencies were in the smaller districts. The only other position mentioned by more than 10 percent of those who enjoyed another job more than the superintendency was the secondary school principalship. Other answers ran the gamut.

The men who said they enjoyed another position better than the superintendency were then "put on the spot." They had to respond to the question, "Everything considered—pay, professional status, community prestige, et cetera—do you now wish

51

you had stayed in the other field of work?" Eighty-one percent answered "No."

It seems clear that generally speaking those who are superintendents want to stay superintendents! It might do the profession a lot of good if this attitude were made public and we could tell the world that here is a group of men in public education who are there because they want to be and because they really enjoy it.

STEREOTYPES IN RETREAT

What has this survey revealed about the superintendents of American urban school systems? The least that can be said is, "More than has ever been known before." It is clear now that many of the stereotypes of superintendents are not true, that the clichés do not hold. Much of what has been discovered should be reassuring to the people of America for whom the superintendents administer our schools.

Among the interesting and important findings of this study are the following:

Superintendents are less mobile than is commonly thought.

The mean time in present position is nine years.

Superintendents were born in families larger than the average and were first children more than would normally be expected.

The median salary is $10,700.

Less than one-fifth of the superintendents majored in professional education in undergraduate school and one-seventh minored in education. Superintendents have a strong undergraduate preparation in the modern liberal arts.

School finance is considered by superintendents to be their most important field of graduate study and physical science, the least important.

Men are beginning their graduate work in administration at an earlier age now than previously.

Superintendents average five years and seven months in graduate preparation.

Approximately 21 percent of the urban superintendents hold doctor's degrees.

The median reported net cost of a doctor's degree is $4400.

Superintendents are generally satisfied with their graduate preparation.

The major strength of graduate programs is thought to be a good faculty. The major weakness is considered to be instruction which is too "ought" oriented.

In the smaller communities the conventional career pattern is teacher—secondary school principal—superintendent. In the larger communities the conventional career pattern is teacher—secondary school principal—central office administrator—superintendent.

Higher salaries are the prime reason given for entering administration.

Conceptual skill is the quality rated highest by superintendents.

If superintendents had to do it over again they certainly would choose school administration as a career.

chapter III

The Current Scene: Professional Preparation

What kinds of preparation programs are there in the colleges and universities at the present time? We have heard much of the Cooperative Program in Educational Administration and of the revitalizing influence it has had on our colleges and universities. One would expect rather widespread use of newer methods of teaching such as the internships, the use of cases, field work, and the like. One would also expect to find greater emphasis on research and the findings of research. While we have no bench mark from whence to measure progress, we might profitably look at preparation programs to see if expectations have been met.

In order to obtain the basic data for this chapter a unique procedure was used. First, 302 colleges and universities which were presumed to have programs for the preparation of school administrators were identified. The Commission then invited selected superintendents of schools to participate in the study. Each was asked to take a questionnaire to a specific institution, to contact appropriate individuals there, and have the forms filled out. The superintendents were instructed to make certain that the completed forms were legible, that all questions were answered, and that the data were as valid as possible. An unbelievable 97 percent return was obtained. Of the 293 returns, 251 indicated programs of preparation in educational administration.

The Commission is indebted to D. Richard Wynn, associate professor of education, and Mary Emerick, graduate student, Teachers College, Columbia University, for the analysis of the data reported in this chapter.

Even though this study was done with considerable care, the content of the questionnaire was of such a nature as to make it very difficult to get reliable data. For this reason, conclusions from the data will be presented in a very conservative fashion.

In describing the programs of preparation in our nation's institutions we shall first discuss standards for admission to the programs; next, what is taught—with the strengths and weaknesses of the curricula; and finally, the major problems faced by colleges and universities in the improvement of the preparation of school administrators.

ADMISSION TO PREPARATION PROGRAMS

On what basis are candidates admitted to programs for the preparation of school superintendents? Are the admission requirements stringent and exacting, or can anyone able to pay tuition be admitted? Are the requirements for programs for the preparation of superintendents different from requirements for those seeking to be principals? Are the criteria for selection valid; that is, are the criteria that are used the best that research has turned up? What would the colleges do differently if they could do what they wanted?

Specific Requirements

The most common requirement for admission to a program of preparation for the superintendency is teaching experience; the next, a teaching certificate; and the third most common, a bachelor's degree of any variety. The frequency with which each was mentioned is as follows:

ADMISSION REQUIREMENT	TYPE OF PREPARATION PROGRAM			
	MASTER'S	SIXTH YEAR	DOCTORATE	TOTAL
Teaching experience	37	10	46	93
Teacher's certificate	32	7	33	72
Bachelor's degree (any type)	35	6	29	70

Since these data were gathered by means of an open-end question, it is not possible to determine percentages. The omission of a requirement does not necessarily mean that a program does not have it.

As in many parts of this study, the responses on this question ran to extremes. Whereas the vast majority of those requiring a bachelor's degree would accept any degree, two institutions require a specific type. One requires a bachelor's degree in education; the other, a liberal arts degree without education course work.

Many institutions have requirements in terms of undergraduate grade averages. The most common average required is "B", although grade averages ranging from "C" to "B+" are acceptable at one or more of the institutions. Many institutions allow a "dry run" if the grade average is not met by the candidate. The student takes a number of courses (two to six), and if his marks meet a standard he is admitted. These courses do not count toward the degree being sought at most of the "dry run" institutions. Other institutions whose applicants do not meet the required grade point average administer a standardized examination such as the *Graduate Record Examination*. A sizable number of institutions (30) reported that they required "acceptable grades," but did not specify what was acceptable.

Forty-eight programs of preparation reported admission requirements consisting of a definite number of credits in undergraduate preparation courses. This number varied from six to 33 semester-hour credits.

A number of other devices are used in the admission of candidates to programs of preparation. Interviews were reported by a surprisingly small number of institutions. Although at least one major study, that done at the Harvard Business School, has demonstrated that the interview is not worth much for selection purposes, one would expect it to be used more than has been reported. "Recommendations" are used by a sizable number (34). In most cases a recommendation is solicited from the chief administrator where the candidate is employed. Numerous studies have demonstrated the unreliability of recommendations, yet they continue to be used. It is another example of the ease with which expediency so often conveniently overcomes reason and rationality.

"Faculty committee action" is necessary before a candidate can be admitted to 18 of the programs reporting. A semester of acceptable graduate work is required by one institution, while a "screening course" is a prerequisite to four programs. A few institutions demand evidence of good health and good character.

Examination requirements of various sorts were reported by several programs, with the *Graduate Record Examination* and the *Miller Analogies Test* being the ones most frequently mentioned. The following statement from one university indicates the extensive testing in effect there:

> Admission to the doctoral program requires passable scores on the *Ohio State Psychological Test*, the *Minnesota Multi-Phasic Personality Inventory*, a general culture test, a written English proficiency test, *Strong Interest Inventory*, and a general educational background examination that is both objective and essay.

As was the case with most institutions which reported the use of tests for admission purposes no cut-off points were given, nor was there any indication as to how the test results were used.

A typical pattern of admission procedures appears to be the one which was in use at Boston University. Although the pattern is now in the process of revision, the procedure is described here to illustrate what appears to be average practice. The requirements for admission at Boston were reported as:

> Three years experience as teacher, recommendations, satisfactory prior academic record, satisfactory score on scholastic aptitude test, satisfactory completion of an introductory course—experience combining instruction with personal-vocational guidance.

Few of the respondents indicated that their programs of selection were particularly strong or that all who applied would not at least be given a "dry run." However, a midwestern institution made a report which should be taken to heart by all colleges and universities in the country:

> The Graduate Council admits only the strongest students with the strongest personalities to graduate school administration, especially to study for the small town superintendency. One-third of the applicants for graduate study are refused admission because of lack of intellectual capacity and attainment. More than half of the admitted applicants are refused admission to study in school administration. Those students who are admitted to graduate study in education, but not for study in school administration, are urged to prepare for teaching careers.

Special Situations

In stock market parlance a "special situation" develops when a set of circumstances is present that predisposes a company's stock to rise in value. The study revealed some procedures at colleges and universities which the Commission believes will bear fruit in terms of good administration in the future. These admission procedures are not recommended to everyone to adopt *in toto,* but they should be studied by all institutions.

Selective criteria for admission. The Administrative Career Program at Harvard University is an example of a training plan based on careful advance testing to insure greater-than-usual selectivity of students. Developed with Kellogg funds, it has been in operation since 1952. It was reported that:

> Admission to the Program is limited in any one year to a small group, including (1) men and women already established and experienced in educational administration, and (2) those with little or no administrative experience who are nonetheless regarded as persons of administrative promise. The Harvard Master of Education for General Purposes degree or its equivalent is prerequisite to admission. . . . Students planning a program of specialization ordinarily must have had two to three years of successful teaching experience. Some experience in educational administration is desirable but not mandatory.
>
> All candidates will ordinarily be required to take the *Aptitude Test* of the *Graduate Record Examination.*

A variation on the Harvard plan was developed at Teachers College, Columbia University. Here, a small number of students (approximately 12) were selected each year. While they were awarded scholarships and student assistantships, they were not given a special program but took their work along with the 600 selected in a conventional manner. These students were selected through a lengthy procedure. Letters were sent to Teachers College graduates holding administrative positions throughout the country. They were asked to nominate persons considered to have an outstanding potential for administration. A list was then compiled and each person nominated was sent a letter explaining how his name was obtained and inquiring as to whether he was interested in coming to Teachers College to do graduate work in educational administration. All those replying affirmatively were then invited to test centers throughout the country. A Teachers College professor was present at each center and he interviewed each candidate and administered a battery of tests. At one time, the battery included the *Teachers College General Examination,* which is given to all who apply for admission; however, the special candidates scored so high on this test that the *Graduate Record Examination* was later substituted. Students selected in this way have tended to be highly intelligent and have done very well academically in their graduate work. Not enough time has elapsed to note their professional success.

Phased admission. A different approach to admission is that which is being used at the University of Buffalo. Here students are "admitted" at the end of each "phase" of the program. As more information is gained about a student, a better judgment can be made regarding his administrative ability. A description of the phased program at Buffalo follows:

The core program in educational administration divides into three phases. Phase I is a two semester course meeting for six clock hours one day each week. Its major focus is the systematic study of a school system on a contract basis under faculty supervision. Frequent field visitations are made in the progress of the study. A final report is published for the benefit of those concerned with the school system and as a summary of the activity of the class on this project. Seven such reports have been published to date.

Phase II is the second core experience in the new program. It is a two semester course meeting six hours, one day each week. Students are expected to have completed Phase I and additional study in education and related social sciences prior to entering this part of the program. Case studies are used as a major vehicle. Individual research is also done by students on topics of administrative importance.

Phase II students also meet in weekly seminars in their areas of specialization. Seminars are presently conducted in elementary school administration, secondary school administration, general administration and the administration of programs in health, physical education and recreation. It is anticipated that seminars will be added in school business management and administration of vocational education.

Phase III is the culminating core experience in the new program. Prior to entering Phase III the student is expected to take advanced courses in various administrative areas such as school law, public school finance and school plants as well as advanced work in social science research methods and philosophy of education. Students accepted participate in a detailed systematic study of a school system. Regular class meetings are supplemented by several weeks of intensive full-time field work.

What Colleges Would Like To Do

Following the questions on present practice in selection, institutions were asked: "Assuming more applicants than you can accept, list (in a general order of importance) the qualifications and experiences you would weigh in making your selections." The purpose of this question was to determine what selective devices would be employed if conditions approached the optimum more closely than they do now. One might expect the colleges to suggest selection criteria of a more rigorous nature than they are now using, and indeed, this is just the way they responded. The responses did not indicate that if conditions were improved they would do anything different, but they would do *more* of the same old thing. The following 10 criteria were most frequently reported:

TYPE OF ADDITIONAL ADMISSION REQUIREMENTS IF CONDITIONS IMPROVE	MASTER'S	SIXTH YEAR	DOCTORATE	TOTAL
1. Academic Record	88	12	57	157
2. Successful Teaching Experience	75	4	36	115
3. Leadership (general evidence, administrative position)	49	9	42	100
4. Recommendations (usually employer)	48	7	26	81
5. Satisfactory Personality	39	3	33	75
6. Successful Experience	32	10	31	73
7. More Tests (unspecified)	26	4	33	63
8. Determine Nature of Student's Motivations, Goals, Values, Etc.	16	9	11	36
9. Ability To Work with People	17	3	15	35
10. Unspecified Intellectual Criteria	18	5	8	31

TYPE OF PREPARATION PROGRAM

In view of the fact that research on the selection of educational administrators has been barren of results, it is difficult to pass judgment on the admission requirements listed above. Many of them seem of such a nature, e.g., "Satisfactory Personality," that one wonders why they are not in use regardless of the conditions now existing. Perhaps it is unfair to raise the question, but are colleges and universities now admitting candidates with unsatisfactory personalities? In considering the added intellectual requirements which would be considered under happier circumstances, one is struck by the apparent offhandedness of the responses. If one actually wished to determine the intellectual ability of the candidate, a standard measure such as the *Graduate Record Examination* could be applied with ease; yet it was mentioned with low frequency. While "Academic Record" was mentioned most frequently, what would be looked for in the record was not clear—the obvious inference is higher grades.

Several criteria which are considered in the literature of administration to be worthy of consideration were mentioned by a few of the institutions. Among these were emotional maturity and stability, health, communicative ability, character, and broad scholarship. With the exception of "character" these are all relatively easy to determine and have both face validity and research backing.

In looking at the picture of admission to programs in educational administration, one should not be too critical of present practice. The situation now is the same as it was in 1957 when Hall and McIntyre said:

> All researchers who have studied the problem of leader selection—be it in education, industry, government, or the military—are agreed on one point: No "answer" has been found.[1]

It does appear, however, that we have more knowledge about selection than we are using. We are using devices of expediency which are easy to administer yet have never been related to success in the superintendency.

Admission requirements for the superintendency are not different from those for the principalship. The more rigorous entrance requirements exist at those institutions where the doctorate is given. In these institutions, students are generally obliged to meet the requirements for admission to the graduate school, and this appears to have a beneficial effect.

The newer developments in admission practices are relatively few in number and include "phased" admission and "high" selection for a few students.

There appears to be little doubt that more research is needed as the basis for the selection of students to be prepared for the position of school superintendent.

PRESENT PREPARATION PROGRAMS

In Chapter VII of this yearbook there is detailed a program for the preparation of school superintendents which, while somewhat idealized, is fully within the capabilities of any adequately organized and financed institution. This program calls for a comprehensive selection process, a core of integrated administrative content, specialized work in the superintendency, support-

---

[1] Hall, Roy M., and McIntyre, Kenneth E. "The Student Personnel Program." *Administrative Behavior in Education.* (Edited by Roald F. Campbell and Russell T. Gregg.) New York: Harper and Brothers, 1957, p. 403.

ing courses in professional education, courses in other disciplines to insure a broad cultural background and acquaintance with the behavioral sciences, an internship, and field work. This content is to be taught using varied methods such as cases, simulated situations, lectures, discussions, and the like, by a competent staff which has adequate secretarial and clerical help and financial resources.

But, before we can evaluate proposed changes in preparation programs, we need to know where we are now. What constitutes a typical program at the present time? What are considered by the respondents to be the strengths and weaknesses of present day programs? What are the programs which now seem to be the closest to the ideal? To what extent do the colleges and universities approach this ideal at the present? These are the questions which the Commission deals with in this section.

Course Requirements

The respondents to the questionnaire were asked if there was a common core of subjects or courses in educational administration required for prospective superintendents. While a large number of institutions were reported to have "cores," a closer examination of their offerings indicated that no confidence could be placed in the responses. The word "core" was interpreted to mean anything from an integrated experience to a set of discrete courses required for state certification.

The "core" at different levels. It was possible, however, to discern the titles of the courses in programs of preparation at the different levels such as master's degree, sixth year, and doctorate. These courses are listed in Table 1 by the titles given by the respondents although, of course, this tells little about the content in each course.

Several conclusions can be drawn from the data on the opposite page. The assumption is made that Table 1 contains the course work that is considered to be most important by the institutions reporting. With this in mind it appears that the most typical program for the master's degree would contain the eight ingredients listed in Table 2.

The courses given in the sixth-year program appear to be much the same as those given in the master's program. The courses listed in Table 3 tend to be required by more institutions on the doctoral level than on either of the two lower levels.

1 MOST COMMON ELEMENTS OF CORE PROGRAMS*

		TYPES OF PROGRAMS			
RANK	DESCRIPTIVE COURSE TITLES	MASTER'S	SIXTH YEAR	DOCTORATE	TOTAL
1	2	3	4	5	6
1	Organization and Administration (General)	94	14	57	165
2	Supervision (General, Secondary, or Elementary)	83	14	47	144
3	Curriculum (General, Secondary, or Elementary)	65	12	39	116
4.5	Social Foundations (including Philosophy of Education)	35	9	39	83
4.5	School Finance	42	11	30	83
6	Research	43	6	19	68
7	School Law (General or State)	34	8	24	66
8	Psychological Foundations (including Human Growth and Development)	34	5	24	63
9	Tests and Measurements, Evaluation	20	5	20	45
10	Guidance	20	5	15	40
11	School Plant	17	6	16	39
12	School Community Relations	19	5	13	37
13	Field Experiences	11	2	9	22
15	Business Administration	6	3	8	17
15	Current Issues, Problems, Trends	10	2	5	17
15	Personnel (General)	6	2	9	17
17	Introduction to Graduate Study	9	1	5	15
18	Thesis (Master's)	13	—	—	13
19	Personnel (Pupil)	5	1	6	12
20	Federal, State, and Local Relations	—	1	6	7
21	Personnel (Staff)	3	—	3	6
22	Case Studies	—	1	3	4

* "Core" is used very loosely to mean anything from an integrated experience to a set of discrete courses. Also note that the totals are given as *programs*, not institutions. Some institutions have two or three programs.

2 TYPICAL COURSES IN MASTER'S DEGREE PROGRAMS

Organization and Administration (General)	Finance
Supervision	Research
Curriculum	Law
Social Foundations	Psychological Foundations

The courses in the core of the preparation programs do not measure up to the program which the Commission advocates in Chapter VII. The core as an integrated experience exists in very few institutions. The absence of internships and the sparsity of field experiences are alarming. After all the discussion of the importance of *people* in administration, it is distressing to

3 COURSES REQUIRED MORE FREQUENTLY ON DOCTORAL LEVELS

Personnel (General)	Federal, State, and Local Relations
Advanced Seminar	Personnel (Pupil)
Business Administration	Case Studies

note that Table 1 is void of a title such as Human Relations, Interpersonal Relations, or their equivalents. There is also a complete lack of course titles referring to theory of administration. The courses currently offered do not reflect, in their titles or patterns of titles, the ground swell of change which is evident in the field of administration.

Additional courses required or recommended. In addition to the core, each respondent was asked to report additional required or recommended professional courses. The responses to this question were very interesting and confirmed the interpretation that the "core" reported by many constituted all of their required courses. Thirty-nine programs reported the absence of any additional professional courses required or recommended, 106 gave no response or unusable responses, while 74 reported "Yes," but said the courses were varied or left them unstated. This is the place where the newer developments might be recorded since it appears that most of the courses were recommended rather than required. Table 4 lists those courses recommended or required by 20 or more programs.

In order to estimate which courses a superintendent in training would be most likely to have been exposed to, Tables 2 and 4 were combined in Table 5, to show the 10 content areas *most* frequently offered. This gives a picture of the courses required and recommended together with the required core courses.

The important finding revealed by the data in Table 5 is that there is little difference in the course titles in any of the three level programs. There are some variations in the frequency of

4   ADDITIONAL PROFESSIONAL COURSES REQUIRED OR RECOMMENDED

		TYPES OF PROGRAMS			
RANK	TITLES	MASTER'S	SIXTH YEAR	DOCTORATE	TOTAL
1	2	3	4	5	6
1	School Finance	26	4	61	91
2	School Plant	20	4	44	68
3	School Law	18	4	37	59
4.5	Organization and Administration (General)	20	8	19	47
4.5	Philosophy of Education	14	5	28	47
6.5	Curriculum (General)	18	3	23	44
6.5	Psychological Foundations	12	4	28	44
8	Personnel	7	4	31	42
9	Research	15	2	23	40
10	Guidance	15	3	20	38
11	Organization and Administration (Elementary and Secondary)	16	4	16	36
12.5	Supervision	19	2	11	32
12.5	Tests and Measurements (Evaluation)	12	5	15	32
15.5	Current Issues and Problems	11	2	16	29
15.5	Other Social Foundations	6	4	19	29
17.5	Advanced Seminars	5	8	13	26
17.5	Curriculum (Secondary and Elementary)	7	—	19	26
18	Statistics	12	2	10	24

course offerings. For instance, Finance has a rank of two in doctoral programs and four in master's degree programs; Supervision ranks two in the master's and seven in the doctoral; Social Foundations fluctuates; Research drops from five in the master's to 10 in the doctorate; and School Plant moves up in frequency from the master's to the sixth year to the doctorate. Personnel is taught with the lowest frequency in all but the doctoral programs where it is ninth in rank.

5 COURSES REQUIRED AND RECOMMENDED FOR THE PREPARATION OF SCHOOL ADMINISTRATORS

DESCRIPTIVE COURSE TITLES	TYPES OF PROGRAMS AND THEIR RANK ORDER			
	MASTER'S	SIXTH YEAR	DOCTORATE	TOTAL
1	2	3	4	5
Organization and Administration (General, Elementary, Secondary)	128 (1)	26 (1)	92 (1)	248 (1)
Curriculum (General, Elementary, Secondary)	90 (3)	15 (4.5)	81 (3)	186 (2)
Supervision	102 (2)	16 (3)	58 (7)	176 (3)
School Finance	68 (4)	15 (4.5)	91 (2)	175 (4)
Social Foundations (including Philosophy of Education)	55 (6)	18 (2)	76 (4)	159 (5)
School Law	52 (7)	12 (6)	61 (5)	125 (6)
Research	58 (5)	8 (8.5)	42 (10)	108 (7)
Psychological Foundations (including Human Growth and Development)	47 (8)	8 (8.5)	52 (8)	107 (8.5)
School Plant	37 (9)	10 (7)	60 (6)	107 (8.5)
Personnel (Staff and Pupil)	21 (10)	7 (10)	49 (9)	77 (10)

It is difficult to draw conclusions from Table 5 because the titles have varieties of meaning. Just what "Organization and Administration" encompasses is anyone's guess. One can observe the remarkable similarity between courses at the master's and the doctor's levels and wonder. The lack of widespread use of course titles such as Human Relations, Administrative Processes, or Administrative Theory is indicative of the lack of program revision in recent years.

Over 100 institutions reported that they required courses outside the field of professional education. There was a great diversity of courses named, none with a frequency greater than five. Most of the respondents did not name courses, but said the requirements were variable, although there were many references to the "social" or "behavioral" sciences. There are two possible interpretations of these data. One is that there is careful guidance of each student and that each is being directed to take courses to remedy his weaknesses. The other is that the professors of educational administration, not knowing what their students should study, are sending them to the social scientists on a helter-skelter basis. In either case it appears that what is needed is to work out the essentials in the social sciences for school administrators and to develop a program containing these essentials.

Internships

Probably the most lauded development in the preparation of school administrators in the past 10 years has been the internship. One would expect that the use of the internship would be quite general by now and would be widely reported in this study. Since the questionnaire did not contain a definition of an internship (see Chapter VII for the one acceptable to the Commission), one cannot be certain that all those reporting an internship program actually had one. In fact, it appears as though any type of field activity was reported as an internship. Thus, the total of 56 shown in Table 6 represents a figure which is probably considerably inflated. But even if it is an accurate count, the situation is discouraging, for 56 represents less than one-fifth of the programs in the country. It appears that for the nation as a whole, the learning of administration is still a bookish chore.

6 NUMBER OF PROGRAMS HAVING INTERNSHIPS

| | TYPE OF PROGRAM | | |
MASTER'S	SIXTH YEAR	DOCTORATE	TOTAL
1	2	3	4
14	8	34	56

Number of Students

There has been much speculation as to the number of graduate students in school administration. Each institution was asked to report the number of full-time students and the number of part-time students. The results are tabulated in Table 7.

It can be seen that the range of enrollments is very great. Full-time student enrollments range from zero to more than 200, while part-time enrollments vary from three to 700. The very large number of programs with few students is striking. Taking 25 as a break point, let us see what the enrollment picture looks like. (There is no empirical justification for 25, but one might reasonably ask what kind of program can be given to fewer than 25 full-time students. For instance, what kind of program could a medical school offer if it enrolled fewer than 25 students?)

A total of 244 programs (not institutions) responded to the question concerning full-time students, of which 215, or 88 percent, have 25 or fewer full-time students. A total of 237 programs reported number of part-time students, of which 46, or 19 percent, have 25 or fewer part-time students. There appear to be far too many institutions with small enrollments in the business of preparing school administrators.

One of the New England universities, in response to the question, "What is your major strength?" answered in a way that should be given serious thought by the multitude of small programs throughout the country.

> I don't think our program has strength. On the other hand, I don't think it needs improvement. We are in an area crowded with universities. In one of our studies we found that there are 25-30 open superintendencies in these six New England states annually and at least 15 universities offering courses which would lead to certification.
> We would like to encourage more centralization and more cooperation in this field.

A total of 1306 students completed a program for the preparation of a school superintendent in 1957-58. The number certified would, no doubt, be much larger. Three states have no certification requirements for administrators, and the majority of states have requirements considerably lower than the requirements of the preparing institutions. As an example, the certification requirement in New York calls for 30 semester hours of courses, yet all of the major institutions in the state have 60-hour programs of preparation.

7 NUMBER OF FULL-TIME AND PART-TIME STUDENTS ENROLLED IN PROGRAMS OF PREPARATION FOR SCHOOL ADMINISTRATION

NUMBER OF PROGRAMS ENROLLING FULL-TIME STUDENTS					NUMBER OF PROGRAMS ENROLLING PART-TIME STUDENTS			
TYPE OF PROGRAM				NUMBER OF STUDENTS	TYPE OF PROGRAM			TOTAL
MASTER'S	SIXTH YEAR	DOCTORATE	TOTAL		MASTER'S	SIXTH YEAR	DOCTORATE	
1	2	3	4	5	6	7	8	9
53	7	4	64	0	3	—	—	3
38	5	16	59	1- 5	3	—	1	4
18	3	13	34	6- 10	2	1	—	3
7	3	15	25	11- 15	5	1	4	10
7	1	6	14	16- 20	10	—	2	12
5	1	13	19	21- 25	11	1	2	14
7	—	13	20	26- 50	38	5	10	53
—	—	3	3	51- 75	12	3	14	29
1	—	2	3	76-100	15	2	4	21
1	—	1	2	101-200	25	4	21	50
1	—	—	1	201-300	6	2	15	23
—	—	—	—	301-400	1	1	4	6
—	—	—	—	401-500	—	—	4	4
—	—	—	—	501-600	1	—	3	4
—	—	—	—	601-700	1	—	—	1

Scholarships, fellowships, and part-time work. Of the 1306 who completed programs of preparation in 1957-58, 420 had received a scholarship or fellowship. This is slightly under one-third of the graduating number. The attempt to ascertain how much money was received by students was not very successful. Most of the respondents failed to report the amount of the scholarship or fellowship. Of the 86 who did report, the range was from under $100 to $5564, with a median of $900.

Of those graduating from a program in 1957-58, 329 did some sort of work for which they were paid. Amount of reimbursement was rarely noted as was the case with scholarships and fellowships. The stipends of only 66 were reported, ranging from under $100 to $3000, with a median of $1000.

Forty-eight institutions reported that some of their students received financial aid from a school district. This is 19 percent of the 258 colleges and universities responding to this question.

It is clear that aid of the order now being given is no great inducement to enter graduate study in school administration.

Examinations

Several questions were asked about the nature of final evaluations of graduates of programs for the preparation of school superintendents. One question asked if a "test of performance" were given. While 65 programs reported using such a test, the interpretation of the test varied so much that the returns are not of much value. Twenty-five programs indicated that they considered the practicum or the internship as tests of performance. The following description of a performance test now being used appears to illustrate a desirable direction.

> Performance in an administrative role is normally the terminal element of the Program. It involves an individual administrative responsibility equivalent to at least three-quarters of a semester's work, involving major responsibility in defining, planning, developing, and carrying out a significant administrative task. This project normally comes toward the end of the candidate's period of study; thus far, in most cases, it is being conducted in the school system in which the candidate is employed following his period of residence study in Cambridge.

Major Strengths

The Commission was interested in knowing what the colleges and universities saw as their major strengths. Respondents were asked to list and describe briefly courses, seminars, workshops, field experiences, internships, and other elements thought to be strengths. Table 8 summarizes the reported strengths.

It is interesting to note that field experience, other than the internship, ranks highest (reported by the most programs). Where such experiences are part of the training of superintendents they have, apparently, been found to be very valuable.

It should also be pointed out that the strength reported with second highest frequency was workshops, conferences, and other types of in-service work for practitioners. This is an acknowledgment of the fact that a program for the preparation of superintendents cannot be effective unless it makes ample pro-

8 MAJOR STRENGTHS OF PROGRAMS OF PREPARATION

STRENGTHS	TYPE OF PROGRAM			TOTAL
	MASTER'S	SIXTH YEAR	DOCTORATE	
1	2	3	4	5
Field experiences for students other than internships, particularly of the action research variety	34	6	43	83
Workshops, conferences, and other types of in-service work for practitioners	30	9	35	74
Superior faculty	38	5	21	64
Internship program	21	5	25	51
Core program or well-balanced, well-integrated program	22	2	26	50
Good relations with neighboring schools and professional associations	19	6	24	49
Specific courses cited	22	2	23	47
Seminars	20	3	19	42
Close student-faculty relations, good individualized advisement, etc.	19	3	18	40
Interdisciplinary work or support of other divisions of the institution	5	2	27	34
High standards of admission	14	2	14	30
Problem or need-centered curriculum	18	1	5	24
Flexibility in student programming	9	1	12	22
Other research opportunities for students	8	—	14	22
Use of practitioners as instructors	10	9	2	21
Bureau or institute of field studies or services	4	2	14	20
Good research services	4	2	13	19
Small classes	6	2	11	19
Good laboratory facilities (curriculum, statistics, etc.)	3	1	7	11
Good library	6	1	4	11
Study councils	—	—	9	9
Student participation in conferences, workshops, etc.	—	—	8	8
Case work	2	1	4	7
Emphasis on improving instruction	—	—	7	7
Number and variety of specializations within the faculty	—	—	6	6
Use of distinguished visiting professors	5	—	1	6
Good student orientation	—	—	5	5
Part-time student body	4	1	—	5
Emphasis on administrative behavior	—	—	5	5
Work in theory of administration	—	—	5	5
Aptitude and final exams	3	1	1	5
Requiring two years of advanced study for superintendents	—	—	3	3
Extension program	—	—	3	3
Program not differentiated by area of specialization	1	—	2·	3
Operational research, i.e., study, experimentation and evaluation of own program	1	1	1	3
No residence requirement	—	—	2	2
Nothing outstanding	8	—	—	8
No response	2	—	—	2
Unusable response	11	—	1	12

71

vision also for the improvement of superintendents on the job. Not only does this help the in-service superintendent, but it improves the pre-service preparation of the student and keeps the professor informed as to problems and developments in the field. A good example of such a program is the one under way at Teachers College, Columbia University, where a professor has been assigned full time to develop workshops, seminars, and conferences for practicing administrators. To date there have been activities in school-community relations, problems of large cities, three-week superintendents' workshops, elementary and secondary school principals' seminars, business officials' workshops, and the like.

The high ranking of "superior faculty" calls for some commentary. Almost two-thirds of the institutions citing superior faculty as a strength were master's degree programs. Some cited full-time faculty while others cited part-time faculty as one of the reasons for the faculty being superior. It is apparent that there is no unanimity as to what makes a faculty "superior." This is a point which could stand much more study.

A few of the strengths reported are puzzling, to say the least. How "part-time student body," and "no residence requirement" can be construed as strengths is rather difficult to understand. The relatively large number of programs which cited the use of practitioners as instructors is also cause for concern. If the practitioners are used to supplement full-time professors in the teaching of a well-integrated set of experiences, this could be a strength, but if the practitioners teach discrete courses in an uncorrelated program, it is inconceivable that this could be a strength.

New developments. Several strengths in the newer aspects of school administration were noted, but practically all of these were in doctoral programs. Some of these strengths were "emphasis on administrative behavior," "case work," and "theory of administration."

A description of the "Seminar on the Nature and Problems of Administrative Behavior" given at the University of Oregon illustrates one type of newer development in the field. The seminar is staffed by five professors from different disciplines.

The purpose of this seminar is to assist advanced graduate students in administration to develop a perspective on the human relations involved in administrative situations. Faculty members from the fields of business administration, political science, psychology, and education are brought together for the purpose of providing orientations to administrative situations from different points of view.

A case-study approach is employed. The analysis of each case is made through group discussions, in which the faculty and student members of the seminar participate. The emphasis is placed upon each person's sharing in the analysis of each case, in order to develop a sound approach to administrative problems. Each student is expected to prepare a case report from his own administrative experience.

The Administrative Career Program at Harvard University is one which incorporates a large number of the elements reported by the institutions in this study. The description from Harvard states:

> The Administrative Career Program was early described as one designed to provide opportunities for study and training for candidates of unusual administrative promise. In entering upon this Program, the School turned sharply from past practice. The Program is based upon the assumption that significant training for administrators implies *acting* upon problems, rather than only studying or contemplating them. It is felt that such action should involve responsible and purposeful behavior on the part of the student as a member of a group committed to the conduct of a task, in a real situation, pertinent to improvement of administration of education. Through such a test of learning "under fire," the candidate may gauge the realities of organized human activity in the administrative realm and deepen his understanding of productive working relationships. Administration is viewed broadly: the administrator is not simply a technical executor, but also a judge of values and frequently a determiner of policies.

Pattern of the Program

> The core of the Administrative Career Program initially consisted of a series of units involving study and clinical field work in areas of the social sciences and administration. In the course of the initial five-year experimental period, this core was successively modified under the prompting of experience. It moved from a pattern of core elements—such as case studies, social science research and studies, administrative problem seminars, field study—in which not one of these predominated, to a pattern revolving primarily around joint faculty-student responsibility for the professional study of a school system under formal contract. Although all of the original core elements remain, the major focus of learning during the main block of time in a year of residence study is the fulfillment of the study contract initiated with the Center for Field Studies by a school system in response to a felt need for assistance.

Fall and Spring Time Blocks

> A unit devoted to analysis of problems in educational administration, together with study and readings in theory and practice of administration.

A unit devoted to study in various aspects of sociology and social relations relevant to school administration.

A sequence of studies of cases in educational administration and of concepts in various fields of knowledge and thought which emerge as significant in the consideration of cases.

For those administratively less experienced: assignment to two administrative posts on a part-time basis, one during the fall and the other during the spring.

In partial completion of work toward the Certificate of Advanced Study, each candidate will write the Certificate special-field examination on a stated day in the spring.

Initial and final phases of participation in contractual study of a school system.

Intermediate Time Block

This is the major period of faculty-student contractual study of a school system along the lines already indicated. This study becomes the core of the Program during this period.

Weaknesses

The same procedure used to gather data on strengths in preparation programs was followed to gain information on weaknesses. Returns were so varied and multitudinous that they were grouped into four tables.

Instructional program. Table 9a deals with the instructional program. The most frequently mentioned weakness is the lack of a good internship. Either no internship at all or a limited intern program was mentioned by respondents of 92 programs. This is an understandable weakness and probably should have been reported by a larger number of colleges and universities. While good field experiences topped the list of strengths, its lack was noted as a weakness in 42 programs. Thus the two most commonly mentioned weaknesses have to do with "in the schools" activities—the on-the-job experiences which the Commission encourages. In comparing the list of strengths with the list of weaknesses, it appears as though the colleges and universities agree to the value of the internship and field experiences yet have not been able to find ways of putting them into operation.

In reviewing Table 9a, it is obvious that most of the weaknesses conceivable have been reported. Some, such as "geographical factors," appear to be unremediable. Others, such as "better research opportunities for students needed," "poor relations with public schools," and "poor cooperation with rest of university" are problems which should be tackled on a local basis.

9a WEAKNESSES REPORTED IN INSTRUCTIONAL PROGRAM

	TYPE OF PROGRAM			
WEAKNESSES	MASTER'S	SIXTH YEAR	DOCTORATE	TOTAL
1	2	3	4	5
No internship or limited internship program	50	9	33	92
Field or laboratory experiences inadequate	23	3	16	42
Gaps in program or narrow curriculum	30	1	9	40
Segmented program, or poor order and sequence of courses	7	1	12	20
Better research opportunities for students needed	9	2	5	16
Only a summer or part-time program	13	1	1	15
Better interdisciplinary support needed	4	1	8	13
Should offer six-year program	10	—	3	13
Too few students	9	1	2	12
More and better seminars	6	1	3	10
Program still too new and undeveloped	4	—	5	9
Should offer doctorate	1	5	2	8
Students' lack of background in general education	4	—	3	7
Poor cooperation with rest of university	0	0	6	6
Geographical factors	1	1	3	5
Need a department of educational administration	2	1	2	5
Need a core program	1	1	3	5
More flexibility in programming	3	2	—	5
Lack of adequate in-service program	1	1	3	5
Classes too big	3	1	1	5
Inadequate theoretical base for program	4	—	—	4
Need operational research on own program	0	0	3	3
Poor relations with public schools	2	—	1	3
Lack of emphasis upon graduate program in the institution	2	—	1	3
Should make better use of practitioners	—	—	2	2

Student personnel services. The second set of weaknesses were tabulated under the heading of student personnel services. The institutions with doctoral programs reported more weaknesses in this area than did the master's degree programs. This should probably be interpreted as evidence that the doctoral programs are more critical of themselves.

9b WEAKNESSES REPORTED IN STUDENT PERSONNEL SERVICES

	TYPE OF PROGRAM			
WEAKNESSES	MASTER'S	SIXTH YEAR	DOCTORATE	TOTAL
1	2	3	4	5
Need better selection of students	17	3	22	42
Part-time or summer student body inadvantageous	12	5	22	39
More scholarships and other forms of student aid	9	1	18	28
Poor student advisement	7	—	10	17
Better recruitment of students	6	2	4	12
Need more student assistantships	5	1	5	11
Too few students	2	—	8	10
Poor evaluation of students	5	—	3	8
Student body is too inexperienced	4	1	—	5
Need follow-up	2	—	2	4

The most frequently mentioned weakness is in student selection. Since this is a problem which has not yet been solved, it is little wonder that it heads the list. Many more institutions should have reported it. A large number mentioned the part-time or summer school student as a weakness. This, too, is a problem which has not been solved. If the colleges and universities continue to struggle along with few full-time students, they will never develop adequate internships and field experiences. The part-time student is much more of a weakness than the frequency of mention indicates, because many of the instructional program weaknesses are traceable to part-time students. This also involves the lack of funds for assistantships and scholarships mentioned in both Tables 9b and 9c.

9c WEAKNESSES REPORTED IN FUNDS AND FACILITIES

	TYPE OF PROGRAM			
WEAKNESSES	MASTER'S	SIXTH YEAR	DOCTORATE	TOTAL
1	2	3	4	5
Poor facilities, general	8	3	4	15
Poor research facilities	5	1	11	17
Poor field services	3	2	11	16
Poor library	3	2	3	8
Poor laboratories	1	1	6	8
Poor equipment	4	—	4	8
Poor lab school, or none	1	1	2	4
Lack of funds, general	5	1	5	11
Lack of money for research	3	—	7	10
Low faculty salaries	3	—	4	7

Funds and facilities. One would expect more weaknesses to be reported in this area than was the case. There were fewer weaknesses reported in this area than in any other as a look at Table 9c will demonstrate.

Staff. The weaknesses mentioned under the heading of staff reveal that, seemingly, the greatest problem is that there are too few professors, with a resultant heavy load. The other major

9d WEAKNESSES REPORTED IN STAFF

	TYPE OF PROGRAM			
WEAKNESSES	MASTER'S	SIXTH YEAR	DOCTORATE	TOTAL
1	2	3	4	5
Numerically inadequate/heavy load	16	5	19	40
Difficulties of part-time staff	13	2	5	20
Staff too small to specialize	5	2	5	12
Little opportunity for research	1	1	4	6
Lack adequate secretarial help	—	1	2	3
Need money for travel expenses	—	—	2	2
Not doing creative teaching	—	—	2	2

weakness deals with the problems involved in working with part-time staff. At two universities it was reported that the staff was "not doing creative teaching."

Of all the "weaknesses" mentioned, one, more distressing than the rest, should be shared with the reader: "Our building was condemned as a public hazard and torn down. The interim finds us without space."

Faculty Experience in the Superintendency

What percentage of educational administration faculties have had experience in the superintendency? Table 10 reveals the percentage of faculties having experience in the superintendency. For example, 28 master's, one sixth-year, and two doctor's programs have professors with no experience as school superintendents. On the other hand, six programs at the master's and five at the doctor's level have faculties on which 91-100 percent have had experience as superintendents. In comparing master's with doctor's programs, it is noted that 50 percent of the master's programs have faculties on which 23 percent or fewer have had

10 PERCENTAGE OF FACULTY WITH DIRECT EXPERIENCE AS SUPERINTENDENT

PERCENT	TYPE OF PROGRAM			TOTAL
	MASTER'S	SIXTH YEAR	DOCTORATE	
1	2	3	4	5
0	28	1	2	31
1-10	8	3	3	14
11-20	31	1	6	38
21-30	17	4	16	37
31-40	17	4	12	33
41-50	16	6	17	39
51-60	5	1	5	11
61-70	6	—	12	18
71-80	7	—	4	11
81-90	1	—	1	2
91-100	6	—	5	11
No response or unusable	8	—	3	11

superintendency experience, whereas 50 percent of the doctor's programs have faculties on which 43 percent or fewer have had superintendency experience. No sixth-year program has a staff with more than 60 percent who have had superintendency experience.

Conclusions are difficult to draw from these data. An adequate program of preparation should draw upon a number of professors for whom superintendency experience is not at all necessary. Among these are those who teach philosophy or psychology of education, or statistics. However, it does seem that *every* program should have at least one professor with experience as a superintendent if for no other reason than to provide a "live specimen" for observation by students. Actually, the reasons for having a person with such experience are multitudinous and need no eloquent statement of justification. In view of the criterion of "at least one," it is discouraging to note that 31 faculties have no former superintendents.

IMPROVING PROFESSIONAL PREPARATION

The real purpose of this study of colleges and universities is to gain information upon which to base improvements. This study has established bench marks so that in the future we can look back and note the progress made. Only a token contribution to progress can be made by describing the *status quo;* definite recommendations must be made and action suggested in order to move ahead. Respondents to the questionnaire were asked to indicate what they thought the major deterrents were to progress, and given the funds, facilities, and staff, what measures they would take to improve their programs in educational administration.

Major Deterrents

On this question respondents were asked to check a list of six deterrents and were also asked to write in additional ones they thought important. Table 11 reports the results.

It can be seen that the deterrent most frequently reported is lack of funds, and it might well be the reason behind the next most frequently mentioned deterrent, "shortage of trained per-

11 MAJOR DETERRENTS TO PROGRAM IMPROVEMENTS

	TYPE OF PROGRAM			
DETERRENTS	MASTER'S	SIXTH YEAR	DOCTORATE	TOTAL
1	2	3	4	5
Inadequate funds	101	16	76	193
Shortage of trained personnel	47	10	31	88
Shortage of buildings and facilities	45	10	31	86
State certification requirements	36	3	20	59
Resistance of staff members and college to change	10	1	25	36
Lack of close relations with school systems	19	2	9	30

sonnel." Colleges and universities are having a difficult time competing with the rising salaries in the public schools.

Of the deterrents written in, none had a frequency of more than nine and these could generally be classified as weaknesses (and do appear in the section devoted to that topic). It was reassuring to note that 10 programs reported "no deterrents."

Desired Improvements

The question was asked, "Given the funds, facilities, and staff, what would you do to improve your program in educational administration?" Forty-six different improvements were suggested, and the range of frequency of mention was from one to 157.

The respondents identified a great many improvements to be made. This is in sharp contrast to the answers given to the question of how selection procedures could be improved. It should be recalled that the institutions reported nothing new, but rather that they would do more of what they were doing. A different picture is presented regarding improvements. One of the goals of the profession should be to obtain the funds to bring about the desired improvements. Those that were mentioned 10 or more times are to be found in Table 12.

12 IMPROVEMENTS WHICH WOULD BE MADE IF CONDITIONS WERE OPTIMUM

		TYPE OF PROGRAM			
RANK	IMPROVEMENTS	MASTER'S	SIXTH YEAR	DOCTORATE	TOTAL
1	2	3	4	5	6
1	Initiate or improve internship program	93	12	52	157
2	Provide more financial aid for students	36	8	36	80
3	Undertake or improve research program	32	7	34	73
4	Undertake or expand field services, study councils, field studies, etc.	26	7	34	67
5	Provide better in-service program for administrators	29	3	12	44
6.5	Broaden curriculum or fill in gaps in curriculum	23	3	12	38
6.5	Lighten faculty teaching load for research, field studies, etc.	16	5	17	38
8	Hire one or more full-time professors or add to staff	16	1	19	36
9	Improve selection of students	15	4	15	34
10	Undertake interdisciplinary work or improve coordination with other divisions of university	8	—	24	32
11	Offer sixth-year or doctoral program	15	5	5	25
12.5	Improve student recruitment	2	2	19	23
12.5	Provide better student advisement	11	3	9	23
14	Redesign program of studies to reduce segmentation	9	1	10	20
15	Improve library	12	3	4	19
16	Develop better relations with local schools	5	1	11	17
17	Improve buildings and equipment	9	—	7	16
18.5	Better placement and follow-up of students	6	3	6	15
18.5	Engage more consultants, resource people, etc.	10	—	5	15
20.5	Develop core program	4	1	8	13
20.5	Provide for more graduate assistants	3	3	7	13
22	Undertake year-round program	11	1	—	12
24	Establish curriculum laboratory	4	3	3	10
24	Expand or improve general facilities	2	2	6	10
24	Pay professors' expenses to meetings	7	—	3	10

The high frequency of the desired improvement, "initiate or improve internship program" is very significant. It was reported with a frequency of almost two to one over the next highest item. Those institutions which have tried the internship appear to be convinced of its value, yet disheartened by its cost. To institute an internship program at an optimum level requires a low professor-student ratio and an expense account to provide funds for the professors to visit the interns. All this is expensive, far more expensive than the usual classroom type of teaching. The internship poses a serious problem to the profession. Without doubt, it is expensive, yet it is a very valuable experience.

In the coming years an institution's willingness to undertake an internship program and to finance it at an appropriate level could well be the test of its existence. The internship is so important that it is the *sine qua non* of a modern program of preparation of educational administrators. If an institution cannot provide internship training, it should not be in the business of preparing educational administrators.

It is encouraging to note that "undertake or improve research program" was ranked as high as third. The need to improve research is urgent and the profession should move rapidly to make it possible to improve research and to initiate programs where there are now none. Several other improvements fit in with the desire to "undertake or improve research program." Some of these are "provide more financial aid for students," "undertake or expand field services," and "lighten faculty teaching loads." These improvements will aid other aspects of the preparation programs also, but they are essential to the prosperity of the research program.

All but 13 of the colleges and universities responded to this question, which is an indication that practically all see things they want improved. One college's response, however, indicated a relaxed attitude: "Everything is o.k. now."

FAR FROM IDEAL

Through the cooperation of superintendents and college personnel, an unbelievably high rate of response was obtained to the Commission's questionnaire. The 97 percent return meant that only nine institutions having programs of preparation failed to send their questionnaires back.

Admission requirements most commonly in use were teaching experience, a teacher's certificate, and a bachelor's degree of any variety. Recommendations were used by a sizable number of programs, while interviews, a faculty action committee, a "dry run," and an occasional use of evidence of good health and character were also reported. Standardized tests were used by some, but no cut-off points were given. The most promising new methods of admission were the highly selective plans of such institutions as Harvard, Chicago, and Teachers College, Columbia University; and the phased admission plan as used by the University of Buffalo.

It seems completely fair to say that the procedures generally employed by colleges and universities are *admission* rather than *selection* procedures. They are ways of getting students into preparation programs, but not on any discernible selective basis. Only a small handful of universities have anything resembling a selection program.

When reviewing the programs of preparation, one is reminded of Whitehead's discussion of the learned world.

> First-hand knowledge is the ultimate basis of intellectual life. To a large extent book-learning conveys second-hand information, and as such can never rise to the importance of immediate practice. . . . What the learned world tends to offer is one second-hand scrap of information illustrating ideas derived from another second-hand scrap of information. The second-handedness of the learned world is the secret of its mediocrity. It is tame because it has never been scared by facts.[2]

No statement ever conveyed the spirit of programs of preparation for school administrators more accurately or precisely. The programs appear to be bookish to the ultimate. What most programs need is to be thoroughly "scared by facts"—the facts of what administration is really like.

The mediocrity of programs of preparation comes from the sterility of methods reported. Instruction is classroom bound; administration is talked about rather than observed, felt, and in these and other ways actually experienced. Where the student should be "scared" by exposure to the facts of administrative life, he is instead bored by the tame fare of second-hand success stories. Where the student should be fattened by a rich diet of multidisciplinary fare, he is starved by the lean offerings of

---

[2] Whitehead, Alfred North. *The Aims of Education and Other Essays.* New York: Macmillan Company, 1929. p. 61.

provincial chow. Generally speaking, schools of education and departments of school administration have not found ways of bringing their students into contact with professors from other disciplines; they have not made use of the public schools as laboratories; and they have not revised preparation programs to include cases, role-playing, field study, simulation, or any other of a multitude of techniques.

Full-time graduate study in school administration is relatively rare. When it does exist the numbers of students are so small as to cast doubt upon the validity of the idea that *bona fide programs* actually exist. Eighty-eight percent of the programs reporting had fewer than 25 full-time students. What kind of an offering can be given to fewer than 25 students?

No category of major strengths was reported by more than a third of the respondents. Field experiences and in-service work topped the list. The major weakness reported was the lack of an internship, followed by inadequate field or laboratory experiences. Other weaknesses were selection of students, part-time student bodies, lack of adequate financing, poor facilities, heavy teacher load, and problems of part-time teaching staff.

The major deterrent to the improvement of the preparation of superintendents is the lack of money. This is substantiated by the indication from the colleges that the things that would be added if conditions were optimum are the expensive ones such as the internship. The seriousness of the financial problem cannot be emphasized too much. At present, only a few can afford a program such as the Commission advocates. These few can raise sufficient funds only through hard work and the utmost of diligence. Where the 75 or so institutions which are needed to prepare the number of superintendents required will get sufficient funds to do the job is the problem now facing us.

This chapter has revealed the rather dismal montage of the preparation of school superintendents. There is a shocking discrepancy between what the Commission recommends in Chapter VII and what exists at the present time. Without doubt, if the investigation of the colleges and universities could have been carried on at a more intensive level, the discrepancy would be even greater. The professional preparation of school superintendents is badly in need of complete overhauling.

chapter **IV**

The Current Scene:
In-Service Education

There is "no rest for the weary" in school administration. Even after experiencing the best preparation program, the school administrator cannot rest on his "Doctor of Ed" and take comfort in having "arrived." There can be no self-congratulation by anyone that he knows enough to do his job well forever; for change in school administration is inevitable, even as it is in the instructional program itself. If we are to presume a competence to guide, direct, support, challenge, yes inspire, we must set aside the notion that administrative devices that worked in 1940 or 1950 will automatically and routinely work today.

To be the profession that our public resolutions and our private assertions describe us to be, we must identify anew the essential materials and knowledges of our profession. The college president cannot, for example, be an able scholar of oriental languages, and at the same time have full command of the swiftly evolving processes of nuclear fission. Nor can the superintendent of schools be expert in the techniques of word attack at grade one and know the intimacies of the amoeba at grade nine or ten. He must, instead, be broadly competent in basic educational principles, and possess high faith in others and the skill to release and guide their creativity. His is at once a lifting, supporting function, and a guiding, challenging function. But the function is *administration* as distinguished from production; *executive*, as distinguished from operational.

We shall confine ourselves here to an examination of in-service education as related to the school administrator *as an administrator*. For, while educational leadership has come to mean an embracing of many competencies which relate to school buildings, teaching, psychology, curriculum, public relations, and finance, we must at some time deal with the administrative role *itself* as an instrument for activating and articulating the many components of the education complex.

Role conflicts in educational administration are perhaps most clearly seen in the college presidency, but the problem is equally acute—and in many ways closely similar—for school superintendents.

For example, on the college scene, when the successful and highly regarded presidents of five distinguished colleges (among many others) chose last spring to separate themselves from the chief executive role, *McCall's* magazine took unhappy note: "From top positions in the educational hierarchy these five men say they have had enough." Harold Dodds, ex-president of Princeton sums it up: ". . . in the minds of a good many people the job is becoming unmanageable, and something must be done about it." [1]

Woven through the many critical observations about the school administrator is the implication that they are becoming managers instead of scholars, public relations men instead of teachers. Whether or not the criticisms hold up in all cases, we have good reason to examine ourselves as professional persons, and to scrutinize what we are doing to keep ourselves professionally fit for the tremendous duties we have assumed. It may well be that the words *management* and *public relations* are indeed increasingly relevant to good administration and are not naughty words at all. It need not necessarily follow that these terms are incompatible with *scholarship* and *professionalism*.

A good definition of administration is the one advanced by Arthur Schlesinger: ". . . the true test of an administrator may be, not his ability to design and respect organization charts, not his ability to keep within channels, but his ability to concert and release the energies of men for the attainment of public objectives. It might be argued that the essence of successful administration is: first, *to acquire the ideas and information*

---

[1] Anne W. Langman "Why are College Presidents Resigning?" *McCall's* 86:64-65; 134, 137-39; May 1959.

necessary for wise decisions; second, to *maintain control* over the actual making of the decisions; and, third, to *mobilize men and women* who can make the first two things possible. . . ." [2] The italics in the foregoing quotation are the Commission's. They speak succinctly the message of this chapter: The administrator, through continuous study, keeps informed of the advancing art and science of education, and keeps himself fit for his behavioral role in leading others.

THE NEED FOR IN-SERVICE EDUCATION

This leads to a basic assumption of this Commission: To retain professional effectiveness, stature, and dignity, the school administrator must continue steadfastly to improve himself; to remain abreast of, often sharing in, innovations; to create for himself a disciplined program of in-service advancement. If he does not do this, swift-changing situations and expectations from the community and the faculty will pass him by. Evidence to be presented later in the text reveals that school administrators in general are ready and willing to accept change, and to contribute actively to its processes, given the opportunity. Hence, we approach the following hypothesis: The superintendency is a profession; it rests upon a dynamic body of information; school administrators want to fulfill their professional obligations of continued learning and growth through one or another instrument of in-service study.

This chapter examines the opportunities presently available to the school administrator for extending his own professional growth — and weighs the worth and effectiveness of these resources. Chapter VIII proposes changes in some present arrangements for in-service education and suggests some new approaches.

APPRAISAL OF IN-SERVICE OPPORTUNITIES

We are, of course, fundamentally a learned profession. If one doubts this, he has ceased to be an educational leader. For, indeed, we must admit that teaching, of all things, is a learned

---

[2] Schlesinger, Arthur M., Jr. *The Age of Roosevelt.* The Coming of the New Deal, Vol. II. Boston: Houghton Mifflin Co., 1959. p. 522.

profession; and if we are to presume to lead teachers we cannot deny the obligations of intellectual discipline that accompany the privilege. We then may well ask, what intellectual disciplines? What resources for in-service growth? We have many, some well used, some not.

The paragraphs which follow describe the resources to which the school administrator may presently turn for the improvement of his own effectiveness. If the observations in some cases are less than benevolent, we must keep in mind that the writers of this book are speaking of themselves, if not of their colleagues in administration.

Without attempting any chronology or ranking of in-service opportunities, we shall list them as they come to mind. There is no particular significance attached to the order of listing.

The National Professional Association

One of the purposes of the American Association of School Administrators is clearly and specifically the furtherance of the professional competencies of school executives. Its publications probably are among the most thoughtful, carefully planned, and broadly representative writings in our specialized field. Typically, each year four or five significant publications in book, brochure, or pamphlet form are published by AASA, aimed precisely and specifically at the improvement of the administrator. Some may, of course, miss the mark. There is reason to doubt, however, how carefully the materials are read, and, more important, how seriously they affect the behavior and beliefs of the readers. These problems are faced by all groups which must rely on the mass media rather than direct, personal contact.

Another function of AASA, treated more specifically below, is the Association-sponsored drive-in conference. This service is of particular value to rural and semi-isolated areas. Its potential as a major in-service instrument for growth is probably yet to be realized fully.

But of all of AASA's varied resources, administrators probably form their major impressions and derive their largest nourishment from the annual convention. This meeting, whether regional or national, draws not only the administrators of all kinds of educational institutions, but thousands of allied professional and business persons as well.

One must, obviously, count the AASA meeting as one of the universal resources for the in-service growth of the administrator. The nature of the growth, however, is likely to be in the direction of stimulation, reaffirmation and exposure to ideas, rather than a depth experience in an important concept of education. The vastness and comprehensive scope of the AASA meeting necessarily impose a surface treatment, assuming a subsequent follow-up in depth by the member.

Some people suggest that the AASA meeting could be redesigned to provide a narrow front with concentrated intellectual offerings in depth. One can conceive, for example, a convention devoted wholly to the field of mathematics, with all the assembled giants of numbers at hand to pour out knowledge over a period of four or five days. Or one can envision the central theme as child growth and development, an arena for the psychologists to draw and quarter each other before our eyes. But it is doubtful that the narrowing of the front would be successful. In the tradition of convention-going in the United States, we would probably find the meeting unrewarding, accustomed as we are to the broad spectrum of ideas and materials adapted to many passing interests and appetites.

One is motivated to do things for reasons important to him. How many school administrators relish eagerly—are motivated by—opportunities for deep intellectual development afforded by the annual convention? Let us admit, rather, that the motivation is one of pleasant anticipation of a needed change (a sea change if you will) having to do as much as anything with the mental health of the administrator. The convention offers a chance to renew old acquaintances, a casual chat with a placement officer or two (either in behalf of the folks back home or oneself), good food, drink, and lodging for a man whose timetable affords these pleasures but rarely. Fundamentally, the purpose is to enliven, enrich, and stimulate the school leader.

We rationalize warmly to the theme "Oh, the meetings are fine, but I get my real inspiration out of the bull sessions in the rooms." Let us observe that one does not have to go to Atlantic City and sit on a radiator in a smoke-filled room, squeezed between a poker game and a book salesman to find a companionable bull session on education. Recalling certain unhappy information from Chapter II, only 16 percent of the superintendents in the survey rated AASA and state administrator associations as among the more valuable resources for professional growth. On close reflection of past convention activities, one does not wonder why. We should not look to the convention for products which our motivations in attending exclude. The convention should, instead, leave the superintendent questioning, interested, charged with ideas. But he should go home to take the next, more demanding steps to further learning on his own. The convention, in other words, is a good platform for launching more specific and diligent in-service work "back home."

State Department of Education Leadership

There is no question but that education in a fair number of states is so organized and led as to provide excellent opportunities for in-service growth of superintendents through the state department of education. Highly qualified consultants, opportunities for state-wide committee membership, and visitations from teams of specialists in one field or another can be very effective resources. At this time, however, conditions of leadership, political arrangements, and policies differ so widely among states that we cannot assume this to be a universally reliable resource.

It is more in the realm of potentiality that this field offers one of the most fruitful possibilities for systematic in-service growth for superintendents. Unlike the large national association meeting, the state provides a relatively compact and uniform setting for an orderly and consistent program of learning. Having full-time staff members at state level, it need not rely on the voluntary services of busy men for organizational and planning chores as is the case in state and local professional associations mentioned later. We would do well to think further in this direction.

In passing, the Commission commends the present trend toward a larger professionalization of state leadership in education. Those states in which the chief state school officer is appointed by a state board of education, and where the professional staff at state level offers a respectable career, unrelated to the ebb and flow of politics, the pattern of in-service leadership is clearly superior to others. It is noteworthy that a resolution on this subject, adopted by the Council of Chief State School Officers in 1947, has apparently borne fruit. In 1947, 32 state chief executives in education were politically elected; eight appointed by the governors; and eight appointed by state boards of education. By 1959, with two new states to account for, only 23 were politically elected; five appointed by the governors; and 22 named by state boards of education.

In states where board appointment is the pattern salaries are higher, both for the chief state school officer and his professional organization; turnover is lower; and the systematization of in-service education is more clearly evident.[3]

Regional and State Professional Groups

To many superintendents this is one of the most valuable resources. Professional meetings and workshops, including drive-in conferences sponsored by area or national organizations, appear to be one of our very important instruments for increasing effectiveness. Undoubtedly, a number of things affect this device favorably. The immediacy of the meeting to home and its relative brevity probably remove the holiday temper that accompanies larger and more remote meetings. There seems to be a "no-nonsense, let's-get-to-the-issues" quality about such meetings that suggests a setting for high motivation for learning. The bull session cherished by the convention apologist can be reproduced in more effective surroundings at such a meeting in a variety of ways, not least of which are carpools, train or plane companions, luncheon visits, and the circumspect, close-to-home cocktail hour.

Typical of the regional and state professional groups described here are the following: state associations of school administrators; regional groups embracing county, township, or other convenient geographic units; metropolitan area groups; or the more formalized study councils sponsored by such groups. There come quickly to mind such examples as the Southern Fairfield County Superintendents in Connecticut, meeting monthly;

---

[3] From: National Council of Chief State School Officers. *Our System of Education.* Washington, D. C.: the Council, 1950. p. 20-21. "In each State there should be a non-partisan lay State board of education . . . broadly representative of the general public and unselfishly interested in public education, elected by the people in a manner prescribed by law. . . . It is desirable that the board select the chief State school officer on a non-partisan basis and determine his compensation and his term of office. He should serve as the executive officer of the board and head of the State department of education. . . . The primary function of the State department of education in relation to local administrative units should be to provide educational leadership, planning, research and advisory services."

the Chicago Area Superintendents' Round Table, meeting twice monthly; the Crawford Notch meeting in New England, gathering annually; the West Suburban Superintendents (Chicago) meeting on call.

Informal, Nonstructured Organizations

Perhaps one of the most effective group activities leading to professional growth for the superintendent is the semi-private, unpublicized, informal group. Commission members are acquainted with a number of such groups, some having a history of 25 years or more. Born of necessity, budgeted on a shoestring, administered with the least possible effort, such groups consisting of perhaps 20 to 50 members are not uncommon.

One such group, organized in the 20's, has met once a year for a Friday, Saturday, and Sunday session in March every year since its inauguration. A few "charter members" remain, but each year new blood is brought in. The same hotel has regularly afforded a room, about 20 by 30 feet, where the members sit around in shirtsleeves. Talk starts with little guidance; a moderator keeps order; the members argue, challenge, listen, make occasional notes, refute, document, and from time to time rise in enthusiasm to press an idea. These schoolmen have been doing it with rich fulfillment for 30 years.

Not much is required to start such a group. Ten or twelve men would be an excellent beginning. One meeting a year is sufficient. The Commission commends such arrangements and the results of such group effort.

Research Participation

There is, perhaps, no more effective intellectual discipline for an administrator than actual personal participation in a research activity covering teaching and learning in his own school system. In such activity one is compelled to inform himself on the literature of the subject and to design an experiment with care and vision, based upon a comprehensive knowledge of what he is about. The stimulation of the staff and the guidance of the research activity demand a knowing touch. True, its demands are heavy for the executive who must keep his many other houses in order. But there are rich rewards in terms of a personal satisfaction and a larger sense of fulfillment which accompany this kind of professional growth.

Closely allied to this resource for professional growth is the university-related study council. This device will be treated more fully later in the chapter.

Public Speaking

The school administrator is fair game for an infinite number and variety of speaking and writing obligations: formal and informal, deliberate and extemporaneous. This suggested in-service endeavor may overlap to a degree with participation in professional organizations. It is treated separately, however, since it implies a more individualized and specific responsibility for research, collection and collation of materials, diligent preparation, and thoughtful delivery.

Knowing he is vulnerable to the call for declamation from many quarters, and knowing his time for this phase of work is limited, the superintendent should accept only those invitations for public speaking for which he can conscientiously prepare. Only such addresses will earn the respectful ear of discriminating listeners. Only such addresses will add to his own in-service growth.

Learning from Teachers and Other Colleagues

Perhaps the most ready-made and rewarding in-service learning opportunity available to the administrator lies close at hand, often unseen, in the teachers possessed of special proficiencies in his own faculty. There are many things that administrators can learn about education from the distinguished teachers present in some measure in all faculties. There should be no reluctance to admit that virtually all teachers in a school system know more about *something* than the superintendent can ever know. The day is past in school administration (if it ever existed) when the chief executive was expected to know more than the subordinate about the specifics of every task performed in the schools.

There are many ways that the chief executive can learn from teachers. One way is through active, shoulder-rubbing, week-in-week-out participation in the work of a curriculum committee. This does not mean occasionally dropping in at meetings to "show the flag." The ubiquitous superintendent who feels that his brief presence is a leaven to the deliberations of the working staff not only exaggerates his own significance, but doubtless serves to delay and distract those charged with the task.

Another way to learn from teachers, of course, is to observe work in the classroom; this is inefficient in terms of *specific* in-service growth, unless the teacher intentionally designs a teaching-learning situation to demonstrate something in particular to the superintendent.

Probably the most profitable way for the superintendent to learn from the teacher is to find the quiet hour in a quiet place and ask honest, unembarrassed questions of wise and experienced teachers. This can happen in the superintendent's office on a Saturday morning or in the teachers' room, with chairs drawn up in a corner as the late afternoon shadows dim the room. It may occur over coffee after a friendly luncheon. Wise superintendents find many ways to learn from teachers. Incidentally, the product of such a communion flows not only to the superintendent. The teacher is generally a better person and a happier person for knowing she has been sought out for her wisdom and insight—if the seeking was genuine.

Cultural Activities

The school superintendent is one of the first to excuse himself from worthwhile opportunities for cultural growth, pleading "too busy." It is true that most superintendents are indeed too busy to engage as much as they should in cultural affairs. A sober assessment of the superintendent's community obligations is critically needed. Many of his "off-hours" tasks have accrued through historic precedent and tradition, until the total presents a forbidding burden. Membership in such worthy community groups as Boy Scouts, Girl Scouts, the Public Library, the Chamber of Commerce, service clubs, veterans organizations, church activities, fund drives, safety councils, and hospitals is often taken for granted. Unquestionably the affiliations serve an excellent public relations function for the schools, and no doubt the agencies prosper under the prestige of the superintendent's name. But the degree to which participation is expected and required, beyond the control of the superintendent to delimit, is unhealthy and in conflict with cultural opportunities.

Superintendents who find themselves "too busy" should find ways to delegate interesting and rewarding opportunities to others. We should keep clearly before us the idea that, by the nature of our work, we enrich the lives of others when we enrich our own lives through worthy cultural pursuits. Many creative outlets are available to most administrators. Study groups, theater, museums, concerts, religious or philosophical discussion groups, important television offerings, and art are among the obvious resources. We cannot, as professional leaders in the world of culture, afford to divorce ourselves from the mainstreams of art and creativity.

University Teaching

One of the most satisfying disciplines that the superintendent should not find himself "too busy" to undertake is an occasional teaching assignment. Often there is a shortage of qualified instructors on the graduate or undergraduate level in a nearby college or university. As the demands for post-secondary teachers increase, the increased opportunity for administrators to lend a hand will follow.

Confronting a class of alert, mature, and professionally well-read students in a classroom is no child's play. The superintendent, for all his experience and his well-worn procedures and principles, finds that he must re-examine what he believes, organize it, and document it if he is to pass it on with effectiveness to others. He must also bring his own bibliography up to date and learn his way again among the library stacks. He cannot conduct a graduate seminar as a "how-to-do-it" show, nor can he rest on the practical cliché, "This is the way it worked for me in East Overshoe."

But the joys of teaching, which in nearly all instances the administrator has known, come swiftly back. He gets chalk on his coat cuffs again, he disciplines himself again through careful preparation, and he relives the deep satisfaction of lifting up a willing student.

University Offerings

When one thinks of in-service professional growth, the image most likely to come first to mind is the formal graduate school.

In treating this subject as an in-service resource for the school administrator, we shall consider only those offerings not related to pre-service and formal preparation. Chapter III criticizes the present preparation program, Chapter VII proposes a new design, and Chapter X analyzes obstacles to setting a new design in motion.

Hence this appraisal shall be limited to the role of the university in directions other than those offered in the catalogue. The continuing growth of the superintendent within the evolving curricular design for advanced degrees is the broad message of this yearbook and of AASA's membership requirements. Society and our profession have come to expect continued graduate study in its formal sense as the obligation of leaders in education. Learning, then, is essential to a learned profession.

Universities are, by definition, communities of scholars. Those scholars concerned with the advancement of public education can be deployed advantageously for school administrators in patterns other than the formal university classroom. Assuming that the school superintendent will, by and large, fulfill the legal and professional expectations in formal study, he can and should remain in close communion with the graduate schools serving his area.

Listed below are at least four devices for keeping the path between the practicing administrator's office and the university well traveled.

The cooperative study council. Many superintendents are heavily and productively identified with research-oriented councils centered at universities, staffed by highly competent professional persons, and financed by assessment or sliding scale membership fees. Typical of such activities are the New England School Development Council at Harvard; the Metropolitan School Study Council at Teachers College, Columbia; and the School Improvement Program at the University of Chicago. Such bodies are in a good position to attract foundation funds for research, since they are capable of embracing a broad spectrum of participating school systems for cooperative research. As in any human endeavor, the values derived from study council membership are directly proportional to the depth of involvement of the school system concerned. Mere membership by the school administrator is unrewarding and futile. Active participation in planning sessions and in subsequent joint investigations and explorations in participating school systems provides a stimulating setting for growth.

The curriculum consultant. Acknowledging that variables in quality of state-level staff (see page 90) make state-assisted curriculum development differ from state to state, the university provides a consistent and dependable resource for consultant services. The superintendent who is moving forward in one or another direction with his faculty, presumably through curriculum development, would find the university consultant a ready ally. Professors enjoy the opportunity to labor in the field, not only because a fee is generally attached, but because they broaden their own scope of influence in subjects for which they wish to become well known. The consultant tends to remove controversial overtones from the superintendent's role, at least by sharing the onus of change where change is somewhat resisted. The consultant is likely to be a specialist who knows more about some area than the superintendent can ever know. The superintendent who uses this resource cannot help but grow through such an affiliation.

The school survey. Many universities provide either formal or informal arrangements for the evaluation of school systems. Again, the "community of scholars" is organized and staffed to bring information and counsel to the superintendent and his teachers. A school evaluation by a university is not something to be entertained lightly. There is much to be said in favor of a systematic self-evaluation by the staff and community concerned. However, the judicious and deliberate employment of university personnel to share in such an enterprise can be extremely effective.

The institute or workshop. Call it by any other name, this device is a meeting of scholars and practitioners. It is generally held on the campus, drawing upon the free services of professors and schoolmen jointly to staff one or more panels. This instrument for in-service education can be very good, or it can be a total loss, depending largely upon the quality of planning and preparation invested.

Independent Professional Reading

The final item in this listing of in-service opportunities is the well-known professional library, however undramatic. This consists of current books on education, in all its many aspects; non-fiction in broader fields of business, philosophy, biography, the arts; reports of research and development in mimeograph or brochure format; and the journals of the profession. This item has been reserved to the end of this section since it calls for extensive comment. In spite of the 10 other opportunities (and there are more) which are suggested for the superintendent's professional growth, selective reading is still the most fundamental, reliable, and efficient resource at hand. It is the purpose of professional reading to equip the leader for independent, creative thinking. It is through the literature that the school executive lives and thinks in the present of a swiftly moving and complex profession, as distinguished from the past.

We have conflicting evidence as to the amount of reading performed by educational leaders, but it is a safe assumption that much more reading will be required as the task becomes more complex and as the knowledge of teaching and learning continues swiftly to grow. It is further observed that the quality of some professional literature, both in book and journal form, leaves much to be desired. Perhaps if publishers were more discriminating in the things they allowed in print, the respectful reading of professional literature by superintendents would increase.

For evidence concerning the reading habits of school administrators, one has only to examine, with some despair, the results of a study conducted by Pharis for *The School Executive*. According to the survey, one-fourth of the school superintendents in the country did not read any book on education during 1958. Only 53 percent read one or more books of fiction; 55 percent, one biography or more. The survey goes on to document and tabulate the apparent indifference to literature prevailing among many school leaders. To begin with, the report states that the response to the survey form was uniquely below expectation. "We are forced to conclude that this unusual silence denotes negative reading habits which school superintendents who normally reply to our questions were too embarrassed to put into writing." It continues, "The findings were discouraging . . . far below what should be expected from a group with a position of intellectual leadership in our society. . . . 'How long can our profession endure in a leadership role if we neglect reading?' " [4]

[4] Pharis, William L., Jr. "Your Reading Habits Are Showing." *School Executive* 78:58-59; April 1959.

Some happier evidence will be offered later in this chapter to suggest at least a guarded judgment that leading superintendents read with considerable zeal.

The fact of the matter is that we must rely on literature as the basic medium for professional integrity, as is the case in any profession. Chapter II reports that 90 percent of the superintendents rank professional reading, periodicals, and research reports their daily in-service resource. We have an obligation, fully as much as the physician or the chemist or the investment counselor, to keep current with our field. "Too busy" is not a valid excuse; we should examine what we have been too busy *at*, and ask ourselves which is more important.

This chapter has so far concerned itself with the assumption that the role of the school leader is ever-changing, and that, to remain fully effective, the school leader must avail himself of a variety of in-service opportunities for growth. Eleven devices for in-service growth were viewed critically, concluding with the assertion that independent professional reading remains the chief in-service resource for the school administrator.

RESEARCH IN ADMINISTRATIVE THEORY

While we have given considerable attention to the various *devices* or *resources* for in-service growth, we have not yet examined in any detail the material or content of the learning that schoolmen might be expected to acquire. It is the contention of this Commission that of all the many areas of knowledge in which a school administrator needs to keep up to date the most crucial, at the present time, is knowledge of administrative theory. This is especially true for most of the administrators currently in service, since administrative theory as a clear body of content is still in an early developmental stage. Furthermore, a number of different disciplines and subject-matter areas contribute to research in the field of administrative theory. This topic has been chosen by the Commission, therefore, for intensive examination in this chapter to show the factors which need to be taken into consideration in planning an adequate program of in-service development for school administrators.

A survey, which is reported in the later pages, was conducted to reveal the extent of concern expressed by school administrators about their knowledge of research in administrative theory. Stated differently, the survey sought to relate the in-service growth habits of school administrators to the evolving research in administrative behavior, and to weigh the concerns expressed by the superintendents about this particular topic. Acknowledging that the many, many parts of education, from the "new mathematics" to improved seating, are subjects about which the superintendent must be adequately informed, we sought only to determine the feelings of the school administrator about *administration*, and to examine whether his in-service professional growth included a study of research affecting the executive role.

Igniting the Fuse of Inquiry

Before reflecting upon the degree of concern possessed by school superintendents on the subject of research in administration, let us examine first just what it is that we are or are not concerned about. Those who are familiar with Campbell and Gregg, *Administrative Behavior in Education,*[5] are aware of a field of exploration and scientific appraisal which began to take form over 10 years ago. As in any movement of national proportions, the swelling of interest in the role of the school superintendency did not come about all of a piece. A number of independent forces seem to have converged at roughly the same time to give prominence to the need for investigation. Among these were the following:

1. The Kellogg Foundation's "discovery" in 1950 that superintendents of schools were very interesting and significant people, resulting in the Cooperative Program in Educational Administration.

2. The formulation of the National Conference of Professors of Educational Administration in 1947.

3. The findings of the Graduate School of Business Administration at Harvard regarding executive role in fields not unlike school administration.

4. The group dynamics movement, as stimulated by The National Training Laboratory and the University of Michigan, and heavily espoused during the past 12 years or more

---

[5] Campbell, Roald F., and Gregg, Russell T., editors. *Administrative Behavior in Education.* New York: Harper and Brothers, 1957. 547 p.

by AASA's sister body, the Association for Supervision and Curriculum Development (NEA).

5. Armed Forces experimentation with leadership and personnel hypotheses following World War II.

6. A new and aggressive search for executive leadership and the techniques for identifying it and developing it in business and industry.

7. And not least of all, our own silent and sometimes anguished admission that for all our confidence in our own know-how the superintendency is becoming more and more complex and less and less a piece to be played by ear, practiced though the ear might be. It is the condition that has recently been described by a very able superintendent: "The superintendency has become untenable."

When the convergence of these forces in time and place ignited the fuse of inquiry into the superintendency, professors of education began to speak to social scientists and, perhaps, even more singularly, *to be spoken to* by social scientists; and schools of education began to draw upon the resources of the schools of business and other schools in the university complex. Funds from the foundations were attracted. Educational administration, for the first time, came under the behaviorist's microscope, and we became the white mice of the social science laboratory.

From Empiricism to Theory

It is astonishing that so much thinking and writing could have been perpetrated in so short a period. But the literature is already extensive. One central theme pervades the content. To those who have let it pass them by the message may be broadly stated as follows: Up to and including the present time, school administration has been based upon empirical foundations; it has evolved as a quasi-professional apprenticeship or folklore, with the techniques and processes handed down from one generation to another, through the trial-and-error and the hard-knock pattern. The administrators are the practical, effective, get-the-job-done men who know what will work and what will not work, because they have tried the solutions available, or they know good men who have. Further, through skill and experience and prestige, they *make* things work, whether or not the same device might work for others.

The social scientists, on the other hand, declare that an educational theory is capable of formulation. This theory would systematize administration, giving a sense of direction to what is now guesswork. The scientist asserts that a cause-effect formula is attainable, as in physics and chemistry. He does not claim this theory is yet at hand, but he is hard at work searching for it. His position broadly stated is that a set of principles can be conceived which will produce known, predictable results from given administrative behavior.

Even more crudely stated, the situation can be likened to the airplane bush pilot cf the 1920's who, without instruments, flew his craft by the seat of his pants. Seat-of-the-pants flying was successful, right, and good for the aircraft being flown at the time. Furthermore, there was little else upon which to rely. But the bush pilot now finds himself in the pilot's chair of a monstrous flying machine of untold power and dimensions. The social scientist tells us that there are buttons to push, levers to adjust, gauges to watch, beacons to reckon, and codes to decipher. He tells us that one cannot fly this craft by the seat of the pants, but that certain levers and gauges, when actuated, produce specific and predictable results in the performance of the craft.

Administration and Change

Another theme that threads itself through the literature is the *inevitability of change* in school administration, and the certainty that school leaders must not only change with a changing culture, but contribute to that change. This notion is not new to us, as it affects curriculum and the instructional program, but have we counted ourselves and our *administrative* beliefs among those things which must change as well? James Thompson states this well, referring to administration in general: " 'Good supervision' of the 1920 variety in America was rooted in a firm paternalism in which fear-inspired discipline had a large role. The same supervisory behavior today is 'bad supervision.' Why? In part, I think, because the individuals being supervised today have more education, are better organized, and place higher value on human dignity."[6]

---

[6] Thompson, James D. "Modern Approaches to Theory in Administration." *Administrative Theory in Education.* (Edited by Andrew W. Halpin.) Chicago: Midwest Administration Center, University of Chicago, 1958. Chapter 2, p. 22.

It is clear that those who have taken upon themselves the scholarly study of our profession agree that empirical administrative processes must give way to theory, and that we must not only be amenable to change, but that we must be its champions.

Pieces of the Mosaic

Let us examine smaller pieces of the mosaic which is gradually being assembled by the social scientists and the professors of school administration. (And it is noteworthy that many of the observations are not identified exclusively with education, but indeed more likely originated in another field and were transplanted for our consideration.) We have taken a number of interesting extracts from the accruing evidence of the theorists, upon which we may ponder:

1. Talcott Parsons, sociologist at Harvard, states that decision making is not the absolute function of the executive. Veto, yes, but not decision. The technical expert (in our case the teacher) participates in the decision. He does not merely display alternatives for executive action. He is involved, responsible, he shares in the consequences. The executive is powerless to implement without the skills of the technician. He can only fire one expert and hire another.[7]

2. Roald Campbell of Chicago's Midwest Administration Center admonishes us: ". . . education, chiefly public education, is a built-in corrective for our kind of society. Only through general public enlightenment can the experiment we call democracy succeed. It seems clear that the administrator of schools charged with such a critical function needs to understand the nature of the charge, and he needs the skills necessary to mobilize people to implement such a concept." [8]

3. Henry Harap, *The Nation's Schools*, June 1959, page 55-57 reported an extensive nine-year survey on morale, conducted by Peabody College. The most significant fact revealed in the tabulation of the strengths of a school system was the importance that teachers attach to good administration. Harap noted that the administrator tended to overrate the degree of good morale of the teachers under his supervision.

4. Testimony from the Associated Public Schools System prods us to be wary of administrative hypotheses . . . based chiefly upon specu-

---

[7] Parsons, Talcott. "Some Ingredients of a General Theory of Formal Organization." *Ibid.*, Chapter 3, p. 46-47.

[8] Campbell, Roald F. "What Peculiarities in Educational Administration Make It a Special Case?" *Ibid.*, Chapter 8, p. 172.

lation or upon apparent success through personal experience. The item continues, "The Sequential Simplex is a statistical tool which assists one in gaining insights into the importance and influence of community forces and administrative arrangements to the school. . . . Once the Simplex is perfected it will be possible to test statistically many administrative hypotheses which up to this time have been left, of necessity, to speculation. . . . Once the Simplex is completed we will be able to give you a deeper and more meaningful analysis of your community, and with greater speed." [9]

5. Walter Crewson, associate commissioner in the New York State Department of Education, has stated recently, "The superintendent was originally viewed as a fine scholar, a man of letters, and a gentleman. As he evolved and groped toward maturity, the superintendent came to be seen as a local leader in educational matters— a wise judge of good education—a supervisor of teachers. As it became apparent that good schools depended critically upon community leadership, the superintendent began to emerge as a community leader, a local educational statesman. . . . (birth rates, more classrooms, tax rates) tended to divert and indeed to fragment the superintendent. Small wonder, then, that the local superintendency came to be a synthesis of salesmanship and managerial skills, to the corresponding exclusion and neglect of . . . instructional leader. . . ." [10]

6. Hollis Moore, in his skillful synthesis of the work of the several CPEA centers of the Kellogg Foundation, asks what differences in school administration have resulted from the expenditure of 5 million dollars by Kellogg, matched by at least equal investment of university staff and resources. "Or have we merely substantiated the hypotheses which were made at the start of the program?" he asks. "It will surprise no one who knows how slowly new concepts become generally known or how qualified are the findings of research in educational administration to see that we have firmed up our convictions more than we have discovered new ideas. Yet, certain shifts can truly be observed in today's perceptions of a school administrator's function compared with those a few years ago." [11]

7. Referring again to Thompson: "Much has been written about the uses of theory in research, less about the potential contributions of theory to the training of future administrators. In my opinion, an

---

[9] Associated Public Schools System, *Newsletter No. 3.* New York: the System, March 1959.

[10] Crewson, Walter. *A Design for State Leadership in Instruction.* Albany, N. Y.: State Department of Education. (Mimeographed.)

[11] Moore, Hollis A. *Studies in School Administration.* Washington, D. C.: American Association of School Administrators, a department of the National Education Association, 1957. p. 27.

adequate theory of administration would go a long way toward preparing students for change. . . . We cannot expect techniques of administration for 1977 to have much resemblance to those current today." He continues: ". . . an adequate theory of administration might . . . allow the administrator to incorporate knowledge produced by the several disciplines. . . . Many administrators have responded to new situations, new conditions, and new opportunities by adjusting or adapting their behavior. These responses have not always been consistent or successful, but could we expect otherwise when administrators are forced to rely on hunch and ingenuity, trial and error? These are expensive tools." [12]

8. Edward Litchfield in the *Administrative Science Quarterly*, the voice of the theorists in administrative research, deplores the confusion attaching to the issue: "The most serious indictment which must be made of present thought is that it has failed to achieve a level of generalization enabling it to systematize and generalize administrative phenomena which occur in related fields. . . . We seem to be saying that there is business administration, and hospital administration, and public administration; that there is military administration, hotel administration, and school administration. But there is no administration." [13]

9. Andrew Halpin, one of the more educationally oriented of the social scientists, and indeed, an earnest sympathizer of the practitioner, says ". . . the practitioner consoles himself with the knowledge that he is on the *real* firing line, that what he contributes to his school system is more important than any misty theory. Talk about theory may be good chatter in a seminar, but the administrator proudly admits that he is no egghead; he is a man of action." [14] Halpin, incidentally, has been more productive of tangible and immediately useful research than most others. His work in establishing certain characteristics of successful leadership through heavy documentation of the two traits examined, Initiating Structure and Consideration, made rewarding reading, even for a working superintendent. He may leave superintendents behind when he says, "The variances tend to be correlated negatively with the magnitude of the means . . .," but he gives us a useful message when he says, "Evidence from the present inquiry and findings from earlier research show that the leader's description of his own leadership behavior and his concept of what his behavior should be have little relationship to others' perceptions of his behavior. In the case of school superintendents,

---

[12] Thompson, James D., *op. cit.*, p. 22-27.

[13] Litchfield, Edward H. "Notes on a General Theory of Administration." *Administrative Science Quarterly* 1:7; June 1956.

[14] Halpin, Andrew. "The Development of Theory in Educational Administration," *Administrative Theory in Education.* Chapter 1, p. 12.

this is especially true in respect to their consideration of others (or their acts of human relations and warmth)." [15]

10. In the *Harvard Educational Review* John Walton deplores the inelegance and proliferation of our literature in educational administration. "In addition to the fragments appropriated from other disciplines, the content of the courses in [school] administration has consisted of a description of practices, the cautious recommendation of promising techniques, personal success stories, and lively anecdotes, all surrounded with the aura of common sense, and often purveyed by a more or less successful administrator. . . . It has not done much for the development of the subject." [16]

11. As a final extract from the literature, let us examine Dan Griffiths' definition of theory in school administration: "A good theory exists when there has been established *a set of principles upon which action may be predicted. These principles . . . constitute a logical and consistent whole built about a single theme or a small number of themes.* . . . As yet, there is no theory of administrative behavior which satisfies this definition. . . . A list of principles is not necessarily a theory. . . . A theory attempts to state in one general form the results of the observations of many different researchers. . . . A theory starts with [scientific] observations which have been made. . . . The observations must be in the form of facts." [17]

The selective overview of the literature of research in the theory of school administration may move you as it has moved us to reconsider our posture as "practical" schoolmen and listen with some respect to the theorists. We have by no means offered a comprehensive overview of the subject. We have simply picked and chosen, here and there, an interesting item from the vast smorgasbord of information available to us. It is worth noting, too, that all the writers and thinkers in this field are by no means johnny-come-latelys to the question, nor are they all by any means "alien" social scientists who have never confronted the "firing line." Many names of distinguished old friends in practical administration can be listed along with theorists Stogdill, Argyris, Simon, Griffiths, Getzels, Barnard, Guetzkow, and many

[15] Halpin, Andrew. *The Leadership Behavior of School Superintendents.* Columbus, Ohio: Ohio State University, 1957. p. 85.

[16] Walton, John. "The Theoretical Study of Educational Administration." *Harvard Educational Review* 25: 169-78; Summer 1955.

[17] Griffiths, Daniel E. "Toward a Theory of Administrative Behavior." *Administrative Behavior in Education.* Chapter 10, p. 359-60.

others. (See note below.) We mention only a few to call forth the images of statesmen in our profession, who, notwithstanding their practical posture and experience, share these concerns about the evolving "science of administration": Ernest Melby, Walter Anderson, Howard Funk, Samuel Brownell, Hollis Caswell, Francis Chase, Walter Cocking, Willard Elsbree, Van Miller, to name a few.

SUPERINTENDENTS' CONCERNS
ABOUT ADMINISTRATIVE THEORY

The above sampling of concerns of our academic colleagues has been presented as a backdrop against which to view the concerns of superintendents about in-service education in administrative theory, as revealed by the survey conducted by the Commission.

To compile evidence on the subject, a questionnaire, of course, was required (that indispensable device for the sharing of educational melancholy). The instrument was developed with the collusion of social scientists who had been thinking deeply about educational administration. Some of them had been thinking about it for years. A total of 140 questionnaires were distributed to a select list of superintendents who had been invited from throughout the United States to a conference at the University of Chicago in November 1959. A total of 115 responses were received. The poll takers would probably call this a very satisfactory sampling of superintendents of schools in the United States, further reinforced by the high selectivity with which the original invitation list was compiled.

Note: For further reading in the field of Administrative Theory, see the following:

Argyris, Chris. *Executive Leadership.* New York: Harper and Brothers, 1953. 139 p.
Barnard, Chester I. *The Functions of the Executive.* Cambridge, Mass.: Harvard University Press, 1938. 334 p.
Getzels, Jacob W. "Administration as a Social Process." *Administrative Theory in Education.* Chapter 7, p. 150-65.
Griffiths, Daniel E. *Administrative Theory.* New York: Appleton-Century-Crofts, 1959. 123 p.
Guetzkow, Harold S. "An Exploratory Empirical Study of the Role of Conflict in Decision-Making Conferences." *International Social Science Bulletin* 5; 1953.
Stogdill, Ralph M., and Shartle, C. L. *Methods in the Study of Administrative Leadership.* Columbus, Ohio: Ohio State University, 1955.

The questionnaire contained four parts:

1. Of 18 items relating more or less to research in administration, the respondent was asked to declare the degree of his concern on the subject: (a) vital concern, (b) some concern, (c) little concern.

2. Of 12 published materials relating to the subject of research in administration, the respondent was asked to declare his degree of familiarity with the publication: (a) in full command of this source; (b) familiar with this source, using it often; (c) familar with the source, but use it rarely; and (d) unfamiliar with this source.

3. The respondents were then asked to describe briefly their understanding of the term "Theory in Administration."

4. Finally, 25 terms,[18] selected by authorities in the field of administrative research as common in the literature, were listed, with the request that respondents check those terms which they fully understood.

Research in Administration

On the opposite page is reproduced the first part of the survey form, with responses of 115 superintendents tabulated by percentages. These responses, without recourse to formal statistical analysis, clearly indicate that in all of the 18 categories concerning research in administration there is substantial, forthright concern. In 10 of the 18 categories half or more of the respondents declared the item was of "vital" concern. In only a few of the categories did a response of "little concern" exceed 10 percent. The *concerns* of superintendents about research in educational administration can be summarized as follows:

1. The majority of school superintendents are greatly concerned about this subject in general, varying in their concern according to their day-to-day tasks. For example, the academic definition of "theory" stirred no particular excitement, but the translation of "theory" to useful principles, the presentation of dependable evidence, and the clarification of the superintendent's role in instructional leadership brought sharp consensus. Techniques for in-

[18] See Appendix.

The following questions may well be raised by administrators concerned about problems posed by the administrator's role. Some may be your concerns; others may not. Please indicate your interest and concern by checking each question according to the following guide:

COLUMN A : This question is of vital concern to me.
COLUMN B : This question is of some concern to me.
COLUMN C : This question is of little concern to me.

Please note: Your response should be a reflection of the **degree of concern** you feel about the question at hand.

	A	B	C
1. How can a practicing administrator **get hold of research findings** relevant to the administrator's role?	52	42	6
2. To what extent does the administrator's behavior have a marked effect on the **achievement** of **organizational** goals?	61	33	6
3. What has research into **administrator behavior** to do with the functioning of the superintendent in the performance of his many responsibilities?	43	47	10
4. Is agreement being reached on what the **superintendent's job** really is?	52	35	13
5. Are **changes** occurring in the **concept** of the superintendent's role?	56	36	8
6. Are **changes** occurring in the **performance** of the superintendent's role?	56	36	8
7. What contributions are basic disciplines such as sociology and psychology making to the field of educational administration?	44	46	9
8. Are there indications that an **interdisciplinary approach** in the **training** of administrators better enables the superintendent to solve administrative problems?	45	41	14
9. What is known about the characteristics of **community decision-making** and the skills administrators need to work successfully with community groups?	62	33	5
10. What role should the superintendent take in **community leadership?**	49	43	8
11. How can the superintendent assist **community groups to express themselves** accurately and effectively in school matters?	52	42	6
12. Has research identified any **dependable evidence** concerning **leadership?** How may such evidence be used in the training of administrators? Are there ways of assessing leadership "dimensions"?	63	35	2
13. How do **variables** inherent in **the local situation,** i.e., "situational factors" determine the type of role desirable in the superintendency?	39	49	12
14. What is the meaning of **theory** in **educational administration?**	16	61	23
15. **How can theory be translated** to be of use to educational administrators?	39	51	10
16. What is known about the **expectations** of major **community and faculty forces** (both within and without formal organization) with respect to the administrator's role?	42	48	10
17. What is the superintendent's role in relation to the Board of Education?	59	28	13
18. What is the superintendent's role in relation to the teachers and the instructional program?	72	21	7

109

formed communication, community understanding, and faculty morale were earnestly sought.

2. Coupled with the expressions of concern is the implication that superintendents are looking for help from their university colleagues in education and related disciplines. There is the further implication that they are not now receiving much help, either through the literature or through direct in-service programs of one kind or another. Otherwise the "concerns" would not be as clearly expressed.

3. The readiness for change is also implicit in the responses. Acknowledging a condition of "vital concern" in the majority of topics by the majority of respondents suggests that the superintendent is willing to be shown, is willing to accept, the in-service growth obligations that follow concern. The small incidence of indifference (no more than 10 percent showing little concern for most items) should be encouraging.

Familiarity with Sources of Information

The second part of the survey was intended to reflect the degree of familiarity acknowledged by superintendents with 12 sources of information in the field of research in administration. (A few of the resources were stretched to meet the criteria for qualifying as expressions of research.) These responses tend to contradict the evidence offered earlier in this chapter which deplored the lack of professional reading by the superintendent.

Summary treatment is offered here to reveal general results of the inquiry. Responses having to do with "familiarity" and "frequent use" of the literature in question were combined to reflect the percentage of superintendents reporting positively. The remaining columns are treated as percentage of superintendents responding negatively, in terms of in-service professional growth. It is noteworthy that a fair number of superintendents candidly acknowledged that they were unfamiliar with the material. Without attempting to prove anything by tabulation, it is noted with interest that 40 percent were unfamiliar with the *Administrative Science Quarterly;* 24 percent unfamiliar with the *Educational Research Bulletin* (Ohio State University) ; 22 percent unfamiliar with reports of such cooperative councils as

Rank	Authoritative Published Works Appropriate to the In-Service Education of Administrators in the Field of Administration	Percentage of Superintendents Reporting Positively on Their Knowledge and Use of the Material	Percentage of Superintendents Familiar with the Material But Seldom Using it	Percentage of Superintendents Unfamiliar with the Material
1	Conant Report—The American High School Today	88	9	3
2	NEA Research Bulletin	85	10	5
3	Rockefeller Foundation Report —The Pursuit of Excellence	72	16	12
4	Administrator's Notebook	62	30	8
5	Studies in School Administration	57	29	14
6	Educational Research Bulletin	52	24	24
7	School Life	51	40	9
8	Journal of Educational Research	50	48	2
9	Reports from Cooperative Educational Councils	46	32	22
10	Review of Educational Research	45	40	15
11	Encyclopedia of Educational Research	44	48	8
12	Administrative Science Quarterly	24	36	40

Metropolitan School Study Council and others; 14 percent were unfamiliar with the summary of the CPEA findings by Hollis Moore.

However, there is evidence of substantial in-service reading going on among more than half of the superintendents in two-thirds of the sources listed. Familiarity with the material, but its infrequent use, as reflected in column 4 may be more complimentary to the respondent's scholarship than the negative implications derived from the survey. For example, an honest response to the query on the *Encyclopedia of Educational Research* could hardly acknowledge a full command of this infinitely complex volume. The same observation can be made of a number of the other source titles, suggesting that conscientious respondents could be professionally well-read people without claiming to have "command of the content," or without "using it often." (A study conducted by Dr. Finis E. Engleman two years ago on the reading habits of successful school superintendents produced positive findings generally suggesting the conclusions of this inquiry; see *The Nation's Schools,* September 1957.)

Understanding of "Theory in Administration"

The third part of the survey dealt with the question, "What does 'theory in administration' mean to you?" Only 33 of the 115 respondents attempted to answer this question. Some of the responses would have pleased the scholars in the field, but most of them missed the purists' mark. Some respondents gave voice to their frustrations (either at having to complete another questionnaire, or at having their administrative linen hung out to view) by such answers as, "Theory isn't worth a darn" or "Not much." Even a generous reviewer of the 33 responses would probably admit that of the total questionnaires returned, fewer than a fourth gave evidence of a good knowledge of the meaning of administrative theory.

Familiarity with Terminology

The fourth and last section of the survey dealt with 25 terms selected by authorities in the emerging field of administrative science as being frequently and authoritatively used in the literature. It is emphasized that these terms relate to administration in its general sense. They are not limited to school administration. The implication is that one familiar with the present literature of research in administration could not avoid a familiarity with these terms. The questionnaire quite specifically asked the superintendents to check those terms "which you fully understand." The results follow. (The meanings of the terms as provided by Steven P. Hencley, Midwest Administration Center, University of Chicago, are furnished in the Appendix.)

RANK	TERM	% *	RANK	TERM	% *
1	Line and Staff Functions	91	13	Initiating-Structure-in-Interaction	43
2	Vertical and Horizontal Organization	86	14	Rational Authority	39
3	Social Mobility	73	15	Zone of Acceptance	37
4	Informal Organization	72	16	Situationist Theory of Leadership	33
5	Unity of Command	65	17	Alter-Group Expectations	31
6	Organizational Effectiveness and Efficiency	65	18	Degrees of Freedom in Organizational Therapy	20
7	Power Structure	63	19	Charismatic Leadership	14
8	Span of Control	61	20	The Hawthorne Effect	14
9	Role Theory	60	21	Nomothetic and Idiographic Considerations	14
10	Urban Fringe	54	22	The Rabble Hypothesis	12
11	Scientific Management Movement	51	23	Invasion and Succession	12
12	Group Maintenance and Group Achievement	43	24	Parsons' Input and Output	9
			25	POSDCORB	9

* Percentage of Superintendents reporting full understanding.

It may be of some surprise and satisfaction to the theorists in the field that a majority of the practical men of education understood at least half of the selected terms of administrative science. However, if the terms are scrutinized closely, one must admit that those most familiar to schoolmen are by no means the monopoly of the social scientist and the administrative research movement. Superintendents would probably have a good command of a fair number of these terms if no such movement had ever occurred. When one examines the responses on the purely technical terms which are restricted in usage to the literature of the field, the great majority of superintendents acknowledge they are left behind.

This survey, admittedly covering only a selected, small sample of superintendents, reinforces the assertions made at the beginning of this chapter that superintendents take their in-service work seriously. While we have belabored at some length the subject of research in educational theory, and drawn rather stern implications for the superintendent as a guinea pig in the social scientist's laboratory, we would not wish to close with the notion that *all* administration is reducible to impersonal cause-and effect formulae, or to purely scientific explanations. While in-service education disciplines are essential, they do not

113

exclude the human, intuitive, unlettered dimensions of school leadership that no amount of contrived in-service work can convey.

We speak of that basic good sense, intuition, if you will, with which we are endowed as leaders. The hunches, the trials and errors, the creative, inspired solutions to problems, the actions prompted by spirit as much as by fact, unaccompanied by scientific management, unguided by the social scientists, have produced a sweepingly successful product. Let us not lose our gift for seat-of-the-pants judgment while we are waiting for research answers to our problems.

For all of the group dynamics involving the participation of many teachers and laymen, for all of the promised devices of social science, for all of the expert help at hand, the burden of the lonesome hours of decision making is the superintendent's own. In other words, his final resources are, yes, his intuition, his common sense, his heart, and the *things he has learned about education through disciplined study.*

CONCLUSIONS

There are changes taking place in school administration and in the function of educational leadership that call for disciplined in-service education of the school administrator. The school administrator's strategic role is being weighed thoughtfully by many competent observers.

Many resources, some more readily available, and some more productive than others, lie within reach of the superintendent. Apart from professional reading and formal graduate study, the most promising in-service opportunity is the small, informal professional group, meeting regularly to exchange challenging ideas, viewpoints, and experiences.

Professional reading is still the most efficient and reliable resource for systematic in-service growth. There is evidence to suggest that among some superintendents, known for their accomplishments, professional reading is relied upon heavily. There is also evidence to suggest that among many superintendents professional reading is neglected.

On the subject of research in the theory of school administration, selected superintendents expressed considerable concern, interest, and willingness to assume the responsibilities for in-service self-education.

The lines of communication between the theorist and the administrator leave much to be desired. Given important information that school administrators should possess, and given an attitude of willingness to learn on the part of the schoolman, we should find better means of insuring simple, reliable processes for effective dissemination of information.

The apparent lack of orderly self-education through disciplined professional reading may spring from the overwhelming volume of materials published. More discriminating selection by the superintendent and more discriminating publishing by editors and authors could relieve the superintendent of the present feeling of inundation in "required reading." The professional association, AASA, might well consider a readers' guide service, calling attention to worthwhile published work, screening out the unimportant or irresponsible writing.

In the specific category of in-service education relating to theory in administration, selected superintendents displayed concern over readiness and willingness to learn. Adequate familiarity with the literature is apparent among the successful practitioners, yet they clearly indicate a wish to learn more, particularly in the categories most realistically related to their day-to-day tasks.

Superintendents should find ways to disengage themselves from the demands of day-to-day time consuming obligations that stand between them and their professional growth. We cannot preserve ourselves in the swift evolution of education unless we establish our own personal standards of intellectual discipline and systematize our fulfillment of those standards. This may mean more assistance for the delegation of duties; it may mean better quality and more discriminating professional publications; it may mean expanded screening services by professional associations to conserve the executive's time through a reading guide. All of these measures would be fruitful. But basically the problem calls for a sense of commitment and determination on the part of the school superintendent to remain a professional person.

chapter V

The Changing Nature
of School Administration

"A man says what he knows, a woman says what will please," wrote Jean Jacques Rousseau two hundred years ago. This Commission (composed of men only) shall not attempt to argue the validity of Rousseau's statement as applied to contemporary society. It is evident, however, that much of what the Commission has thus far said it knows about the preparation, selection, and in-service education of school administrators is far from pleasing. Serious deficiencies in each of these areas have been revealed and discussed. This appraisal of current practices has been presented, not as an end in itself, but rather to provide background for recommendations for improving the professional experiences of school administrators. Such recommendations are presented in following chapters.

If these recommendations are to be realistic and practical, they must be attuned to the actual job of the school administrator as it is today and as it is likely to be in the predictable future. This chapter, therefore, attempts to "tune in" on the day-to-day work and problems that absorb the time and effort of the contemporary school superintendent.

ADMINISTRATION AND CHANGE

To discuss the everyday problems of the administrator in the public schools today would seem to require, at the outset, some consideration of change. Unquestionably school administration is changing. This is a basic assumption of this yearbook and a

116

major reason why preparation and in-service programs for administrators deserve continued scrutiny. One reason why school administration is changing is because its social setting is changing. Every major issue and problem of the schools has its source in the community.

If one takes up school problems one at a time, he finds that every problem has two aspects. What seems at first glance the exclusive concern of the schools invariably today turns out to be rooted in the community. Since schools are an instrument of society, new demands on school leadership are resulting from change which is occurring along a broad front. Chase says:

> Within the past forty years man has catapulted himself into a new era through his application of science and technology to the release of energy, the processes of production, the means of transportation, and the mechanics of communication . . . . Change has been so rapid as to demand within a single generation new concepts of time and distance and a readjustment, if not a reconstruction, of social institutions and values.[1]

There is every reason to believe that the period of history immediately ahead will be something different from the present, perhaps fantastically different, as man becomes increasingly involved with automation, atomic power, and the penetration of space. In the meantime we find ourselves living in a transition period characterized by concepts that are both old and new. An economist quotes Peter Drucker as follows:

> We live in an age of transition, an age of overlap, in which the old 'modern' of yesterday no longer acts effectively but still provides means of expression, standards of expectation, and tools of ordering, while the new 'post-modern' still lacks definition, expression, and tools, but effectively controls our actions and their impact.[2]

In order to see some ways in which the new age is having its impact on schools we have some exhibits to look at. We need only to observe such items as the blueprints for curriculum change that are being drawn, innovations in the teaching of major subjects, and the new tools of learning such as television and language laboratories.

Changing Expectations

In the first place, as school administrators are aware, public expectations of them are changing. Sputnik Number One

---

[1] Chase, Francis S. "New Conditions Confront Education." *The School Review* 65:3-11; Spring 1957.
[2] Means, Gardiner C. "Requiem for the Modern Age." *Saturday Review* 42:55; January 17, 1959.

appeared on October 4, 1957. Immediately citizens began to increase their expectations of school administrators. As the education editor of the *New York Herald Tribune* wrote on October 20, "The public is awakening to education as never before, and education is at last awakening to the public demands."[3]

Recently some thousands of articles per week dealing with math and science alone have appeared in our newspapers and magazines. Few of these have approved what was being done. This ground swell of concern for education has created a whole set of new loads for school administrators to carry. Renewed public interest in education, however, has brought additional aid and support from federal sources such as the National Science Foundation and the National Defense Education Act as well as from local sources now better disposed to vote bond issues and approve tax levies.

In the second place, school administrators find themselves in a climate of changing expectations as far as their professional colleagues are concerned. In an earlier era the top administrator was inclined to be accepted as the sole decision-maker. Today teachers, principals, and central office staff members expect to have increasingly important shares in molding the decisions that affect them. The top administrator finds that he needs to rely more and more on their technical knowledge and skill. It is presumed that school administrators will use a fair proportion of their time in planning and consulting with staff groups. The administrator of today is expected to exercise his roles in the interest of instruction itself as well as business affairs, with instruction receiving top priority.

Administrative status and position have changed in character as central staff, teachers, and principals have gradually come into their own as spokesmen for themselves in matters of salary and welfare. It is not unusual today for a teacher's salary committee to become the bargaining agent that deals directly with the board of education in setting salaries instead of depending upon administrative recommendation.

Moreover, expectations of school administration are being remodeled as wider responsibilities are assigned to the schools. The school administrator today is expected to take a larger part in the total community-wide program of education. The scope

---

[3] *New York Herald Tribune,* October 20, 1957. Section 2, p. 3.

of the public school enterprise now extends beyond the range of kindergarten to grade twelve. Adult education, community colleges, preschool programs, and special services for the mentally, emotionally, and physically handicapped are becoming the accepted province of the public schools. More and more the public school administrator is obliged to provide educational leadership in his community, not only through his administration of the public schools, but also as a leading participant in many educational and cultural enterprises.

All that we are saying is that school administration is affected by many kinds and varieties of social change. To find the evidence one could go to such fields as the shift in living patterns, technological change, or readjustments in our system of values. Let us outline a few developments in these areas beginning with changing living patterns.

Shift in Living Patterns

We are witnessing a national population explosion with a fabulous increase in the number of people to be provided for. All past forecasts of population growth have been too conservative. One expert says:

> Remember that the projections of the 1930's based on the marriage and birth rates, which were prevalent then, indicated that the maximum population of this country would be approximately 165 million persons; that this maximum would be reached about the year 2000; that we would probably have a declining population thereafter.

> The Bureau of the Census now expects the national population to increase to between 207 million and 228 million by 1975.

> This means that in the course of 25 years we are faced with the necessity to expand goods and services to meet the needs of a vast addition to the American nation.

> In only 42 years—about the year 2000—the continuation of these trends indicates a possible population of as many as 300 million Americans.[4]

Our contemporary culture displays many varieties of change in living arrangements. Paradoxically, science is bringing us closer together and at the same time expanding our communities. There is much talk about the "metropolitan areas," a convenient designation for a city somewhere near the center of a given area. Suburban rings are surrounding and spreading

---

[4] Hauser, Philip M. An address delivered at The National Conference on Metropolitan Growth. Washington, D. C., November 24-25, 1958.

outward from the old central cities. It is true, of course, that efforts at urban renewal are getting under way in certain cities and many new central cities may be eventually created, particularly if federal funds are available to help.

This population shift has been called by the editors of *Fortune* the "greatest social upheaval in the world today." During the last decade, as rural population has moved to urban centers, there has also been a rush from the cities to the suburbs. Every social level is involved, not just the middle classes which supposedly have the means to live where they choose. The new pattern of population growth in broader areas is described by Gulick as "concentrated dispersion." He says:

> The major revolutionary fact of American metropolitan growth for our generation is concentrated dispersion.
>
> Homes are being spread out, suburbs have no apparent shape or limits, city densities are dropping, factories arise in the open country, and shopping centers cluster about the traffic interchanges.[5]

School administrators are well aware of growth and shifts in population. Some of their most difficult problems are concerned with the empty classrooms that appear in the center of the district and the overcrowded classrooms on the growing edge. Expanding districts require extended transportation lines and increased services. District annexation problems are found in every region and are usually complicated by legal and psychological factors. School financing is rendered more difficult as industry locates outside of the school districts that receive the employees' children to educate.

It has been commonly said that education's three biggest problems are how to get (a) more and better teachers, (b) more and better buildings, and (c) more and better instructional aids and equipment. All of these problems are a direct result of the population changes just noted.

Growth and the School Organization

To understand the changing tasks of the school administrator it is important to recognize that in many school systems these tasks have emerged as a by-product of community growth and expansion. School units, saddled with the responsibility of caring for more and more children, have necessarily grown

---

[5] Gulick, Luther. An address delivered at The National Conference on Metropolitan Growth. Washington, D. C., November 24-25, 1958.

larger. Today, as everybody knows, there are more and more large school districts with increasing transportation of pupils and provision of added school services. This, as we have said, is one of the effects of the urbanization of our country, the growth of suburbs, and the desire of citizens for school units large enough to provide a variety of services and programs.

In a community that originally had a single high school, two junior high schools, and a half dozen elementary schools, today there may be three high schools, eight junior high schools, and 16 elementary schools. As this state of affairs develops it becomes necessary to reorganize the central administrative machinery. The superintendent's office moves out of the senior high school where it has always been based and achieves independence as a separate administration center. It expands as staff members are added to take care of special services and the increased number of school units. Concomitantly, the central office must relinquish or delegate many of the controls over the detailed operations in individual school units and classrooms. As more classrooms are added the control of teaching tends to migrate to the periphery of the organization. System-wide responsibilities such as purchasing, food service, transportation, and maintenance move toward the center. There is thus a tendency for the center to become detached and aloof from classroom teaching and learning, the purpose for which it was originally devised, and to concentrate more of its effort on the over-all business activities of the district.

As the superintendent adds staff members, he is likely to get technical specialists who possess particular abilities and to whom are delegated the special jobs of handling the technical aspects of administration. The new staff members are likely to see their jobs as specialists. In many cases they have come up through the same kind of experiences the superintendent has. They have worked in a single school or they have worked in a job which gave them a relatively narrow view of the total range of administrative responsibility. As was noted in Chapter II, many administrators are working in districts larger than the ones in which they began.

The superintendent soon finds that he has a job to do in coordinating the efforts of these staff members. It is his responsibility to help staff members to see how their jobs fit into the total organization and how their functions in the organization affect the operation of related departments and the organization as a whole. The dynamic character of this net of relations is not represented by an organization chart. The communication of information and attitudes among staff follows psychological contours and topography regardless of the location of official channels on the chart. One of the administrator's major problems is to help each staff member to see his task as a component part of the total organization and as contributing to over-all organizational goals. Lacking an appreciation of the importance of integrated staff effort, the individual members may engage in departmental feuds without ever surmising that the major organizational goals are being jeopardized. Administration has the job of tying together loose ends, of organizing team effort, of communicating goals, and of stimulating leadership effort of the sort that subordinates personal ambition to group effectiveness. Population growth and shift are complicating these already difficult tasks.

Technological Advance

One could easily show that technological change has preceded and contributed heavily to the population changes just outlined. Everybody is familiar with the inventions that have led to our vastly improved transportation and communication systems. The mere mention of the expressway, television, and refrigeration suggests ways in which advancing technology affects our life and thought. But technological advance has done more than create labor-saving devices and household gadgets that modify our way of life. With technological change have come moral and philosophical problems. From the H-bomb to artificial insemination, technology has created problems of readjustment.

As we have already suggested, the classroom itself has been transformed by new devices for teaching that have come into being. With the increase in the number of scientists and engineers devoting full time to research in the service of industry and government, new educational needs for those doing the technical and subprofessional work have arisen. Automation and the mechanization of industrial processes have created new occupations requiring new skills. The current interest in area vocational schools springs from a concern to serve new educational needs arising from the impact of technological change.

Our Changing Value System

Schools have little protection from social and cultural change. Their local ownership and control make them sensitive to variations in the local climate. As new and old elements combine in the social scene, schools are caught in more conflicting demands and crosscurrents of pressure than in any other historical period that we know anything about. The American value system is being shaken. Because of the problems of our changing value system, the task of education in the mid-twentieth century is infinitely more complicated than that of even a century or two ago.

Many writers have offered an analysis and description of our changing values in these changing times. One attempt to classify the values in our society led to this conclusion:

> ... we have, side by side in the community and in the educational institutions, a kaleidoscope of shifting and confusing, if not absolutely contradictory, assumptions about life and the values that are really ours.[6]

Since the teaching program of every school is necessarily based on some value system, the choosing among competing goals and values must fall to the lot of somebody in the leadership role.

Aims can no longer be clearly perceived and defined. In earlier times, man at the worst had to choose among competing sets of values, but today we face the difficulty of deciding whether there is any possibility of reaching generally recognized landmarks or universally held values at all.

The values of the home are brought to school. As the schools attempt to teach all the children of all the people, some children come to school with conscientious objections to certain activities in the school program.

In a community which has had a relatively homogeneous Protestant population, Jewish and Catholic groups may acquire strength as they grow in number; and as a result, public school practices regarding religion are challenged. Discussions may ensue respecting the teaching of religion in the schools. A high school course in Bible History may draw criticism. The motives of certain teachers will be called into question. Religious observances in schools at Christmas and Easter are opposed by some citizens. A newspaper story about a Christmas program given

---

[6] Getzels, J. W. "Changing Values Challenge the Schools." *School Review* 65:92-102; Spring 1957.

by a kindergarten group may draw fire from non-Christians. Some of the clergy may contend that baccalaureate sermons at commencement time are Christian in emphasis and hence an offense to students and parents of other faiths. Other clergymen will assert that the relatively homogeneous composition of the community justifies a continuation and even an extension of the practices that are being questioned.

Related problems present themselves. There arises the question of pupils who refuse to participate in the pledge of allegiance because of conscientious objections, and of pupils forbidden by parents to don gym clothes or to attend school dances. Parents may disagree with the supervision that students ought to have on graduation night. Some parents will have no objection to an all-night class trip to a distant resort while others will insist on close adult supervision of all the student activities. Meanwhile, editorial comment in the newspapers may criticize the schools for failing to teach moral values.

The school administrator thus finds himself "in the middle." Time was when a single value system had sufficiently general acceptance to indicate what the schools were to do in particular cases. Today the traditional values have lost sway, and we appear to be less sure of what we believe about the right and wrong and the good and the bad.

With a cursory description of a few areas of change and a hint of the buffeting that administrators are taking, let us look more closely at the administrator's behavior on his job, beginning with a consideration of his psychological orientation toward the job itself.

THE ADMINISTRATOR AND HIS JOB

Administrators largely agree on the question of where their responsibilities lie as far as the relatively inescapable jobs are concerned. It is the consensus that the major tasks of school administration are to facilitate learning, develop staff, advise with the board, organize the school system, interpret the schools to the public, prepare budgets, and provide funds and facilities. The literature on administration sometimes divides the field into four parts: finance, personnel, curriculum improvement, and community relations. University programs for administrators reflect this division.

The Administrator's Perception of His Job

Although much has been written about these responsibilities of administration and how they should be met, in the last analysis how an administrator performs on the job will depend mainly on the way he sees his task. Realization of this fact accounts for the current interest in the administrator's philosophy and his perception of his role, as the following indicates:

> The study of the behavior of the school administrator has usually been focused on examining factors affecting his behavior such as intelligence, experience, personality, his personal life, human relations skill, job expectations and the like. Variables within the school system itself that affect administrator behavior have been studied. These have included such variables as communication structure, teacher effectiveness, participation, morale, non-instructional expense, the amount and type of equipment in the administrator's office and the like.

> The effect on administrator behavior of variables outside the school has also been investigated. The effect of the level of education of adults in the community, the legal structure of the school system, the level of community expectations for education, and the total amount of taxable value of property in the school district (true value) are examples of this type of variable.

> Although these studies reveal many things about the man and the matrix in which he operates, they indicate very little about his perception of the task of education despite the fact that his perception of the task is the key factor in his behavior. How he "sees" the organization's job and his role in relation to this will influence his choice of the problems to be solved and of the available alternatives.[7]

To repeat, the "perception of the task" is important because how a person performs on his job will depend ultimately upon his view of himself in relation to the work he believes he is commissioned to accomplish.

G. K. Chesterton said that if a man were considering an apartment to rent, the most appropriate question to ask the landlady would be, "What is your philosophy of life?" On her answer to this basic question would hinge everything else of importance to a prospective tenant. Applying Chesterton's statement to school administration one might say that the school administrator's performance will be largely a matter of his personal value system because he will set his administrative goals accordingly. These values vary, of course, with the administrator because he is, like the poet, a "part of all that he has met."

---

[7] The University Council for Educational Administration. *Perception: Its Relation to Educational Administration.* New York: the Council. n. d. p. 1.

Improving Teaching and Learning

In a welter of change the school administrator must go about his job of improving teaching and learning in the public schools. The central focus of his efforts concerns three aims: (a) helping the board who hired him and the other citizens of the district to select goals and policies that support and enhance teaching and learning, (b) leadership of the staff that he is employed to organize and supervise in the service of teaching and learning, and (c) management of materials and personnel required in an organization designed to further the aims of teaching and learning.

The precise connection between day-to-day behavior in the administrator's office and the processes of teaching and learning is not always obvious. A time and motion study of any administrator's job would reveal a varied range of activities and problems. In the course of his daily duties the school administrator might be observed to attend to almost anything from federal aid to phonics, mathematics to merit ratings, internships to integration. In one office the official day might include the following items:

A phone call from the school attorney about proceedings in acquiring a site for a new school.

A principal's report of a burglary in his school.

An appointment with the Executive Committee of the city-wide PTA Council, who were offering to help with a study of delinquency.

A call from the business manager about the purchase of athletic supplies.

A visit from the chairman of the Policy Committee about a recommendation concerning smoking in high schools.

A telephone reminder of a speech to be made at a civic club.

A question from a newspaper reporter regarding the agenda for the next board meeting.

A request from the chairman of the Long Range Planning Committee for an appointment to talk about school district annexation problems.

A curriculum guide to read.

Extend this list of items to cover a week, a month, or a year and one would get some impression of what the range of problems is and what the administrative task currently entails. Such items, of course, do not define the job. The question, On what should an administrator spend himself? is not answered.

The administrator has some important questions to answer:

Which tasks deserve the most time?

Who can be trusted to make what decisions?

Which programs should receive the most budget?

How can the parts of the system be interrelated?

How will staff members react to a given idea?

Will this plan foster staff compatibility?

What is the best way to counsel with the board?

How shall a better staff be built?

Defining the Difficult

Because it is difficult to identify what it is that an administrator really does as he goes about his work, we have been slow in establishing criteria for selecting administrators and for evaluating their performance.

Administration has been described as problem solving, as a social process, as decision making, as a complex of interrelated processes. It has been defined in terms of structure as well as function. In addition, we have case studies that reveal administrators in action, reports of observers viewing the tasks from different angles, and a sizable literature about the job requirements. The administrator's problems have been classified and his roles and relationships defined. His skills and qualifications have been identified. Studies have been made of the way he spends his time, what he worries about, and what occurs in his problem-filled days.

The 1955 AASA Yearbook describes administration as follows:

Administration, then, may be defined as the total of the processes thru which appropriate human and material resources are made available and made effective for accomplishing the purposes of an enterprise. It functions thru influencing the behavior of persons.[8]

8 American Association of School Administrators. *Staff Relations in School Administration.* Washington, D. C.: the Association, a department of the National Education Association, 1955. p. 17.

Using the structure-function analogy, Getzels says:

Let me say then that we may conceive of administration *structurally* as the hierarchy of subordinate-superordinate relationships within a social system. *Functionally*, this hierarchy of relationships is the locus for allocating and integrating roles and facilities in order to achieve the goals of the social system. It is here, in these relationships, that the assignment of statuses, the provision of facilities, the organization of procedures, the regulation of activity, and the evaluation of performance takes place.[9]

Another student of administration employs a "three-skills" approach. He says that the behavior required for administrative performance consists of the exercise of *technical* skill, *human* skill, and *conceptual* skill.[10] This division of skills is used also in Chapter VII of this yearbook.

The 1952 AASA Yearbook presents an analysis of school administration in terms of eight functions with *planning* and *evaluation* overlying the whole process.[11]

Almost any observer of administrative activity has to conclude that the administrative process is composed of such ingredients as decision making, planning, stimulating, coordinating, and evaluating. There are others that could be named such as programming and allocating resources.

In the remainder of this chapter a few administrative tasks and obligations are discussed as examples of the school administrator's day-to-day activities. The first to be considered is decision making, sometimes called the essence of administration.

Making Decisions

Every administrator makes certain decisions and every major task area is involved in the decision-making process. For example, when an administrator faces the problem of preparing a salary plan he begins by making decisions. How will the problem be attacked? Will the money be spent in annual raises across the board? Or will minimums and maximums be treated differently? Will the credit allowable for experience be changed?

---

[9] Getzels, Jacob W. *Administrative Theory in Education.* (Edited by Andrew W. Halpin, Jr.) Chicago: Midwest Administration Center, University of Chicago, 1958. p. 151.

[10] Katz, Robert L. "Skills of an Effective Administrator." *Harvard Business Review* 33: 33-42; January-February 1955.

[11] American Association of School Administrators. *The American School Superintendency.* Washington, D. C.: the Association, a department of the National Education Association, 1952. Chapter 4, "The Organization of the Superintendency," p. 65-102.

If the salary minimum is increased how will teacher recruitment be affected?

A dozen such questions have to be answered even before other basic decisions can be made. To get the answers, the administrator is likely to enlist the help of his staff. The range of technical skills available to him through staff members, of course, will vary greatly with the size of his school system. Time was when the staff served as a channel to funnel up to the top the questions to be decided. Less so today. If an administrator finds that day to day and hour by hour staff members are coming to him to get his decisions in all matters, it is time for him to look for better ways of decision making.

The effective administrator organizes and supervises the decision-making process so that responsibility for deciding questions is placed close to their point of origin. Thus he may make few decisions himself. Some of the most important decisions that an administrator makes are decisions that govern the decision-making process. He is effective in the degree that he can delegate the decision-making responsibility and assist others to carry it out. The task of the top administrator thus becomes one of engineering and overseeing the decision-making machinery.

Thelen warns against being too tightfisted with the decision-making function. He says:

Methods of thinking in administration are based on concepts of authority. Thus, the man who sees himself as the authority, who uses only his own experience as the basis of decision, tends to set up his own private theories of administration, and these are generally not very well articulated simply because they are private. . . . The person who bases his action primarily on his own experience, interpreted by his own private theories, also tends to limit the range of his experience. He surrounds himself with yes men, which means that he uses other people simply for the reassurance that he is adequate. In effect, such people talk to themselves because they are basically afraid to talk with others. Their approach to management is likely to be in terms of pressure.

The man who believes that the source of authority is the experience of all those concerned in the operations he governs, has to make his methods explicit so that others can give him relevant information. In the process of this communication, his theories get tested and ironed out, and they become part of the rationale of the group rather than his private property.[12]

---

[12] Thelen, Herbert A. *Dynamics of Groups at Work.* Chicago: University of Chicago Press, 1954. p. 106-107.

It might appear that deciding questions is an activity for which an administrator must have a special gift. This is implied in the pride displayed by some administrators in being able to make quick decisions. The best decisions, however, are usually made slowly and deliberately for the simple reason that decision making is laborious work. In the course of a day's activity, an administrator generally is confronted by numerous problem situations which are difficult and frustrating. He finds that solutions to real problems do not come easily and automatically. Usually it is necessary to spend a great deal of time and effort in getting facts, talking with persons, evaluating recommendations, and assessing people's feelings. Conscientious decision making keeps in mind a set of values, of which first and foremost is a consideration of what is best for boys and girls. Action is based on the best information available. It results from the fullest possible use of the best brain power in the organization.

Today's school administrator, like the modern industrial executive, the modern coach, or the modern military leader, merges his talents and his energies with others in the organization in ways to promote the common goals. The most effective administrators seem to be people who surround themselves with the best associates they can get; who freely admit they cannot decide everything; and who learn to use the ability of others. When associates bring in conflicting counsel, decisions are left open, as far as possible, pending the testing and evaluation that experience will provide.

Real problems are complex. Answers to serious problems are seldom obvious even when the goals of the organization are clear and consistently accepted by the whole staff. Suppose, for example, a school staff is considering the revamping of the foreign language teaching program. They have discussed the question of using federal funds to expand the teaching of foreign languages and to add instructional equipment. They have an opportunity to get several language laboratories at part cost to the local district, the balance to be paid from federal funds through the National Defense Education Act.

A basic question arises: What is the purpose of foreign language in the public schools? Downtown businessmen are saying to the superintendent, "You should teach conversational Russian." One staff member counters, "With whom is a student going to converse in Russian?" A teacher claims, "The purpose of foreign language teaching is to promote language skill. Children should master a second language." A curriculum consultant argues, "Little skill can be acquired in public school. If you teach a foreign language you can justify it only on the ground of its general educational effect. It can create an awareness of another culture." A mother insists that French is the "most cultural language" and therefore the best choice. A world traveler advises, "If you teach a foreign language, teach Spanish. The next generation will be doing a lot of business with South America." "But," a local importer remarks, "you can get translators of language at starvation wages whenever you need them. Besides nobody can learn enough language in the public schools to possess any worthwhile proficiency for business purposes anyhow."

Take any area of school operation and it is found to have its problems. These almost always involve conflicts, dilemmas, and complex effects. Persistent problems in personnel, for example, include: What kind of in-service programs will really result in development of an abler staff? How can you select the best persons for administrative assignments? In what ways can a limited salary budget be used to motivate staff members, and perhaps to reward outstanding performance without damaging general morale?

In finance, questions such as the following arise: What long-range plans will best meet the financial needs of the district? How can one tell whether the budget is appropriately divided among competing departments and requirements? How much money can be afforded for educational television?

The area of pupil personnel presents equally difficult problems: What efforts should be made to keep teen-age students in school? What should be done with children of compulsory school age who are released from correctional institutions? What program is needed for feeding and clothing indigent children? Are special schools for incorrigible boys and girls advisable?

The list could go on indefinitely. Buildings, salaries, criticisms and attacks, federal aid, plant operation, athletics, desegregation, parking facilities, high school fraternities, summer school, student achievement, college preparation, vocational training—suggest a few broad areas each of which presents a wide range of administrative problems in every school system.

School administrators are showing an increased awareness that decisions can be made on a better-than-chance basis even when they deal with extraordinarily complex phenomena. The administrator who must predict how a teaching staff will react to a change in sick leave policy or how the public will respond to a bond issue is dealing with problems of human nature that are far from simple. The predictions that he makes about the results of applying particular techniques require an understanding of human behavior. Beyond this he has a remarkably broad range of technical knowledge and skill to employ in handling the many different materials and services necessary to operate a public school system.

Human Relations

An administrator generally works with and through other people. The Riverdale School Board in Chapter I insisted that their superintendent must be "skillful in working with school personnel, school board, and community organizations." The superintendents in Chapter II themselves prized the capacity for an "unusual understanding of people." Argyris says that the administrator ought to be basically interested in the question, "Why people behave the way they do in organizations,"[13] because, if understanding is achieved, prediction and control of behavior become possible.

When administrators have been asked by interviewers what they do on the job and what problems they encounter most frequently, they usually mention human relations problems. One team of interviewers after talking with a sample of superintendents about "critical experiences" arising in their careers reported that the two major problem areas encountered were "personnel relations" and "public relations."[14]

Another interviewing team who summarized the problems reported by a different sample of superintendents said the administrators' problems consisted of relationships, first, to the school board; second, to the public; and, third, to the school staff.[15]

---

[13] Argyris, Chris. *Personality and Organization*. New York: Harper and Brothers, 1957. p. 5.

[14] Moore, Hollis A., Jr. *Studies in School Administration*. A report on the Cooperative Program in Educational Administration. Washington, D. C.: American Association of School Administrators, a department of the National Education Association, 1957. p. 35.

[15] *Ibid.*, p. 37.

A school staff is a social organization and behaves as such. Interpersonal feelings in a staff are of crucial importance to the goals of the organization. As Thelen points out, top leadership has a special responsibility.

Human relations problems in organizations are likely to be posed by the "top" people. The coldness of a department head, for example, presents the rest of the department with anxieties and inhibitions in their friendship relations. A dogmatic boss sets the stage for undercover revolt and a desire to outmaneuver him by his men. A hesitant or reluctant administrator engenders in workers much anxious conflict over their own roles in the organization. These phenomena are reactions by subordinates to the way their superiors relate to them. The existence of bad feelings within the superior is in itself evidence that he has false expectations about the relationship. False expectations by the top level present subordinates with a prediction of failure, and this strains the relationship further. The existence of false or inappropriate expectations indicates that false prophets have been used—i.e., wrong, inadequate, or inappropriate authority.

The existence of *confused* expectations, in which nobody knows what to expect from himself or anybody else, is an even more serious problem, for it indicates a confusion of the relationships between power and authority. And without clarity in these matters there is no machinery for dealing with any other problem.[16]

The character of staff relations depends heavily on what the superintendent is, and also on what he does. It is a matter of both being and doing. The kind of person the superintendent is can be gauged less by what he says than by how he behaves. He may talk about democracy but practice something else. Concepts of democracy, as will be noted later, seem to be especially subject to distortion. If the superintendent conscientiously believes in the worth of the individual, this belief will show in everything he does. It will deeply affect the way he treats others—not just those whom he likes and who like him, but all others with whom he deals.

Working with a Staff

Like a good class, a good staff has common objectives. Goals are clear. Limitations are recognized. Just as no teacher ever taught a good lesson without painstaking preparation, so no good staff planning session was ever held without thoughtful leadership. The diagnosis of a thousand poor staff meetings—or a

---

[16] Thelen, *op. cit.*, p. 101.

thousand poor classes—would reveal a common lack of planning. However, the staff of a school system is more diversified in its interests, knowledge, and skills than any class of pupils in a school building. This means that a superintendent needs to work with many subgroups in order to release and apply the technical resources available to him.

Mechanics of operation. A well-led staff, like a well-taught class, varies its procedures according to its needs. It creates subgroups for special tasks, uses consultants and other resources when appropriate, and adjusts its mechanics of operation to improve its performance. While a classroom group too frequently uses artificial problems, a staff deals with real problems.

A staff works best and profits most when it is enabled to define and satisfy its own needs. While it is the responsibility of leadership to set certain demands and requirements, the work group itself has a right to participate in the leadership process. Its goal setting and evaluation of progress are necessary to productivity and morale.

Good staffs provide for self-evaluation. Unless a group can decide when it does well and when it does poorly, it cannot improve. The staff itself can best judge what it takes to get at its own evaluation problems.

It takes time for a group to work, as school people are usually aware. Because the process of group thinking takes place in time, no staff can think through a hard problem in 30 minutes. Differences must be talked out. Creative effort in problem solving includes a time dimension to be taken into account by the administrator.

There is no more important administrative task for a superintendent than to find time for a staff to think and plan together. For their regular meetings they probably should decide upon a schedule and commit themselves to it. Once set, the meeting time ought to be jealously guarded since canceled meetings can injure morale. But meetings ought to be devoted only to important problem-centered types of work that cannot be handled in other ways. The administrator needs considerable face-to-face contact with his staff as a group, in subgroups, and individually in order to keep in touch with what goes on.

The selection process. An administrator in the course of time invariably has the opportunity to select some high-status staff members. Selection is the key to good performance in administration as in teaching or any other assignment. Careful thought given to the characteristics demanded in administrative positions is necessary. Problem-solving ability is basic. It must be remembered, however, that problem solving is seldom a matter of simply choosing between one or two alternatives. The process usually includes working with others as well as clear thinking. The field of selection is a fruitful area for research.

Verbal facility is important inasmuch as communication is an indispensable part of the administrative job. Broad acquaintance with the community is also a requisite. Successful administrators are those easily accepted by other people—hence personal likability is to be considered.

No one can say that a high "score" in such characteristics is a guarantee of a good administrator. At the low end of the scale, however, selection seems fairly uncomplicated. It is probably easier to say who will not make a good administrator than who will. Demonstrated inability to work with others, inability to function in a problematical situation, inability to communicate, lack of adequate training, or a retrogressive philosophy of education are all disabling characteristics and should disqualify applicants for administrative jobs. Special educational competence is demanded, including understanding of the learning process, knowledge of developmental levels in children, as well as knowledge of administrative techniques. As a capstone to his qualifications an administrator needs an orientation toward people that squares with the general purpose of American schools. A progressive attitude toward the education profession must be coupled with a humane attitude toward children.

Any study of the process by which leaders are chosen calls into question the soundness of the judgment exercised by the selecting person or board. There is no assurance that the abilities required for delegating responsibility, opening channels of communication, and managing the processes of group decision are those actually sought and found by persons making these personnel decisions.

What is democratic? Consideration of human interaction usually brings up the question of what is democratic. This much-abused term has many meanings and serves many purposes. There is a prevailing fogginess about our view of democracy in staff relations. Some fallaciously equate democracy with happiness. Good feelings have little to do with democratic attitudes and procedures. A staff may abound with good morale and still achieve little or nothing. Staff productivity depends on organization and leadership as well as morale.

Carried away with the zeal to be democratic, administrators have too often failed to develop an adequate working concept of democracy. Halpin, speaking of "democratic leadership," says:

> . . . the notion of "democratic" leadership, as this idea has been applied in education, has degenerated into an empty slogan and has immobilized more leaders than it has liberated. A "democratic" leadership relationship between the superintendent and his staff is good, but let us remember, too, that the primary responsibility of a leader is to lead, and that by doing so he becomes no less "democratic." "Democracy" is a political concept that has accumulated so many diverse and loose connotations that its meaning is no longer precise even in the political sphere. . . .
>
> Yet we repeatedly encounter superintendents who fear to take a stand, who hesitate to initiate structure, lest they be accused of being antidemocratic. This is nonsense, for the superintendents who adopt this attitude eventually lose the respect of their staffs; teachers can quickly spot the phony who tries to hide his own ineptness in the soggy oatmeal of a pseudo group-process.[17]

Unclearness as to the meaning of democracy in a staff relationship is evidenced by such common comments as, "This may not be democratic but it's effective." "He was too democratic." "It's all right to be democratic but we have to get the job done."

Kurt Lewin showed long ago that democracy does not occupy one end of a continuum at the opposite pole from autocracy but is something qualitatively different.

More than feeling good. The books that deal with personnel relations are likely to indicate that the administrator who would get along well with his subordinates and who would have a smoothly working staff must observe certain principles of group action and be mindful of certain basic rules of organization and administration. The books, however, can not say what to do in a particular situation. When the superintendent decides that for the good of the organization a certain department head should move to a different post and attempts to implement the decision, he may encounter difficulties that he could not possibly anticipate. The person may have some connection with a prominent figure in the community who is in a position to exert pressure to thwart the decision. Perhaps the person by virtue of having been for many years in a particular spot has developed a following of

---

[17] Halpin, Andrew W. "The Superintendent's Effectiveness as a Leader." *Administrator's Notebook* 7:1-4; October 1958.

colleagues and associates who are loyal to him and who will be determined to protect him against any threat to his position and status. How does an administrator find effective ways to deal with a defensive staff member or to console one who is resentful? Maybe the reason that some administrators are inclined to concentrate on good feelings rather than on getting the job done is to be found in the difficult and complex problems they face in personnel.

The staff in which there is the best feeling may be the staff that is accomplishing the least. Any administrator who will pursue the goals of the organization and lead his staff in a forthright manner to achieve these goals will find himself at cross purposes with some of his staff and at times with his board and his community. Changes have to be planned and almost every change affects somebody in a way that he sees as unfavorable to him.

Administration, therefore, is notoriously involved in the feelings of people, and solutions to personnel problems are not always a matter of following the well-known principles of group action or generalizations regarding human nature. To understand the Frustration-Aggression Hypothesis and to know that frustration situations breed aggressive behavior is useful but will not provide the answer to the question of what to do about a disappointed candidate for promotion.

How do you work with a department head whose self-insight is limited? What do you do for his in-service growth? What can be done to make him feel secure in trying new ways of doing things? The administrator who is most successful is probably the one who first of all keeps his eyes on the goals of the organization, and in the second place, is as considerate as possible of every person with whom he has any dealings at all.

Advising and Assisting the Board

To achieve the end of better teaching there is nothing more important for the administrator to do than to help his board, and other citizens, set goals and policies that promise to improve teaching processes. To say that the school administrator is the board's executive officer is trite but true. He is also the counselor and adviser to the board, and other citizens, on educational matters in which he is presumably expert. Boards of education have a right to expect their administrator to perform the roles for which he was employed.

Essentially a group of laymen, a board can not be expected to do the creative thinking that leads to educational progress. Nor is there reason to expect that the best ideas for improving teaching and learning should suddenly come to the members of a board of education. One would not necessarily expect a school board to propose that district money be spent to develop potential staff members or to engage in curriculum research. It is part of the administrative role to do such thinking and to present such proposals to the board. The chief reason why more boards do not approve funds for such worthy purposes is that they have not been asked by their administrators.

Boards have only limited ways of knowing about sources of assistance and stimulation available to school systems such as membership in school study councils, participation in research ventures, and other professional growth opportunities for staff members. To inform, plan, and recommend such means to staff improvement is a responsibility that only the chief administrator can discharge.

Relationships with boards of education are necessarily a major concern of the top administrator.[18] School boards are likely to be representative of various community groups and to reflect divergent outlooks. Religious groups, labor groups, racial groups and others strive to get the ear of board members and to influence board decisions and policies. Board members coming from different sides of town may have different attitudes with respect, say, to the social life in schools as a result of pressures exerted upon them. These differences can become particularly acute in relation to such problems as desegregation, pupil transfers, athletics, social clubs, school activities, and even questions of what ought to be taught in classrooms.

Living with Pressures

The school administrators whose views are summarized in Chapter II indicated that their work in considerable measure consisted in handling pressures. The management of pressures becomes an administrative concern in connection with many kinds of problems. In a study to which we have already referred,

[18] The AASA Yearbook of 1956 deals with these relationships quite fully.

a sample of superintendents reported that the pressures they consistently experienced were:

(a) pressures exerted on the superintendent to act on grounds other than the educational welfare of the children,

(b) school districting problems,

(c) the pressure of not enough time, and

(d) economic conditions beyond repair.[19]

Suppose a civic group is promoting an essay contest. The rules are set and the money for the prizes has been budgeted before the schools are approached. How can the administrator turn this offer into something more beneficial, but much less appealing to the publicity-minded members of the organization?

A neighborhood with a newly desegregated school becomes a battleground where issues concerning school achievement, changing real estate values, pupil transfer policies, and faculty morale are involved. There is always the possibility of offending a powerful group if a recommendation or decision goes one way, and the likelihood of offending an opposing group if a contrary decision is made.

A classic example of recent times is to be found in the case of the Little Rock fight on desegregation. As Superintendent Virgil Blossom said,

When I say I was a central figure, I mean it both literally and figuratively. I was superintendent of schools at Little Rock when that capital city of Arkansas became the battleground on which die-hard segregationists of the South chose to oppose the Federal Government. As a professional educator, I was the 'man in the middle' of an emotional and fundamental civil-rights struggle that all the world witnessed—and still watches anxiously.[20]

The Number One Task

The preceding paragraphs have given cursory treatment to several areas of administrative responsibility and concern. By no means do they endeavor to present any such systematic analyses of school administration as those to be found in earlier yearbooks of the AASA. The present selection of tasks and problems is intended to indicate the need for substantial preparation and in-service experiences for school administrators.

---

19 Moore, *op. cit.*, p. 37.
20 Blossom, Virgil. "The Untold Story of Little Rock. I Was The Man In The Middle," Part One. *Saturday Evening Post* 231:19-21; May 23, 1959.

In contemplating the administrative assignment one would conclude that the administrator's number one task is thinking. He must think about his job as a whole. Thinking, of course, both precedes and accompanies doing. Unless an administrator contemplates his job in its totality he will fall into the rut of relying on shortsighted expedients. Failing to find, or to make, time to look carefully and deeply at the job as a whole, he resorts to the convenient, normally accepted ideas and answers. In order to achieve his purposes the administrator uses a conceptual framework for his job. He is the one person in the organization who is in a position to organize the major processes of decision making on which action can be based. Unless he sees as one of his key roles the patterning of staff resources to serve the organizational goals, he runs the risk of spending himself on the less consequential demands of his job.

No administrator today can work long on hoarded intellectual capital. Once he has completed a program of formal graduate study he is not a wound-up mechanism that will run perpetually on stored energy. On the job he ought to work at least as hard as he did in the university to add to his knowledge and to develop his professional skills.

This will be necessary if we as a professional group live up to the goals of the 1959 AASA Resolutions Committee. They said:

> The Association further believes that improvement in education is so im-important that it cannot await the ideal circumstance or the perfect climate. Now is the time to exercise wisdom, insight, imagination, and creativity so that continued improvement is made in organization, finance, curriculum, instruction, teacher training, recruitment, and administrative leadership.[21]

CONCLUSIONS

Consideration of the kind of position that the school administrator holds sheds some light on the kind of preparation and professional growth programs that are needed. If there has ever been any question that the school administrator should be a broadly trained professional person, there is no question about it any more. The signs of the times and the demands of his job

[21] American Association of School Administrators. *Your AASA in 1958-59.* Washington, D. C.: the Association, a department of the National Education Association, 1959. p. 247.

leave no doubt as to the professional stature that it takes. An administrator working in the public schools finds himself faced with problems ranging in character from the purchase of school sites to the selection of personnel, from the making of a budget to the assigning of a department head. To deal with these problems, he needs some familiarity with the whole range of knowledge in such areas as buildings, personnel, finance, as well as the psychology of teaching and learning. He must understand the skills of persons specializing in a number of technical fields even though he may not be himself highly competent in the techniques they use.

It is apparent that school administration requires the skill of seeing the task broadly. The administrator should understand the public schools as a component part of the social complex in which they operate. This same breadth of outlook is needed in coming to grips with the administrative job from day to day. Successful administration requires the capacity to "see the whole picture."

This yearbook stresses the point that professional preparation for school administration should provide grounding in educational and administrative theory. Theoretical approaches to administrative problems are proving their value as different chapters in this yearbook point out. However, there are many specialties within school administration, and theoretical formulations pertinent to one may be of little use to another. This suggests a need for selective specialization in the school staff and the over-all administrative judgment at the top to coordinate and release it.

It is easy to see why school administration should include knowledge in other fields important to education. The school administrator should have better than a passing acquaintance with areas to which his own work is related. Recognition of this need, of course, underlies the provision for strong supplementary work in related disciplines recommended in Chapter VII as well as elsewhere in this yearbook.

The mere need for facts in decision making shows why the school administrator should be familiar with a wide range of research tools, methods, and procedures. Much of his work is applied research. He must rely on research techniques to locate sources of difficulty and to get data necessary for evaluating possible solutions to problems. In the larger school systems, at least, the critical skill is not so much in the execution of the technique (for example, the setting up of the payroll on the IBM machines) as in judging the relevance of various applicable methods for doing the job. But today's administrator should be research-minded in his approach to all problems. He must do a good deal of investigating in order to make wise decisions.

We live in times of accelerated change with rising expectations of school administrators. A golden opportunity exists to justify the vast confidence expressed by the public in school administrators generally. If school administrators are to live up to public and professional expectations for them, they are obliged to look to the whole range of their responsibilities, not the least of which is spotlighted in the topic of this yearbook—*the preparation of administrators*. Every administrator on the job had better take a deep look at his own school system in this regard, decide on next steps, and insure the wherewithal to proceed. The public schools have a greater stake in preparation programs than do the universities. What schools themselves do today in cooperative effort with university programs of preparation and in-service growth will affect education for a century to come.

chapter VI

Better Ways
To Select Administrators

Though demands on schools and schoolmen bear close watching because they change so rapidly and with such occasionally devastating effect, there is one demand which needs no unblinking scrutiny, because it never changes. This durable demand—and a Gibraltar among demands it is—may be phrased in most simple terms:

Schools need leaders.

The continued strength and vigor of any institution is dependent in large measure upon its ability to provide a continuous supply of creative leadership to its critical points of control. Fortunately for the peace of mind of those who must concern themselves with this demand for leadership, it is likely that, one way or another, it *will* be met. There are those who like to work in schools, and (see Chapter II) there are among them those who like—even prefer—to lead. What is more to the point, there appears to be no shortage of those who would aspire to administrative positions in education.

This abundance of aspirants confronts school boards like Riverdale with the difficult task of choosing wisely the most likely candidate from among a field of 65 applicants. The superintendent who is chosen must then take his turn at the same numbers game, by helping pick the best applicant for each of many critical points such as principalships and central staff positions. Though he may verbalize glibly about the kinds of men he prefers for his key posts, and though he may set up certain criteria for selection, as his board did before him, still, when it comes to the actual choosing, he is all too often guilty of the same tea leaf techniques which were used to make him the *unum* out of the *pluribus*.

With the fact in mind that means of identifying and selecting prospects for school administration are often difficult to apply, this chapter will nevertheless make some attempt at discussing various ways now known for winnowing out the best available talent. Along the way an effort will be made to include a few pointers as to how these means might be put to best use.

Two assumptions are implicit in the discussion which follows: First, that the number of persons aspiring to leadership positions in public education is greater than the number of positions to be filled; and, second, that those persons possessing whatever it is that is required for truly creative leadership are in short supply. These assumptions suggest two dimensions for the task of choosing people to administer the schools, and two lines of effort related to them. The first of these is *identification*—the early recognition of potential talent, and systematic effort to direct the interests and aspirations of the persons possessing it toward educational administration. If indeed there does exist a plethora of people who long to administer, certainly it is only wise for those who choose administrators to have some means of sifting the lot and identifying the best. "Systematic effort to direct the interests . . ." implies nothing more nor less than determined recruitment of those who are identified. Since recruitment, to some, brings to mind a picture of Uncle Sam pointing his finger, the more descriptive term *attraction* will be employed occasionally, because it is a bit more seemly. It means the same thing—a desperate battle to the finish for this profession's share of the sum total of talent available for the nation's work.

The second dimension for the task of choosing is *selection*—deliberate, informed, and intelligent choice among a group of applicants for a particular position. It might be best, here at the outset, to distinguish between identification and selection, since both terms will appear consistently throughout the chapter. Though the two tasks are not the same at all, certain tools quite useful in their performance are identical, thereby causing possible confusion. Herein lies the difference: Many people, including the individual himself, are capable of identifying a potential administrator, while only those who employ or who operate preparation programs are equipped to take the further step of selection. Chronologically speaking, attraction comes somewhere between these two steps, and is the obligation of all those who function as identifiers.

IDENTIFYING POTENTIAL LEADERS

The most common identifier of potential talent to date has been the individual himself. That such self-identification does not always insure a flow of the best potential into school administration is obvious. For altogether too long, the profession has relied on haphazard choice and random mobility, among those who would like to lead, to provide for the leadership needs of the schools. That this has allowed a certain amount of mediocrity to creep into the ranks of practicing administrators is evident to even the most starry-eyed members of the profession. It is even more evident to certain pundits from outside the ranks. William H. Whyte's documentation of his opinion that those who can't, enter education, is a case in point. His discussion in *The Organization Man* of the type of person who prepares for the education profession is disturbing even though it is written for popular shock appeal.

Although self-identification has brought some of the most excellent talent available into the schools, along with the less gifted, it still is obvious that a planned, determined, and intelligent program involving many people would do a better job, and would make for a better batting average.

As Early as Possible

Such a program would begin farther down in the school systems than most would suspect—it would begin in the secondary schools, in fact. No research has been directed toward testing the practicability of this suggestion, but there are some capable thinkers in education who insist that identifiers could profitably commence their efforts at this level—the same one at which most prospective teachers should be found. Certainly many of the attributes which would cause a young person to stand out as a likely candidate for the teaching profession would also cause him to be recognized as a possible future administrator. It is

145

true that secondary school students are as yet immature, and that he who would identify will run afoul of almost all of the problems of recognizing talent which are inherent in any such endeavor. Still, common sense would indicate that the better students, the academic and social leaders of the schools, will stand out and will be identified. It is to be hoped that teachers, local school administrators, and guidance counselors will make a practice of encouraging such people to consider the education profession.

Other sources of outstanding young people who might be attracted to administration as a life work are the junior colleges, undergraduate schools of education, and other schools and colleges of the university. Even though the study reported in Chapter II indicates that, with school administrators, it's four to one in favor of their taking undergraduate degrees in some field other than education, still these practitioners must have had at least a smattering of hours in beginning education courses before they could teach in their chosen fields. Here, at the undergraduate level, then, is where identifiers need to be on constant alert for signs of leadership talent.

In Our Own Back Yards

Besides searching through the scholastic ranks in order to identify top-level students, those teachers and administrators in the field need to be watchful for potential talent among their own colleagues and faculty members. The most likely prospects for the jobs of administering schools do not always identify themselves, for various reasons, sometimes because they lack the funds required for further preparation. Such talent, if it really *is* talent, needs to be encouraged, brought to the fore, and, if necessary, provided with the means of getting prepared. Recommending such people to the faculty of a nearby graduate school of education is the very least that a local school talent scout can do. Teachers possessing personal and professional fitness must be identified and prompted to pursue training programs in preparation for administrative roles, if schools are to be provided with capable administrators and not just saddled with those whose only real qualification is availability.

For the most part, identifiers have overlooked the largest source of prospective administrators by clinging to the notion

146

that women cannot be successful school administrators. It requires little research effort to discover that women outnumber men in the teaching ranks, and hence must, by sheer weight of numbers, include more outstanding individuals than does the male group. Identifiers will do well to bear this fact in mind while engaged in ferreting out likely candidates for administrative careers.

An Organized Approach

Here, then, are recommendations as to what needs to be done to avoid the slipshod identification procedures which have allowed too high a proportion of the outstanding young people in the schools and colleges to drift into other professions simply through default on the part of those of us in education:

1. Identification should begin at the high school level and should be a responsibility of school administrators, teachers, and counselors.
2. Further identification should take place during the teacher preparation period.
3. Identifiers should not overlook administrative potential among the women.
4. Local school systems can aid in the identification and recruitment process by setting up machinery which allows talented people to be identified from within the teaching ranks, and which affords these talented ones special incentives and possibilities for preparing themselves while on the job.
5. Graduate schools in education need to make identification procedures much less casual than they have been.
6. Graduate faculties can employ tactics such as appointment of recruiting officers from among their own ranks, encouragement of alumni to recommend likely candidates, and better interdepartmental communication regarding the existence of promising prospects.

ATTRACTING POTENTIAL LEADERS

Teacher organizations at local, state, and national levels have constantly made deliberate and well-planned attempts to attract young people into their ranks, and must continue to do so. Future teacher groups have been quite successful, as have career planning sessions, publicity campaigns, and simple word-of-mouth advertising, in presenting to young people both the problems and rewards which are the lot of the educator. Unfortunately, only a very small percentage of this recruiting effort has been directed toward attracting people to educational administration as a particular part of the teaching profession. Administration and its rewards and possibilities as a life work have been more than a little bit neglected.

In an effort to be fair and to present both sides of the picture, those who engage in teacher recruitment have attempted to keep the inherent idealism of the group liberally laced with some hard-bound realism in the form of warnings about the meager salaries and lack of room for advancement which are often the fate of the teacher-to-be. These warnings, though well meant and indeed necessary, tend to have a particularly adverse effect upon a certain ambitious group of young persons who aspire to be successful *leaders* at whatever career they choose to follow. If this group could be apprised of the fact that classroom teaching, though an especially admirable lifework, is not the only possibility for a trained educator, it would seem likely that more of the talented and ambitious young people might be attracted to the profession.

It is true that it is not usually possible for an administrator to bypass the necessary years of teaching experience as an essential part of his career line. Heretofore, the school administrator has come chiefly from the ranks of the teaching profession, and the study reported in Chapter II provides no evidence to suggest that a change in this basic screening requirement is imminent.

It is just as true, however, that this teaching period might well be considered as an apprenticeship for the aspiring administrator. If properly conceived and planned, such a program of comparatively brief teaching experience, coupled with possibilities for advancement into the field of broader and better paid service in administration, could attract and hold some eager youths who would otherwise not become interested in professional education as a lifework. Too, if properly identified, vigorously recruited, and carefully selected, these potential leaders will go a long way toward allaying the often well-founded suspicion that professional education fails to attract its share of the most talented.

148

The College Attracts

Institutions which prepare educators can play a role of particular profit, both to themselves and to the profession, by engaging in determined efforts to attract prospects who have been identified at the high school and junior college level. "Senior days" and "career days" in which secondary school graduates visit the campus are already bare-faced recruiting devices—why not be just as blunt with a positive, considered effort to present the charms of educational administration while the audience is captive? Certain college counselors and consultants are often in the public schools—why not charge them with a mission to seek out and attempt to attract qualified and promising students into the profession? Certainly recruiting attempts by a responsible, respectable, and absolutely essential profession can be at least as sophisticated, and partially as successful, as the measures employed by the Armed Services in attracting senior boys to a military career.

Other recruiting measures employed by training institutions involve the wide distribution of guidance leaflets exploring the area of administration and the enlistment of key alumni for nominating potential leaders and encouraging them to enter the field.

By far the most successful attracting devices—other than the quality of the program itself—make use of some form of financial assistance for the talented recruit. Though the young men and women identified as potential administrators may be willing to spend some comparatively lean years while preparing themselves for increased income in the future, they will hardly be willing or able to forego such pleasures as food, rent, and clothing. Few especially bright young persons possessed of the leadership attributes so much in demand will consider a "garret and candle" type of existence today, when so many more attractive possibilities are in evidence. When institutions can provide scholarships, assistantships, and like aids to the most qualified prospects for educational administration, then will the profession become an able competitor in the race for talent. Luckily, the foundations and other organizations able to provide assistance are cognizant of this fact and are beginning to provide financial help for some few prospects.

State-Wide Groups Attract

Although state education agencies must perforce take cognizance of the need for recruiting talented administrators, the attracting role of such state organizations is as yet a rather hazy and difficult one. The state agencies' job of *certifying* administrators could possibly militate against any determined recruitment activities at this level. Such possible conflict of roles, however, does not preclude the agencies' creating proper conditions which will encourage other state-wide groups to engage in active recruitment. State school boards associations, for example, could exert considerable positive influence, through their own journals and other mass media, toward bringing about increased public acceptance of education in general, and administration in particular, as desirable careers for young people. Such school board groups, joined by the state branch of the school administrators association, could conceivably offer scholarships, or encourage others to do so, in the same manner that the national association offers the S. D. Shankland Memorial Scholarship through the contributions of convention exhibitors. Both state-level groups—the school boards and the administrators organizations—stand to benefit greatly from successful recruitment practices, and both are in an advantageous position to bring large-scale advertising and publicity guns to bear upon the problem.

Local Schools Attract

Some administrators will remember the fable of the potentate who, being waited upon by a group of lesser kings, was asked by them how he managed to maintain his position of power in a kingdom noted for its numerous aspirants to the throne. The crafty old despot merely led them to his largest wheat field and strolled among the not-yet-ripened grain, pinching off a wheathead or two occasionally as he strolled. "This is my answer," he replied to the questioners, and they understood him not, until they saw that he was destroying only the *tallest* and *strongest* stalks of the growing wheat. . . .

Certainly no modern-day administrator (or administrative team), no matter how authoritarian, can afford the practice of "squelching" talent, like the monarch. Quite the contrary, it is the local school which must be the most potent single force in locating prospective administrators and in encouraging them to prepare for the profession.

A tried, and often true, means that schools may use to attract students of outstanding capabilities is the Future Teachers of America organization which is affiliated with, and encouraged by, NEA. Cadet teaching opportunities and provisions for guidance help and occupational information to those pupils evincing an interest in a teaching-administrative career can also be of considerable impact in a full program.

Far more important to the local district, because of the greater immediacy of the need, is the process of attracting talented teachers with demonstrable aptitude for administration into a program of preparation for leadership responsibilities. Ideally, of course, these talented ones will then proceed to practice on home grounds, right where they were identified in the first place. As has been indicated, no problem exists in finding persons *willing* to take such posts, but in locating persons *capable* of filling such positions—"aye, there's the rub!"

An aggressive, active, and planned policy of recruitment has become extremely essential to those school districts which are growing rapidly. This need for attracting prospective principals without delay stems from the fact that many school systems are constructing buildings faster than they can find proper people to administer a program of education in them! "Bait" that schools may use to attract such persons from among their own corps of teachers ranges from provision for special training programs to be undertaken on the prospect's own time to leaves of absence coupled with some financial assistance for advanced study in graduate schools of education. A more and more common—and quite successful—practice involves the district's offering qualified teachers positions as "trainees," or "head teachers," which allows them to spend part or full-time training on the job, under the tutelage of experienced practitioners. One such plan, which has achieved considerable success over a period of years, will be discussed in greater detail later in this chapter.

Suffice it to say, in concluding the current section regarding attraction of talented prospective administrators, that only those local school boards (and top-level administrative staffs) who make administrative positions sufficiently enticing, and who organize and implement and *finance* a determined recruiting effort, will be able to attract the best prospects to positions of responsibility.

SELECTING PROSPECTIVE ADMINISTRATORS

Frederick Lewis Allen once concluded that "everything is more complicated than it seems to most people." It would appear, even to a somewhat casual observer, that this business of selecting candidates for preparation or practice in the field of educational administration is certainly no exception to Mr. Allen's rule. Indeed, research and literature in the field of leadership indicate that the task is growing increasingly complex, as more and more is learned about the intricate phenomena of personality, group structure, communications, perception, and many other aspects of the problem. Let not those who must select despair, however. Some guidelines for intelligent choosing are emerging from the mists of the numerous inquiries so far undertaken. It is the purpose of the section which follows to point out as many of those guidelines as seem appropriate to the task of selecting prospective—or, as one wag put it, "expectant"—administrators.

The Profession Selects

Assessment by the profession is a potent factor in the selection of administrative talent. Higher standards for membership in the professional associations (see Chapter XI) suggest that the influence of the profession will increase. However, since only those who will award degrees or certificates or who will employ can take the final step and actually *choose* among applicants, the profession *per se* will need to spend its time and effort in such activities as are exemplified by the present volume. Such efforts will include encouragement, and perhaps even sponsorship, of research into the leadership function as it applies to educational administration, the study of selection techniques, and the promulgation of findings resulting from both endeavors. Other than encouraging, prodding, providing ideas, and setting high standards for entrance into its own ranks, the profession will be forced to rely on other agencies to employ adequate selection devices.

The Preparing Institution Selects

Colleges and universities may perform a preliminary screening upon admission to their programs of teacher education, and another upon admission to, or retention in, their programs for graduate work in administration. This situation, which allows the institutions to take at least two selection swings at every candidate before anyone else gets a chance at choosing him, has not resulted in the elimination of significant numbers of dubious contenders.

Part of the reason for this unwillingness to turn away even some of the obviously unsuited candidates stems from the fact that the graduate schools must compete for students, not only with other institutions, but interdepartmentally, with themselves. Such competition, made ridiculous by the emphasis on departmental size as a measure of effectiveness, has caused training agencies to fail to apply some of the selection devices at hand.

Another reason that selection by the institution is sometimes less than impressively effective arises from a kind of uncertainty as to which selection criteria to apply. It is true that selection must be made on the basis of some value system, but college teachers are not at all ready to admit that they possess the one and only "correct" value orientation. Of course, this question of values is a touchy one, and can be dealt with here only by suggesting that much cooperative endeavor be engaged in by all concerned—the state, the profession, the schools, and the colleges. These endeavors should lead to some tentative agreement, at least, concerning what criteria to employ.

Even after reaching tentative agreement on these criteria, a third reason which might cause institutions of higher learning to be less than rigorous in their selection processes involves their justifiable reluctance to employ devices which are not yet of proven validity. To date, as was indicated in Chapter III, no one procedure or set of procedures has been developed which can claim infallibility in separating the most capable candidates from their less talented fellows. As Hall and McIntyre so succinctly put it, "there is no simple shibboleth that will unerringly identify the unfit. . . ."[1]

---

[1] Hall, Roy M., and McIntyre, Kenneth E. "The Student Personnel Program." *Administrative Behavior in Education.* (Edited by Roald F. Campbell and Russell T. Gregg.) New York: Harper and Brothers, 1957. Chapter 11, p. 406.

Luckily, however, a number of institutions have maintained an unflagging zeal in their search for measures which might help select. Researchers from these schools have continued to refine existing techniques, and have even produced a new one or two in the past few years. As was strongly hinted above, none of the evidence is yet conclusive, but a few facts are now known about how institutions might best select from among the many applicants for preparation programs in school administration. Some of the most pertinent and promising of the techniques studied will be touched upon here, along with some *im*pertinent and *un*promising ones.

Tests. It is agreed, among men who know selection best, that no battery of tests, much less a single test, is sufficiently accurate and discriminating to warrant its use as the *sole* selection device for measuring applicants for preparation programs. It is possible today, even simple, to test a person's ability to study advanced mathematics with some acceptable degree of accuracy. It is possible today to test for visual acuity, muscular coordination, reading rate, and speed of reflexes. In short, many of the readily definable activities of mankind are susceptible to measurement by means of tests. Unfortunately, leadership and the related concept, ability to lead, are not yet clearly definable—except in a merry-go-round way which produces such inanities as, "Leadership ability is that which an individual exhibits when he leads."

Since it is not yet possible to "test for" leadership talent, it would seem that some graduate schools (again, see Chapter III) have thrown up their hands in dismay and concluded that if tests cannot do all the job they are not able to do any part of the task of choosing. This conclusion is a patently false one. There *are* some helpful tests, which will do a part of the selection job quite well. Their chief usefulness, quite often, is not in skimming off the most talented from a group of applicants, but in draining off those at the bottom of the distribution barrel— those least likely to succeed.

The most familiar types of tests are those paper-and-pencil devices which attempt to measure certain traits of the individual. Let it be admitted at once that *just* a study of traits has proved to be fairly fruitless. There are simply no specific identical traits universally possessed by all leaders and *not* possessed by nonleaders. There are, however, extreme deviations that are intolerable to even the most undiscriminating selectors, and these deviations can be identified or at least suggested by appropriate written tests.

It is unfortunate that the first trait that comes to mind is usually intelligence, because mental ability is one of the peculiarities of mankind most difficult to define and measure. Still, research has proved that there is some relationship between leadership and intelligence. However nebulous it may be, the institutions of higher learning would certainly have difficulty denying this relationship, because their whole *raison d'être* is based on it. To be truthful, about all that is known about the intelligence of leaders is that they are usually a bit brighter than their average followers, and probably should be. If these findings are to be accepted, then it certainly behooves a graduate school to attempt to take some measure of a candidate's intelligence before setting out to prepare him for school administration. Since teachers, on the whole, rank well above the average mentally, the odds are heavy against their accepting and following an educational leader much less well endowed than they.

Scores on certain tests are known to provide something more than a wild guess as to the examinee's mental abilities. Among these are the *Miller Analogies Test*, the *Watson-Glaser Critical Thinking Appraisal*, and the aptitude section of the *Graduate Record Examination*. There is research evidence to the effect that any one of these tests would exhibit some power to discriminate between the best and the worst of a group of applicants, and it is also demonstrable that ordinarily all three will give a similar picture of a person's mental prowess. Still, it is here recommended that more than one be administered as a double check, and to increase the accuracy of the estimate. No arbitrary cut-off point is recommended, although each institution might well consider setting a point, preferably a composite score on at least two reputable tests of mental ability, below which it would be unwilling to assume the risk of selection. Such a cut-off point would be necessarily somewhat arbitrary, and should be rather low.

Tests of knowledge can also be used for selection purposes. The *National Teacher Examinations* include tests of professional information, English expression, and knowledge of several broad fields (social studies, literature, and fine arts; and science and mathematics). An administration and supervision test is also available. Because of the nature of these tests, they might be used more appropriately for job selection than for screening in the training situation.

Another set of traits which undeniably bear some relationship to leadership is most often lumped under the portmanteau term "personality." There are several objective-type, paper-and-pencil inventories which purport to measure these traits, and these instruments are all available, even though they require a capable analyst for interpretation. As yet, no convincing case can be made for their use in selection, other than in screening out extreme deviants. Such measures may, however, prove to be of considerable value for counseling efforts during a preparation program.

Much the same can be said for instruments which measure interests, attitudes, preferences, and values. There must be some relationship between these traits and the ability to lead—at least common sense would tell us that no leader could possess interests and values and attitudes which are at extreme variance with those of his followers. Such measures, though of value to the psychologist and the counselor, are of questionable value when used in a selection battery. Most of the tests of this breed are so susceptible to "bending" by the examinee, particularly if he is somewhat "test-wise," that the selector can never be certain that the score does not indicate only a strong desire to get selected rather than what it was supposed to indicate.

Up to this point, we have been discussing the measurement of certain general traits that are assumed to have some relationship with ability to administer educational programs. Little can be claimed for the trait approach to selection, for reasons mentioned previously, although certain tests of ability and knowledge might be useful as small parts of the big picture.

It has been known for some time that *situations* affect behavior in significant ways. This knowledge has led many authorities away from the "traitist" and toward the "situationist" point of view. The latter approach assumes that performance, or what an administrator *does,* is the important thing. The difficulty here lies in the problem of placing candidates in situations that are both relevant and sufficiently controlled so that behavior can be scientifically studied. A promising recent development, however, might prove to be a highly significant one: the construction and use of situational action tests.

156

The task of the situational action test is to determine what the candidate *does* in specific situations, in contrast with the traditional test, which determines what he *says he would do* if certain conditions were present. These measuring instruments place the examinee in some type of hypothetical situation (made as real as possible, by every device available) and attempt to scale his reactions, methods of operation, and leadership tendencies by use of skillful observers. This process has some of the attractive advantages of the ubiquitous Link Trainer of World War II notoriety—it allows the examinee every opportunity to make fatal mistakes without anything like fatal consequences. It also provides a unique opportunity to place many applicants in an identical situation, in order that their reactions may be compared systematically. Such identical situations just do not occur for the rater's convenience anywhere outside of such a hypothetical arrangement.

Among the very few devices[2] of this type which are specifically concerned with educational administration are those detailed and painstakingly constructed ones employed in the Criteria of Success Project administered by the University Council for Educational Administration. Aided by the Educational Testing Service of Princeton, New Jersey, this group has developed a week-long situation-type test to be applied to elementary school principals. Intended as an approach to the development of the dimensions of school administration (and, incidentally, to the classification of candidates for beginning administrative positions), this test is the most concentrated effort made to date to avoid some of the shortcomings of traditional selection devices.

Preliminary validation studies of a comprehensive and exacting nature have caused the sponsors of this project to be cautiously optimistic regarding the discriminatory powers of the procedure as it now stands. As yet the device has not been applied to groups of candidates (for either jobs or preparation programs), but has been used largely with people already filling the position of elementary school principal in many parts of the nation. At no place in their plans do the sponsors of this procedure intend it to substitute for all other selection devices now extant;

---

2 Several different types of test situations are employed, including a heavy emphasis on "in-basket" items, so called because most often these tests place the examinee in a make-believe job and then thrust upon him an in-basket full of problems to solve, usually under pressure of time.

it is not a cure-all. Rather, it is a promising device now under study for filling in the great gaps in the knowledge which selectors now possess.[3]

Rating scales. Also available for use in the selection of talented school leaders are those despairs of the statistician known as rating scales. Though it is true that the continuum which each of these devices measures is almost never divisible into the nice even scale steps which are so dear to the mathematician, still the most carefully developed and applied of these scales exhibit an undeniable ability to help separate the good from the not-so-good candidates.

Extreme care must be employed in the constructing and weighting of these devices to allow for the fact that raters nearly always use the upper end of the scale, to the complete exclusion of the lower ratings available for their choosing. There are two ways to avoid this overrating, but neither is easy. The first involves the training of the raters. If those who use the scale are thoroughly familiar with it; if they are trained observers who know exactly what they are looking for and how to interpret what they see in a uniform fashion, then much of the tendency to overrate is eliminated. Such a corps of trained raters must not only be familiar with the scale but also be well acquainted with the usually quite heterogeneous group of candidates to be rated. Since a group of unbiased raters who meet both criteria is particularly difficult to form, this cure for the problem is a difficult one to administer.

Another means of reducing the tendency to overrate is the forced-choice technique. This involves offering the rater the task of choosing between two (or among several) descriptive statements of equal value-tone—either good or bad, as long as they are equal in his (the rater's) eyes. He then chooses the statement which best describes the ratee or the ratee's mode of operation. Only one of the alternatives is relevant to effective performance in educational administration, but it is most important that the rater *not* be able to tell which is the relevant statement. If he can "see through" the device, he will be inclined to select the "better" one. As is fairly obvious, the constructing of two equally attractive statements for each

---

[3] Griffiths, Daniel E. "Development of Criteria of Success in School Administration." Report to the American Educational Research Association, Atlantic City, New Jersey, February 1959.

judgment to be rendered is a task for experts in scale construction. Difficult as they are to build, forced-choice scales applied by a group of raters (peers, superiors, and subordinates of the ratee, if possible) are among the most promising devices for picking out really talented applicants for graduate training in educational administration.

Also of considerable value to those who must select for the graduate schools is the peer rating ("buddy sheet") which the Armed Forces have successfully employed for some years. This device requires a group of people who know each other quite well, through working or training together, and allows for each member to rate all other members of the group. As a preliminary screening device, of course, it is impossible to administer, because no such group exists until the preparation program has actually begun. During and after an "admission phase" or block-of-time program as described in Chapter VII, however, the peer ratings have proved sufficiently discriminating to be among the more useful instruments available to selection committees.

Traditional selection devices. Educators often exhibit a somewhat deplorable tendency to equate the concept of "traditional" with "fusty" and "outmoded," or (even worse) to place that which is traditional, i.e., "bad," at the opposite end of a scale from that which is progressive or new, i.e., "good." No such semantic sally is intended here. There *are* selection devices which are traditional: they have been in use for a long time. They have been in use for a long time because they possess some good features, and because they have been known about for a long time. Some are good; some are not so good. All have some merit, if properly used. The only lamentable thing about the whole situation is the fact that only recently have any of these devices, good *or* bad, been subjected to any sort of scientific scrutiny to determine their efficacy as discriminators between good prospects and bad for educational administration.

As a case in point, one of the most traditional of the traditions among selection procedures is the letter of recommendation. As was hinted with sledgehammer delicacy in Chapter III, the value of this device lies almost entirely in its ease of administration. It seems possible that if such letters were confined to some sort of structure, and if the respondent made some forced choices or filled out a comprehensive rating scale, the letter of recommendation could perchance be converted to currency of some value. As it stands, this time-honored process is valuable only when the selector knows the respondent (and can evaluate his integrity and powers of discrimination) or when the respondent makes blatantly negative statements. And flatly negative statements are enough to raise questions in the reader's mind about both the recommender and the recommended. To repeat, as long as the letter of recommendation is in its traditional form and says the traditional things, then it can wisely be judged in the way that Alice's King of Hearts rated a similar missive. "If there's no meaning in it," said the King, "that saves a world of trouble, you know, as we needn't try to find any."

Another tradition of long standing involves the requesting of a complete personal history of all applicants. This makes considerable sense from the standpoint of efficiency and for purposes of supplying needed data about the applicant's experience, background of training, marital status, and other personal matters. There is a dearth of evidence to show that this information will predict leadership tendencies, however, no matter how vital the personal statistics so gleaned. If scientifically constructed, and interpreted by experts, a biographical data sheet *can* be used as a projective device for determining certain traits of personality. Its value for this purpose lies in the fact that an applicant does not normally perceive a threatening test situation in a personal history form, and thus he is less likely to bend his answers.

One of the traditions which still bears considerable promise as a selection device is the interview. The standard, groping half-hour's discussion does little but waste time, but a focused interview accomplished by a trained interviewer can yield some highly relevant information for selection purposes. If such an interview does nothing but identify the language lacerators and extreme deviants in other respects, it will have been worth the trouble involved in placing it in the selection routine for prospective school administrators. Panel interviews and leaderless discussion sessions are variations which can elicit much that is significant about applicants, again only if observers are trained and if the approach is carefully planned. In every case, whether the interview agent be single or multiple, the whole procedure should involve a studied comparison of the applicant's reactions with a standard with which the interviewer is thoroughly familiar. To be more explicit, the interviewer's bias should be eliminated wherever possible.

The last of the selection devices of long standing to be mentioned here is the practice of evaluating the prospect's academic record and background of training. Once again, this is a tradition which needs to be preserved because the information it yields fills in some of the gaps in the selector's total knowledge about the applicant. Unfortunately, research has not discovered a *high* correlation between grades and success at anything, except making more grades in similar courses. There is a relationship between grades and intelligence, and between both of these and leadership in certain types of groups. There is not enough evidence, though, to warrant many bold and definitive statements about what grades a prospective school administrator must have before he should be admitted to advanced preparation. Extremely low grades throughout a whole undergraduate career would certainly be sufficient cause for further checking on the applicant or for summarily rejecting him. Bluntly demanding an unrealistically high grade point average of every applicant, on the other hand, requires an assumption regarding the accuracy and standardization of grading systems which would be difficult to defend. Suffice it to say that grades usually need to be backed by further evidence before being used as a basis for either selection or rejection of an applicant.

The State Selects

Short of harking back to the days when certification was commonly determined by state-administered examination, the state agency today has little choice but to rely on institutions of higher learning and local public schools for the initial screening and selection of prospective administrators. While reserving the discussion of accreditation for a later chapter, it is appropriate to recognize here that the insistence of the state-level agency on excellence in all things will contribute greatly to the effectiveness of the separate institution's selection procedures. To put it more simply, if the states do not require high standards for teacher and administrator certificates, then the training institutions will probably not impose high standards on themselves. Through cooperation in research, and by serving as clearing houses for dissemination of bits of research evidence as they are mined, these all-important state level groups can aid immeasurably in the search for, and universal application of, better selection devices. A combination of rigid policing and sweet reasonableness is the difficult role of the state agency in improving the level of administration of the local schools, by improving the level of the administrators.

The Local School System Selects

All of the efforts of the profession, the colleges and universities, and the state agencies will be futile unless the local school systems are convinced of the need to employ sound procedures in their selection of prospective administrators. Here, at the local district level, is the final proving ground for all the identification, recruitment, and screening devices which have gone before.

Much of the detailed discussion of selection devices included in previous sections could be repeated here. Repetition will be limited, however, to those places where it is needed for emphasis.

Criteria for selection. No claim is made at any point in this chapter that the selection of qualified people is a simple process. Clearly, it is a quite complex procedure, and one which has been accomplished in extremely diverse ways by many different people. References to personal and professional qualities deemed necessary for successful administrative performance are numerous, but, as a rule, these qualities are stated with all the precision of an advertising blurb for a DeMille movie. Above-average intelligence, reasonably attractive appearance, good health, successful experience as a teacher, and graduate study in education are some of the typically general criteria which are used to identify administrative potential. The limited usefulness of this order of generality, as a guide in the down-to-earth choosing which must finally be done, is self-evident. These selection criteria must be couched in far more tangible and applicable terminology before they will become useful for anything other than material for journal articles.

Some research is being beamed in this direction. Briner[4] and

---

[4] Briner, Conrad. *The Identification and Definition of the Criteria Relevant to the Selection of Public School Administrative Personnel.* Doctor's thesis. Stanford: Stanford University, 1958.

Marshall[5] produced two studies illustrative of determined efforts to move from generalities to somewhat more objective behavioral qualities which a candidate either does or does not exhibit. While identifying what criteria superintendents *do* use in selecting, Briner concluded that superintendents already know more about selection then they use. He found, in addition, that basic prejudices of the selector tend to outweigh any help he might get from an outside agency in this choosing procedure. Of course, this is no real surprise, since superintendents are human. Briner also notes that the selectors claim to compare candidates in terms of what generally can be construed as a leader stereotype. Though they are generally agreed as to what this stereotype is, the applicants they select do not always match the stereotype.

Assessment of administrative potential—the sum of personal and professional qualities bound up in the "leader stereotype"—represents one possible set of desired potential standards for administrative candidates. Other sets of standards can (and should) be created to fit local needs. To what extent a quantity of administrative potential exists among the teaching personnel of a given school district can be determined only by a formal assessment program. Such an assessment plan, as might be expected from what has gone before, would include an analysis of transcripts and other records, certain observational and interview data, measurements by means of rating scales, tests, and in-basket devices, and a certain amount of good, honest guesswork.

The first step in the assessment process is the construction of a set of goals for the school which is to be administered, and a clear understanding, by those doing the selecting, of just what the candidate's role would be in the accomplishment of those goals. It is trite, but necessary, to insist that a person's potential for fulfilling a certain task is not capable of evaluation until the task is fully defined. Too, the candidate needs to know of what the job consists, and what its requirements are, before he can be sure he wants to apply. The necessity of this step—that of listing expectations for the job—cannot be overemphasized, because it is here, right at the starting gate, that so many

---

[5] Marshall, Stuart A. *Differential Perceptions of the Criteria for the Selection of Administrative Personnel.* Doctor's thesis. Stanford: Stanford University, 1959.

selectors lose out in their attempts to choose wisely among prospects.

It must be emphasized, too, that no two situations will require identical job descriptions. Some portions of the task are similar for all administrators everywhere, it is true, but other parts differ with the job and the school system. For example, one job analysis[6] (of commendable completeness) indicates the school system's expectation that each of its elementary principals will organize and direct the group testing program in his own school. It is entirely conceivable that another school system will expect this task to be accomplished by members of the guidance staff, and perhaps will expect the principal to aid the testing program only by setting up schedules for it.

The Fresno system, for example, requires that each principal organize cafeteria services for his own school plant. Other schools, in describing their principals' jobs, may expect that the principal be responsible only for student deportment in the cafeteria.

Though all job descriptions of this nature will have a great many identical elements, it is still fairly obvious that each system's requirements will be unique in some aspects. It is this uniqueness, small though the differences be, which makes it essential that each school system develop its own job analyses.

After such expectations are defined, the selector can go ahead with whatever procedures are available to him, in an attempt to find the people best capable of meeting these expectations. One of the means available to the selector in the public schools is the rating scale. Though still subject to the ills of overrating discussed in a previous section, this device is of considerable value, provided the raters are sufficiently familar with the ratee's work. Scales employed must be carefully constructed, should measure specific and observable dimensions of behavior, and should measure behaviors particularly relevant to the job of administering a school.

Observation of a planned type, with definite goals in mind, is another tool available to the selector who would evaluate candidates at work right in his own system. In addition to evaluation of teaching performance, these observations involve a review of personal and professional qualities deemed essential

---

[6] Fresno City Schools. *The Elementary School Administrator.* Fresno: Fresno Board of Education, 1958.

to successful administrative performance. Particular attention is paid to the candidate's relations with students, faculty, administrative staff, and parents, always with administrative potential as the prime consideration.

Also worth more than fleeting consideration are the health and physical stamina of candidates. No studies have measured the amount of energy output required of an administrator in his daily rounds, but it is obvious that even the most healthy and energetic are taxed almost to their limits, on occasion. For this reason, those with serious health problems or debilitating physical defects should probably be eliminated from the roster of candidates. Observation is about the only means available for ascertaining whether or not candidates possess the required stamina and general fitness. One good clue for observers: If the applicant can survive the rigors of a full teaching schedule, chances are good that he is physically strong enough to be an administrator.

Pertinent records available to the selector in the public schools include placement records and evaluations of teaching. Often these records are not complete enough for screening purposes, so some school systems develop a special personal history blank for applicants. Such forms are specifically arranged to elicit certain information needed by those who select. Typical supplementary information of this type would include physical and health characteristics, job experiences in and out of education, academic training, personal and professional activities and interests, and personal goals and ambitions. Warnings about the use of personal history blanks as *predictors* of administrative success, rather than in their intended function as evidence-gatherers, need to be reiterated at this point.

Some much-needed information about the candidate is nearly impossible to secure from peer ratings, observation, and previous records. To acquire this additional information about certain capabilities and traits, the selector can turn to a number of commercially available formal tests. The results of these tests are used as supplementary data to those bits of information gleaned from all other sources.

Districts using such test results are to be both commended and warned—tests should not be the sole basis for appointing or eliminating candidates. Their primary purpose is that of guiding the selecting committee in gathering additional data

165

and in making further observations of the prospective administrator. The function of the tests, then, is mainly one of raising questions, the answers to which are obtained from firsthand acquaintance and from observation of behavior. The testing program does not relieve the school district of its responsibility for becoming thoroughly acquainted with the candidate, for knowing what sort of person he is, and for making a decision as to his potential for a leadership role.

One general caution which selectors should employ involves the avoiding of "premature" selection. In a profession which prides itself on certain of its equalitarian aspects, the premature formation of a group of "chosen ones" or "fair-haired boys" can cause disastrous effects on the faculty morale of a school system. Too, such a practice of anointing prospective principals too long in advance of their actual appointment can both hinder the anointed ones' growth and destroy administrator-faculty communication at all levels. The proper time to select future principals, in most cases, is that time at which their on-the-job training begins. Any time earlier than this can be dangerous.

Another *caveat* which selectors must observe concerns the adoption of a rigid policy of selection of prospective administrators solely from within the system, regardless of the qualifications of those so chosen. There are many good arguments which should be heeded for giving preference to qualified people already employed as teachers in the system. Nevertheless, an invarying practice of promoting only local talent to administrative posts can prove to be stultifying to any program—especially if the quality of such talent is already quite low. Careful selection procedures will weigh the candidate's employment within the system as a part of his qualifications, but will not place undue emphasis upon his presence on the spot as a major recommendation.

APPRENTICESHIP PROGRAMS

Having identified, recruited, and selected the best possible prospects for administrative positions, many school systems take one more step, and provide them with on-the-job preparation for their eventual role. Such provision, in the form of an apprenticeship or "head teacher" position, is both a recruitment device and a real-life learning situation. A formalized administrative trainee program in a school district provides capable faculty members an opportunity for assessment, recognition, and encouragement from their own administrators.

No formula has been devised for the development of an administrator training program. It can take many forms and can be aimed at any number of different goals. Each district must examine its own needs, personnel, and finances, and then construct its program to satisfy such criteria as are developed from the situation. Techniques used successfully in other districts, however, can provide cues which will assist an interested district in moving efficiently into the development of its own program. The following presentation describes in some detail the programs now operating in two districts in California. Both districts have had considerable experience in such administrative trainee programs and have found careful planning of procedures to be highly essential.

A Trainee Describes the Campbell Program

An administrative trainee who is an eighth-grade teacher[7] has summarized the program in Campbell, California, in the following statement:

To become an administrative training candidate at Campbell, one must have completed two years of satisfactory teaching experience, finished his military obligation, been accepted for graduate level work at college, completed six units of upper division work, and been awarded a California teaching credential.

The candidate then makes a formal application to the selection committee of district administrators and is given a series of tests by Stanford University. The selection committee interviews each candidate, observes his classroom teaching, evaluates him with his building principal, and rates the candidate on the basis of what they have learned about him. After all the candidates have been screened, the committee then selects five for the program.

Each trainee is assigned a principal for an advisor. The advisor helps him plan his program of visitations, informs the trainee of helpful experience available as the semester progresses, and evaluates the work of the trainee.

The trainee is given one day of released time every two weeks during the first semester of the program. This time is spent visiting each school in

---

[7] Peterson, Fred. "An Administrative Trainee Looks at the Program." *Administrative Training Bulletin*, 1958. (Santa Clara County, San Jose, California.)

the district, the superintendent, the assistant superintendent, and the business manager for a half-day each.

Through these visits, the trainee becomes better acquainted with the administrators, the schools, the teachers, and the general policies of the district. While the first semester is mainly a "familiarization" period, the second semester is more flexible, and the trainee can schedule work which will suit his particular needs and interests.

In the second semester, most trainees try to spend the bulk of their time in actual teaching and curriculum work in areas with which they are least familiar. In 1958, for the first time, trainees have been accepted for a third semester and are working with the district curriculum coordinator in improving and evaluating the courses of instruction.

The trainees actually participate in many other phases of the total district program, especially in areas in which they feel the greatest need. To name all the activities would be difficult, but some of the more common functions are attending all board meetings; attending principals' meetings, working with PTA and other community groups, classroom teaching on all levels; assisting their own principal in pupil accounting, budget preparation, student counseling duty, and class schedule preparation, substitute and student teacher orientation, teacher evaluation, etc.; inter-district visitation; house counts; and participating in and leading educational discussion groups and workshops.

Developmental Plan in Fresno

The Fresno City Unified School District of Fresno, California, has been developing a plan for the selection of elementary principals since 1952. The plan, though not presented as a model, has several notable features worth mentioning here.

Purpose. The Fresno plan has been initiated to find the best potential administrators within the district and develop them into elementary principals to be employed in the rapidly expanding school system.

In Fresno, an expanding concept of education demands an increasingly competent school administrator. Because of tremendous community concern with early childhood education, the elementary school administrator is at a strategic threshold.

In cooperation with the board of education, the superintendent, the assistant superintendent in charge of elementary education, and all the department heads, the elementary administrator in Fresno is responsible for developing and executing the local school district program. He also assumes the responsibilities of instructional leadership, curriculum formation, and interpreting the school program to the community. His is the concern for aiding children in establishing the foundation for desirable habits, attitudes, personal adjustment, home-school relations, and fundamental skills. He is looked to for leadership in classroom instruction, individual pupil guidance, curriculum planning, staff coordination, and school and community relations. He is also responsible for supervision of the noninstructional staff and for competent plant management.

The purpose of the Fresno plan is to encourage the development of a career elementary school administrator able to shoulder these responsibilities. Such responsibilities require a special kind of preparation. The administrator needs to bring a background of wide interests and insights to the job, along with the ability to deal effectively with people. He needs to be broadly educated in the sense that he is not unfamiliar with such major fields of learning as social understandings, science and mathematics in the modern world, religion and philosophy, political science, economics, and the arts. He needs to bring a background of professional preparation to the job, including such qualifications as successful classroom teaching experience, graduate work in school administration with special emphasis in group dynamics and human relations, and a desire for participation in professional organizations. Therefore, a well-organized program of preparation directly related to the role and responsibility of the career elementary school administrator is considered imperative.

Testing. With help from the consultative service of Stanford University and the Cooperative Program in Educational Administration, a test battery is administered once each year to those teachers who plan to apply for the preparation program. This battery includes the following tests:

1. The *Miller Analogies Test,* for measuring abstract verbal ability.
2. *The Cooperative Test of Contemporary Affairs,* for measuring general nonprofessional information.
3. *The Minnesota Teacher Attitude Inventory,* for measuring attitudes toward pupil-teacher relations.
4. *The Public Opinion Questionnaire,* for measuring attitudes toward authority.
5. *The Allport-Vernon-Lindzey Study of Values,* for measuring the relative strengths and importance to the individual of various social values.
6. *The Edwards Personal Preference Inventory,* for measuring the relative strengths and importance to the individual of various needs or motivational factors.

The testing program is open to all teachers within the school system, and principals are asked to encourage any likely prospect to take the tests. Formal application for consideration for an administrative position may be made any time following the tests. Letters of recommendation are obtained and invariably include letters from the principals with whom the teachers have worked. Information obtained from these letters is supplemented by means of conferences involving the principals and the assistant superintendent who directs the training program. As soon as is convenient, following the tests, individual scores and interpretations are given to each teacher who participated. Individual conferences follow for those who request them.

Selection. Test results are also made available to the assistant superintendent, who, by then, has quite a complete record of each applicant, including a health history. He has also had opportunity to make field observations and to obtain, through conferences with teachers, informal peer ratings of those candidates showing the greatest potential.

A minimum of four years' service within the district is required. No upper or lower age levels have been established. The program is open to men and women, but of the 20 principals selected through 1959, only one has been a woman.

Development. Selection by this process removes much of the guesswork in administrator selection, and appointments can be made with greater assurance. One trainee is selected for each projected position to be filled, and one extra trainee is added to the group so that the selective process can be continued up to the date of actual appointment. The selectees or trainees are designated as "head teachers" and are assigned to certain schools for one year training. The developmental program is designed to train prospective administrators in both the procedural skills of administration and the human relations skills involved in working with people.

Primary responsibility for the portion of the program devoted to procedural skills rests with the regular principals of the schools to which trainees are assigned. These principals follow a special check sheet of suggested experiences for trainees, and meet with their trainees once a month for a three-hour evaluation of progress. Consultative help and periodic workshops are provided to give special attention to the trainee's development in the area of human relations.

SELECTION OF A SUPERINTENDENT

As we have noted before, the normal career pattern for top-level school administrators is a sort of three-base hit—from teacher to principal to superintendent. This chapter has spent considerable time and effort in discussing ways and means of identifying, recruiting, selecting, and even "apprenticing" prospective school *principals*. It would seem only fair that one final step be taken, and that a few hints be given to aid selectors in choosing prospective *superintendents*.

There are those who sagely contend that a school board can accomplish no more important task than the selecting of a top administrator for its school system. There are also those who bitterly maintain that boards, composed as they are of laymen untrained in selection procedures, are all too often guided more by emotions than they are by wisdom when they set about to refill their superintendencies. A very few ways of avoiding this criticism are suggested here.

In the first place, the best step a board can take in the selection process is to provide itself with a *plan* for selection and with some written procedures and policies of selection to which all members subscribe. Boards will do well to seek consultative help from nearby training institutions and from their local faculty and administrative staff in setting up these procedures.

The second suggested step is identical with one in the principal-selection process—the drawing up of a detailed list of expectations, or job analysis, for the position to be filled. Here, again, this should be far from a superficial attempt at deciding just what the job entails for the particular school system in question. Consultative help will be in order at this stage of the process, too. Once the job analysis is made, it is possible to set up a list of qualifications a candidate must possess before his application will receive serious consideration. This list of qualifications will aid immeasurably in the screening process which must follow the receipt of the many applications with which the selectors are usually inundated.

The third hint for boards who seek a superintendent could well apply to all their labors as school governing bodies. It consists of this plea: Throughout the selection process, the board should act as a unit, with the serving of the best interests of the school system held as the ultimate goal of all concerned. When boards act as loosely organized groups of individualists, allowing personal wishes to outweigh any group goals, they tend to fail miserably in selecting the best man for the superintendent's post.

The information needed by selectors for wise choosing between prospective superintendents is much the same as that needed by those who select principals. The means of gathering such information are not always available to a school board, however, so that it is most often necessary for these untrained selectors to rely on training institutions for the gathering of some of the necessary data about a candidate. Such institutions are becoming increasingly accustomed to providing dossiers on applicants, and as their training programs get better (see Chapter VII), the quality and quantity of information they can provide will no doubt improve.

The one data-gathering device which school boards may legitimately arm themselves with is the interview. Once again, it must be admitted that the unstructured, unplanned, and uninformed type of "visit" in which boards and candidates often indulge is unprofitable in the extreme. Such groups need to plan their interviews, and each individual interviewer needs to be certain what questions he will ask of the applicant. Each question should be carefully planned and worded so that all needed information is elicited. Questions need to be approximately uniform for all candidates so that some sensible comparison of results from various interviews is possible. Interviews need to be unhurried, as well, and probably only one applicant should be invited for an interview at one board "sitting."

Since there are several excellent sources available to school boards which desire detailed lists of suggested steps in the selection process,[8] no attempt is made to include such a listing here. Rather, let it be emphasized here that boards of education need to employ such lists as starting points for the development of their own selection procedures, adapting any or all of the suggestions to fit the local situation. Like all good business and

---

[8] See, for example:

American Association of School Administrators. *Choosing the Superintendent of Schools.* Pamphlet. Washington, D.C.: the Association, a department of the National Education Association, 1949. 12 p.

Baker, John E. *The Selection of Superintendents of Schools by Boards of Education.* Doctor's thesis. Chicago: University of Chicago, 1952.

Neagley, Ross L. *Recruitment and Selection of School Administrators.* New York: Teachers College, Columbia University, 1953. 51 p.

educational procedures, the entire selection process needs to undergo constant evaluation both before and after the actual selection is made, so that the procedure can be bettered, if need be, at any stage from job analysis to contract signing.

A NOTE OF URGENCY

This Yearbook Commission feels that a chapter on the current topic would not fulfill its mission completely if it did not conclude on an urgent reminder regarding the immediacy of the need for application and improvement of the processes here outlined. When talented people with administrative potential are identified earlier, recruited more determinedly, selected more rigorously (with constantly improved procedures), and trained with more care, then the profession can begin to compete with the other professions for high-quality manpower.

It is not necessary to document the fact that stiff competition does exist for those who are capable of leadership. Neither is it necessary to prove that education, by and large, has found it difficult to bid competitively in the talent market, for various reasons (only some of which are financial). Only when the profession of school administrators becomes sufficiently aroused to begin a concerted effort to encourage better identification and recruitment, and to demand better selection for its ranks, can any hope be held for an improved competitive position. The profession, with its national association in the van, can begin with some of the ideas herein presented, and can improve its position appreciably, provided that every individual member responds to the call to arms.

chapter VII

A Proposed Program
of Preparation

A serious contemplation of the enormous responsibilities connected with school administration might
easily lead one to the conclusion that the administrator's lot, like that of Gilbert and Sullivan's police-
man, is not a happy one. The contents of Chapter V
should be enough to impress or frighten all who
approach the graduate schools of the nation with a
career in educational administration in mind. Were
the timorous schoolmaster, Ichabod Crane, to be
delivered incarnate to assume the superintendency of
the Sleepy Hollow schools in 1960, he would undoubtedly, during the first day, remount his steed
and return to the legendary exile from whence he
came—thankful to escape with his head. School
administration is truly no haven for seekers after
the soft touch, for timid souls, or for minuscule-
minded men.

In Chapter VI the problems of identifying, recruiting, and selecting strong candidates for preparation
programs were discussed. The position taken in that
chapter was that effective educational leadership is
not a blessing that "droppeth as the gentle rain from
Heaven" upon all who do not know enough to come
in out of it. Getting prospective administrators of
the highest quality into the preparation programs is
an essential step in the process of improving our
schools.

Assuming for the moment that educational administration will be able to attract its rightful proportion
of the nation's outstanding young manpower in the
years ahead, the awesome task of providing prepara-

174

tion programs that make sense will be our next concern. The purpose of this chapter is to suggest some of the elements of such programs.

ESSENTIALS IN A PREPARATION PROGRAM [1]

First, we must prepare the administrator-to-be to handle the technical aspects of his job with effectiveness and efficiency. The most obvious characteristic of school administration is the job's uncompromising insistence that a host of things *get done*. The almost inevitable list of Competencies That Every School Administrator Should Possess, dutifully developed by nearly every department of education administration during the past 10 years, attests to a common agreement on one point: School administrators are expected to *know* and to *do* a lot. The reader will be spared the task of having to slosh through another such list on the assumption that the point has been made that a school administrator must be much more than just a good fellow.

Technical Skills

In giving due attention to the important technical skills that must be mastered before a school administrator can claim to be fully prepared, we are not referring to the "administrivia" that too often keep the superintendent or principal from doing his real job. We need no courses in How to Count the Lunchroom Money. We *do* need to insist on proficiency in such performances as organizing instructional programs, scheduling classes, accounting for money, procuring supplies, making budgets, projecting enrollments, assisting (or finding assistance for) teachers with specific instructional problems, and many others.

As with most of the other demands upon school administrators, the list of needed technical proficiencies has grown constantly longer as new responsibilities have been placed upon the schools. In comparatively recent times many school superintendents have assumed the *additional* burdens of transporting and providing

[1] The categories presented here are those developed in Katz, Robert L. "Skills of an Effective Administrator." *Harvard Business Review* 33:33-42; January-February 1955; also discussed in Griffiths, Daniel E. *Human Relations in School Administration.* New York: Appleton-Century-Crofts, Inc., 1956. p. 8-12.

meals for more people than are served by any transit company manager or restaurateur in town.

Human Skills

A second, and in most respects a more difficult, category of proficiencies to develop in a preparation program is that of the human skills. The crucial task of the school administrator is that of helping people to make good decisions. The well-prepared school administrator, then, not only must understand people and how they work and live and get along together; he also must be able to use that understanding in getting the best out of people, individually and in groups. It is doubtful that this ability could ever be successfully developed by a recluse, regardless of the nonhuman resources at his disposal. Without seeking to make an Organization Man of every aspirant for a position in school administration, colleges and universities might well place those aspirants in learning situations in which constructive relationships with people are intrinsically and centrally established in the curriculum.

Conceptual Skills

The school administrator who is proficient in both the human and the technical skills could still fail if he is deficient in a third category, the conceptual skills. Well-developed conceptual skills enable one to see the totality of an enterprise as well as its parts, to grasp the interrelationships among the elements in a complex situation, and to establish and maintain the delicate balance that fosters both unity and diversity in an organization. The conceptual skills become relatively more and more important to an individual as he ascends the hierarchical ladder to the superintendency.

The preparation program that could seriously presume to develop the conceptual skills would be characterized by activities leading to: (a) adequate functional knowledge in each of the major areas of the curriculum, (b) thorough grounding in all of the services required in a program of modern education, (c) understanding of the social order in which schools operate, (d) understanding of the psychological makeup of the children, youth, and adults with whom school leaders come into contact, and (e) a strong and consistent philosophical basis for action. It is at the conceptual skill level that a prospective school administrator is most likely to be found wanting. It is at this level that the difference between *training* and *education* is most apparent.

Characteristics of Model Program

The type of preparation program that would be required to develop the technical, human, and conceptual skills, even to a minimum level of adequacy, would seem to have these general characteristics:

1. At least two years of graduate study would be necessary, assuming that the individual already had strong undergraduate foundations in the social sciences, the natural and physical sciences, the communication arts, philosophy, and one or more of the fine arts.

2. The program would be designed for individuals who have been discriminatingly selected (as proposed in Chapter VI).

3. The necessary resources, both human and material, would include a strong faculty with demonstrated competencies in scholarly pursuits, in teaching, and in the practice of educational administration, together with adequate libraries, laboratories, materials centers, and space for classrooms and offices.

In order to have before us some of the specifics that a desirable and yet feasible preparation program might include, the following fictitious account of the program at State University is presented. Although State does not exist, most of the activities ascribed to it can be found in one or more institutions today.

HOW THEY DID IT AT STATE U

The State University story really began in the early 1950's, when the departmental faculty undertook a critical examination of its entire program for preparing school administrators. Stimulated by some of the projects of the Cooperative Program in Educational Administration, and troubled by an uneasy feeling that many of their practices were ineffectual and pointless, the professors set up an advisory committee to assist them in studying the program and in planning needed improvements. The group consisted of representatives of the University administration, related disciplines, and the State Association of School Administrators.

What the study revealed was even more disturbing than was anticipated. State's prospective school administrators were preparing for some of society's most responsible and demanding positions by feeding upon a succession of three-semester-hour courses, constructed with a jaunty disregard for the demands upon educational leaders at mid-century and thrown together in a tasteless potpourri called a Master's degree. There was virtually no selection system in operation. Those who started in educational administration generally finished and were sent forth with the Master's degree and the Administrator's Certificate, there being no logical or systematic process for culling the doubtful cases or even the obvious misfits.

Teaching methods in general provided excellent demonstrations of what the students had been advised *not* to do in their previous education courses. In most courses, the professors were placing great reliance upon the lecture method; their activities could be described, more often than not, as Frank Moore Colby depicted the teaching of his tutor in French, Mme Carnet— "jealous, relentless, unbridled soliloquy."

The Department of Educational Administration and its advisory group realized that not all of the desirable changes could be effected in a hurry, but priorities were established and initial steps were taken to remove some of the obstacles and to create a climate conducive to change. Obviously, where degree or certificate requirements were at variance with sound preparation program elements, something had to be done about those requirements. An even more time-consuming and difficult task facing the faculty was that of changing its own way of doing things. Although the professors could see that their program was outmoded and inadequate, the problem of revising it became increasingly formidable as noble sentiments were probed for specific ways to proceed.

Slow but persistent improvement of the State U preparation program has resulted in something of which those connected with the institution can be justifiably proud in 1960. Some of the important aspects of the present program are described in the following section.

Recruitment of top-level prospects for educational administration begins with the identification and counseling of those prospects as they appear in the undergraduate courses at State University. In addition, regular and systematic contacts are maintained with school systems throughout the region; through this process teachers with outstanding leadership qualities are located and encouraged to look toward careers in educational administration. There are no rigid requirements concerning the undergraduate preparation of candidates for admission to the program, although transcripts are examined for evidences of weakness in scholarly pursuits or gaps in background. The question is not so much, "What courses has he had?" as it is, "What capacity and potential has he for developing into an effective school administrator?" The candidate must, however, meet the state's requirements for a teacher's certificate, including the possession of a master's degree that is appropriate for the teaching field.

Ordinarily, prospective school administrators are identified soon enough to permit planning the master's degree to mesh with the requirements of the administrator preparation program. In such cases, the master's degree consists of 15 semester hours of work selected from cognate disciplines, together with an equal amount of work specifically designed to build competencies in the candidate's teaching field. In any case, the 15 semester hours in cognate fields constitute a foundation upon which a three-phase program in educational administration is built.

Phase I: The Admission Core

Once the recruitees complete the cognate work and satisfy the requirements for admission to the program, including a minimum total score of 1000 on the *Aptitude Test* of the *Graduate Record Examination,* they are enrolled in the Admission Core, a block-of-time program that occupies the student's full time during an entire nine-week summer session or a major part of his time (all of the mornings) during a regular semester. The purposes of the Admission Core are many, including the following:

179

1. To get a large amount of information about the student, including sociometric, situational, and psychometric test data, not only for the student's own benefit but also for the use of the department in helping the student or in advising him to drop out of the program;
2. To expose the student to the content of the field of educational administration through a large number of experiences encompassing all of the major areas of responsibility, with particular emphasis on the principalship;
3. To develop the capacity for leadership in each individual by freeing the Core group to plan, organize, and execute its own learning experiences, with faculty members serving in a consultative capacity;
4. To provide a learning laboratory in human relations, where the difficult lessons of group processes can be learned in a realistic setting;
5. To develop in each student the habits and the attitudes that will lead to in-service growth;
6. To improve abilities in the location, interpretation, evaluation, and application of pertinent research evidence on educational problems; and
7. To help the student to make progress toward developing for himself a consistent philosophy of life embracing a consistent philosophy of educational administration.

Much of the screening that takes place at State is done in the Admission Core. Although all of the participants were admitted to the program initially because of unusual promise for success, it is only through performances in the Admission Core that strengths and weaknesses are sufficiently exposed to permit screening the good enough from the almost good enough. About 25 percent of those who are granted admission to the program are eliminated in the pruning that takes place during the Core.

The central activity in the Admission Core is a comprehensive community study. The Core group contracts with one of the communities in the region, agreeing to make the study and provide 25 or more copies of a report in return for payment of all of the expenses involved in making the study.

The community study includes the gathering and analyzing of all pertinent data on the community's historical background, geographical features, economic life, political life, recreational facilities, power structures, religious and ethical influences, formal organizations and informal associations, provisions for education, and other aspects of community life. In addition, the entire group spends three to five days in the community itself, conducting an opinion poll on civic and educational questions that are of concern locally. The assistance of professors from several departments, particularly those in government, economics, sociology, and psychology, is invaluable in planning the community study and in interpreting the results.

Subsequent to the completion of the study and the report, the Admission Core group uses the survey information as raw material for further studies. For example, the development of enrollment projections, class schedules, and budgets is no longer artificial, unrealistic busywork, as it tended to be at State in years gone by. Students in the Admission Core know the community and its problems and they have actual data from which to project enrollments, schedule classes, make budgets, and do many other administrative tasks.

The Admission Core has certain important and specific functions in the total program at State—the functions that can best be realized in a block-of-time operation. At the conclusion of the Core, those who have survived the screening process are ready to engage in further studies of educational administration through other means.

Phase II: Advanced Studies

Phase II of the prospective school administrator's work at State U carries him into more penetrating studies of the content and processes of the job. This part of the program varies somewhat according to the type of position being sought and is also flexible enough to adapt to individual preferences and to correct deficiencies in individual backgrounds. By this time the student has revealed the extent of his powers of critical, independent thought, his strength of character, and his keenness of perception, and he has demonstrated his familiarity with and appreciation for the contributions of the great bodies of knowledge that are the foundation for a truly liberal education. Any clear evidence of major weakness in knowledge or ability that would adversely affect performance on the job is used in guiding the student into appropriate Phase II activities.

Much of the work at this point is done through the familiar three-semester-hour approach. One continuous academic year of residence study is a requirement of the State U program, and with few exceptions this year of study includes Phase II. Occasionally courses are taken outside the College of Education in such departments as economics, sociology, speech, and business management. More frequently, courses are offered within the

College of Education, but are taught by professors who are ordinarily assigned to other colleges of the university. In other instances, professors from several departments jointly offer seminars for groups of students representing school administration, business administration, and public administration.

As stated previously, the program at State provides a general survey of the entire field of educational administration. The work in cognate fields, the Admission Core, and most of the content of Phase II comprise a common base for all prospective school administrators. Specialization for specific positions consists of six to nine semester hours of work designed with the particular positions in mind. This is the point at which the prospective educational administrator *in general* starts to become *specifically* a school superintendent, or a business manager, or an elementary school principal.

An observer strolling through the halls of State University would see many different methods being employed. He would see some lecturing, of course, but he would get the impression that the lectures were all planned, designed for definite purposes, and delivered with enthusiasm and effectiveness. He would see many small discussion groups, but he would notice that the discussions were *about* something and that the faculty members were subtly but unmistakably insisting on depth, critical analysis, and relentless exposure of froth and fallacies, while being equally concerned about the processes of group activity as such. He would see many and varied uses of the case method, to provide experiences in problem solving and decision making in a context approaching "the real thing." He would see ingenious uses of the in-basket technique, through which administrators-in-the-making must make decisions on a series of specific problems, with the background of the problems supplied by films, recordings, printed materials, or a study of the situation itself. He would see a heavy emphasis on situational activities, as contrasted with out-of-context prescriptions. He would see role-playing demonstrations, evidences of field trips, panel discussions—most of the methods known to modern pedagogy—not in a bread-and-circus fool's holiday to make the students happy, but in a deliberate plan to fit methodological means to clearly defined ends.

Much of the content of State's program has been implied in the processes that have been described, but special attention to content as such would be appropriate at this time. Following are some of the content emphases that give the "new look" to the program:

Administrative skills. Preparation for educational administration in 1960 must include many of the *topics* that have been included in courses traditionally, such as accounting for funds, making budgets, leading discussions, organizing programs, studying the community, interviewing applicants, and explaining ideas to a group. The difference is that skills are taught as *skills to be performed* and not as chapters to be read or lectures to be heard *about skills.*

Instruction. The faculty at State is in complete accord with the cliché-laden principle of instructional centrality in the workings of a school, and attempts to demonstrate its precepts through the preparation program for school administrators. In Phases I and II, students are given a thorough grounding in the processes of formulating objectives, building curricula, improving instruction, and evaluating outcomes. Through numerous opportunities to assist professors as they work with in-service education programs, future administrators get practice in providing leadership for curriculum and teaching improvement. Later, in the internship or apprenticeship programs of Phase III, instructional leadership is emphasized once again in the stern realities of the field situation.

Group processes. A growing belief that successful school administration is largely a matter of working effectively with groups has made a significant impact on the preparation program at State. The Admission Core is particularly well suited to the development of understandings and techniques that are needed in group-centered operations. During the Core phase of the program, students become thoroughly aware of the meaning of the term *group* through intimate contact with an aggregation of individuals in the process of becoming a group. Through sociometric measures and other analytical devices used by the group to study its own composition and dynamics, students become impressed with the possibilities of using scientific procedures in improving the effectiveness of groups. Through repeated use of such techniques as role playing, brainstorming, buzz sessions, and demonstrations—generally followed by a study of the process itself, with the assistance of social psychologists who are specialists in group processes—the Admission Core provides a laboratory in group work that serves as a foundation for Phases II and III of the program.

The community. Much of the content of Phase I is organized around the community study. By using an actual community as the subject of intensive study, the Core group gets firsthand contact with the realities of socioeconomic class and caste, power structures, formal organizations and informal associations, communication networks (formal and informal), and role expectations, as well as with the relationships among these variables and the behavior and opinions of people. Many of the other skills and understandings that are normally textbook-centered in school administration courses are developed in Phase I out of the raw materials of the community study.

Decision making. Good school administration is, to a great extent, a process of getting good decisions made. The making of good decisions involves many of the content areas that have been mentioned previously or that will be in the following paragraphs. The process of decision making is essentially the process of problem solving, which involves defining the problem, gathering information, setting forth the various possible solutions and testing each one, selecting the best solution, putting it into effect, and then evaluating it. The State University program contains not only serious study *about* decision making as a process, but also considerable emphasis on practice in decision making. This practice is secured through the way the Admission Core and certain other courses are organized, with the students being responsible for making most of the decisions and studying the results, and through such decision-centered activities as case discussions, in-basket exercises, and on-the-job learning in Phase III.

Human relations. Although much has been said already about the subject matter that is essentially human relations in content, the State program contains many other elements that belong in that category. By the time a student has completed his preparation, he is thoroughly familiar with motivation and the way atmosphere and incentives operate to affect the performance of school personnel. He understands morale and how it is affected by different patterns of administrative behavior. He recognizes the futility of attempting to influence the behavior of other people without considering differences in perceptions of roles, problems, and many other phenomena. He knows about the problems of communication and has spent much time in the study and practice of the communication arts. He understands authority, its delegation, and its use in a democratic organization.[2] In short, his preparation has taught him well that success in school administration includes success in working with people.

Theory. Running through the entire preparation program, as well as in planned emphasis in certain courses, is evidence of the State faculty's concern for theory in educational administration. Theory makes its presence felt not only in new content, but also in a new approach to the study and practice of administration. The program attempts first to develop clear understandings of the meaning of the term *theory,* and then sets out to equip students with good theory—not a *particular* theory but various complementary systems that generate inquiry and provide sound frameworks for approaching problems. Aware of the inevitability of rapid change in the modern world, the preparation program looks to theory to supply rational bases for changing behavior to meet changing conditions.

The traditional contents of preparation programs—budgets, bonds, buses, buildings, and the like—are not neglected at State, but are streamlined and to a great extent approached through contacts with "live" situations such as field studies and surveys. Integration of such experience is provided through seminars.

Phase III: On-the-Job Learning

The third major phase of the State preparation program takes place in the field and consists of either a full-time internship for one semester or a part-time apprenticeship for one school year. Under the internship, the student is placed in a school system under a capable superintendent or other administrator who is responsible for guiding him through a series of experiences representing every major aspect of the job to be learned. A supervising professor from State University has general responsibility for placing the interns, orienting the sponsoring administrators, overseeing the day-to-day activities, and holding a weekly seminar for the interns.

---

[2] For a more complete discussion of these topics and others dealing with human relations in school administration, see Griffiths, *op. cit.*

In some cases, it is more feasible and advantageous to follow the apprenticeship route, especially for principalship training in the larger systems. Over a period of years, the Department of Educational Administration at State has worked with several of the school systems in the region in setting up jointly sponsored on-the-job learning programs for appointees who are soon to be placed in principalships and for novices who are in their first year as principals. As in the internship, the trainee is assigned to a sponsoring administrator, a master principal who has been carefully selected and groomed for the role he is to play. In contrast with the intern, however, the apprentice works in his own school system and is usually released from only half of his teaching duties. Each system works out a schedule of activities that the apprentice must perform during the year. At biweekly seminars, the principals-to-be, the first-year principals, the master principals, the coordinator from the central office, and a consultant from State discuss the problems that are being encountered.

The field work phase of the program at State, whether it be in an internship or an apprenticeship, is designed to deal with content that is uniquely adapted to the field situation. One special province of Phase III is the area of administrative skills, particularly those of a routine nature, such as the handling of records and reports. Although these matters are not entirely avoided in Phase I and Phase II, they are given much less attention in the campus courses at State than in most other institutions. It is true, too, that the field work program is not entirely devoid of the theoretical aspects of administration; in fact, the biweekly seminars function largely as synthesizers of theory and practice. The relative emphasis, however, is deliberate and unmistakable, and a competent observer would have no difficulty in perceiving the special purposes of Phase III.

Figure I on the following page shows the structure of the State U program, starting with the cognate foundational work and extending through Phases I, II, and III.

At the conclusion of the internship or apprenticeship, the candidate is ready for an administrative assignment. Most of the apprentices and some of the interns are placed in administrative positions in the systems in which they served their apprenticeships or internships. The State University Placement Service works closely with the Department of Educational Ad-

FIG. I

THE STATE U PROGRAM

9 SEMESTER HOURS	ON-THE-JOB LEARNING	PHASE III
6-9 SEMESTER HOURS	PREPARATION FOR SPECIFIC POSITIONS	
18-21 SEMESTER HOURS	ADVANCED STUDIES	PHASE II
9 SEMESTER HOURS	ADMISSION CORE	PHASE I
15 SEMESTER HOURS	FOUNDATION WORK IN COGNATE FIELDS	

ministration in an attempt to find the position that most closely fits the competencies of each individual seeking employment. The folder for each student contains complete transcripts of all undergraduate and graduate work; a comprehensive record of biographical data; forced-choice ratings of past performances in educational undertakings; scores on standardized tests and inventories of mental ability, general knowledge, professional knowledge, personality, interests, and values; standings on sociometric measures; performance ratings by faculty members, including judgments concerning the student's ability to speak and write effectively; and all other relevant evidences of the student's capabilities that come to light.[3] After placement, the Department of Educational Administration makes regular, systematic follow-up studies of its products and attempts to provide leadership in their in-service development.

Stamp of Quality

Looking at the State University preparation program as a whole, one sees certain features that make it stand out. Several

---

[3] The Riverdale board (see Chapter I) could have eliminated much of the guesswork in its quest for a superintendent had all of the placement agencies been able to supply the type of information available at State University.

have been mentioned: the assistance of practicing school administrators in planning, executing, and evaluating the program; the active recruitment and selection of highly promising young people for the program; the Admission Core, a block-of-time program designed to induct and orient graduate students into the program, provide learning experiences in human relations, and develop leadership qualities, in addition to surveying the field of educational administration; the community study and the activities growing out of it; the wide variety of teaching methods, discriminatingly and skillfully used; the internship and apprenticeship programs; and the placement and follow-up services.

An influence that helps to give the program at State the stamp of quality is the availability of campus laboratory facilities in almost every major aspect of educational work. The student of school administration is given firsthand experience with the most modern supplies and equipment—everything from electronic data processing machines to the newest gadget for cleaning commodes; he participates in the planning and designing of school buildings, working with professors of architecture and school administration; he learns to supervise instruction through such activities as observing student teachers in the laboratory school and working with them to improve their teaching; in short, he learns by seeing and practicing the best that is known of the science of school administration.

It is recognized at State that "education is not a single science. Rather it is the application of many sciences to the task of modifying human behavior."[4] Bringing about a genuine interdisciplinary program at State has been one of the most difficult undertakings, but important beginnings have been made. One of the first successful endeavors involving representatives of other disciplines was in the field of research. A few professors from other departments were impressed with the possibilities of conducting significant studies in which their fields of knowledge were closely related to the problems of public schools. Through these investigations, foundations were laid for subsequent cooperative endeavors, such as interdisciplinary seminars, joint instructorships, and the community study.

---

[4] Hall, Roy M. "Cooperation: Essential to Research." *School Life* 40:2; May 1958.

With regard to student research, the products of the Department of Educational Administration at State University are expected to be able to function at a high level in designing and conducting investigations of school problems. Every phase of the program at State contains activities that are planned for purposes of developing in students a keen sense of relevance and validity, sensitivity to fallacious reasoning, and habits of scrupulous avoidance of bias and carelessness. Much of the time that was formerly spent on busywork is now devoted to individual or team investigations of significant educational problems, with the expectation that products of the program will be able not only to *use* the research of others, but also to get research done through guiding experimentation in their own schools. Much of their experience with research is gained through being assigned to field studies conducted by the Office of Educational Surveys and Studies. Graduate students are also involved in the research projects of professors, not as leg men or orderlies but as partners in everything from planning the initial design to writing the results. During the internship or apprenticeship phase of the preparation program, each student is responsible for bringing about and reporting for publication a piece of cooperative research that will survive the scrutiny of a committee of specialists representing educational administration, curriculum, research methodology, and the particular subject or area under investigation.

Special attention is given at State to the development of skill in communication, with particular emphasis on speaking and writing for public and professional consumption. The credo of the Department of Educational Administration is that dullness in educational literature is not a necessity—it is merely a long-standing tradition. Students who have difficulty in expressing themselves are assisted in setting up appropriate corrective measures with the Department of Speech or the English Department.

Great emphasis at State is placed on continuous evaluation rather than on final examinations. Initial selection procedures and the screening that takes place in the Admission Core are rigorous enough to eliminate the poor risks, and subsequent measurement activities are primarily carried on for guidance purposes. Each student has a supervisory committee which not only assists him in many ways but also evaluates his progress periodically. The committee can, and sometimes does, advise the student to drop out and pursue some other type of work, even during Phase II or Phase III of the program.

WHAT WILL BE NEEDED?

The preceding section, describing the preparation program at State University, is a fictional account of what *could* happen at any good institution of higher learning in 1960. The State story is probably better than most, if not all, programs that are actually in existence; it is in no way unrealistic, however. In fact, many of the elements of the State program were adapted from such existing examples as the University of Oregon's interdisciplinary seminars; Stanford University's work in the development of on-the-job training programs; certain aspects of Harvard University's Administrative Career Program; internship programs at the University of Maryland and at Teachers College, Columbia University; the three-phase core program at the University of Buffalo, with particular reference to the use of the case method and the systematic study of a school system and the community in which it is located; and the community study and leadership development aspects of The University of Texas' block-of-time program, Foundations in Educational Administration. Other equally good examples could undoubtedly have been found, but these are sufficient to show that any institution that persists in using 1940-model preparation programs in 1960 will be hopelessly and conspicuously outclassed by her more imaginative and courageous sister institutions.

Obviously the quality program of the future will not be adequately financed through box-top and green-stamp fiscal policies. The recommendations in Chapter IX make this quite clear. The financial outlays for such essentials as adequate libraries and laboratories, properly supervised internships and other on-the-job learning experiences, significant research projects, and fellowships or scholarships large enough to attract many of the most able people into graduate programs in educational administration—to mention only a few of the necessary elements—would be far in excess of the amounts now devoted to such preparation programs in most institutions.

A special aspect of the money problem, and one that goes beyond money alone, is that of getting faculty members who can

190

dream as well as sleep. Higher salaries will help, in the long run, but in addition to pecuniary considerations something must happen in any institution where faculty concepts have not gone beyond the level of preparation by exhortation. Perhaps the greatest obstacle to improvement in education, from kindergarten through the graduate school, is inertia. Francis MacDonald Cornford once contemplated the opposition that faces any public action that is not customary, and facetiously concluded that "nothing should ever be done for the first time." Too many colleges and universities that purport to prepare educational leaders for tomorrow's schools seem to have adopted Cornford's cynical witticism as organic law.

The type of preparation program envisioned in this chapter is not radically different from the best that is now offered in a few leading institutions. It is doubtful, however, that such programs could or should be provided in more than 20 percent of the institutions now attempting to do the job. The human and material resources that are, or will likely be, available for the education of prospective school administrators could well be concentrated in a small number of centers where the chances of success are high enough to justify the cost. Other institutions could, in turn, develop specialties in other fields. In this way, the dissipation of resources on the extravagant luxury of maintaining hundreds of impoverished institutions, competing with each other for the privilege of exposing a little circle of graduate students to a mediocre program, could be turned to the advantage of all concerned.

The improvement of preparation programs is a responsibility of the profession at large; it cannot be left to the professors alone to accomplish. No person connected with school administration should shrug his shoulders at the existence of an inferior program any place in the nation. Only when practicing school administrators, boards of education, and professors of educational administration join forces to insist on quality preparation programs will mediocrity become conspicuous and be driven from the field.

chapter VIII

Continuing Education
for the Administrator

In all of the fairy tales with which we are nurtured in our youth, one constant is always present—"and they lived happily ever after." This is a comforting thought and one that lulls us into complacency. It means, in the words of today's younger set, "we've got it made." The only thing wrong with this theory is that it isn't true, and it won't be even partly true unless certain other things transpire.

In the preceding chapters, this Commission has recommended ways to select and prepare the most able and promising people for careers in school administration for what is obviously a demanding job. If these things are done, and it is apparent that they are being done in some places, can we assume that administrators will thereby be properly recruited, magnificently educated, carefully selected, and ready to "live happily ever after"?

Instead of "living happily ever after," many an administrator has failed in his work because he did not seek the assistance he needed to keep up to date or didn't know what to seek or whom to ask, or the agencies that should have been helpful to him were unable to offer anything of real value.

It is the purpose of this chapter to recommend in-service education opportunities that should be available to school administrators. Some of these suggestions are drastic; some cannot be adopted immediately; some are practices that exist in a few places; a few, perhaps, are obvious. This Commission has hypothesized in Chapter IV that "school administrators in general are ready and willing to

accept change, and to contribute actively to its processes . . . .
School administrators want to fulfill their professional obligations of continued learning and growth through one or another
instrument of in-service study."

ASSISTANCE FROM MANY SOURCES

If this is true, where can the administrator turn for assistance? What agencies should, and must, be interested in his continued competency? It is the position of this Commission that
the in-service education of school administrators is a profession-
wide responsibility and that a profession-wide plan for it must
be evolved. Attention will be given in this chapter to the administrator's own role, that of his board of education, the university, the U. S. Office of Education, the state department of
education, and the professional associations. These are the
principal organizations that must work together in evolving any
comprehensive plan that provides in-service opportunities for
school administrators.

The Administrator

There is considerable justification for beginning a discussion
of in-service education with the part the administrator should
play in it. After all, it is *his* competency that is in need of
attention, and it is through *his* efficiency as a leader that we
expect progress and improvement in our school programs. The
following actions are recommended to the school administrator,
neophyte or experienced, degree candidate or not.

1. *Subscribe to the premise that everyone must continually
   seek to improve himself.* This is a rather large order, probably equal to or even exceeding the amount of determination needed to give up cigarettes or to remain true to a
   self-imposed diet. This is not an attribute which will
   spring, full-born, into a man's consciousness once he says
   the words "I will improve." Rather, it comes as he interacts
   with his community and with the other agencies that are
   (or should be) seeking his improvement. Exactly as we
   attempt to convince students of the value of intellectual

inquiry, so must a school administrator come to convince himself that he needs to strive for continued improvement. Other agencies have the job of dinning this in his ears, but he is the one who must accept it.

2. *Realize that one cannot improve himself without the assistance of others.* It is permissible to give lip service to the idea that men are self-made, or that anyone can lift himself by his own bootstraps, because such statements have just a germ of truth in them. It is time we realized, however, that the practicing school administrator must, in addition to the things he can do strictly by himself, become involved with others in activities that are deliberately planned for his benefit. The man who belongs to no professional association, attends no regional or national meetings, and asks no assistance, either in planning or in problem solving, will become a vanishing breed. Maybe soon.

3. *Spend time wisely.* There is an old proverb which says, "There is just so much water in the jug." Equally true, there is just so much time in a day or a year, and just so much that one man can accomplish. Beyond the time needed for rest, and a limited amount of recreation, there are still a number of hours left in a day for productive effort. How should it be spent? This is a determination which each man must make for himself, but he should weigh the following factors: (a) Am I doing things that could be delegated to others? (b) Does this particular organization permit sufficient time for planning and policy making, or does it keep me involved in trivia? (c) Have I, as William James phrased it, "pushed back the limits of fatigue"? (d) Am I spending too much time with things and not enough with people? (e) Am I accepting too many engagements or speaking too often on matters of little importance? (f) Am I finding time to lead a reasonably normal family life, recognizing all of my children by name without obvious effort and even remembering my anniversary? (g) Have I time for reflective thought? These, and many others, are the questions we must ask ourselves as we examine our use of time. We have little enough of it to afford its continued poor use.

4. *Read.* This point is related, of course, to the first one made, but is set apart for a specific reason. A man may not be

able, for financial reasons, to take advanced degrees or go to conventions or attend three-week workshops in Human Relations. He may not have the time to see what other school systems are doing or to visit his state department of education or the U.S. Office of Education. His personality or beliefs may be such that he refuses to identify himself with a professional association. But he can read. Selected reading has been identified in Chapter IV as "the most fundamental, reliable, and efficient resource at hand." Any administrator who would set aside and rigorously keep a single hour a day for selected reading would inevitably improve both his education and his performance. Some administrators say, "I can't afford the time to read." Others, far wiser, "I can't afford not to."

5. *Carry on research and use research findings.* School administration is long past the day when good sense and a faithful attention to the distribution of paper was enough to assure longevity in a given position, if such a day ever existed. More attention is being paid to the science of administration (see Chapter IV) in many fields of endeavor, and there is great promise in the studies that are being undertaken. "Research" is not a scary word. Even though many reports of findings make for heavy weather in reading, this is less frequently true today than yesterday. Research has made our beef cattle heavier, our hens more prolific, our dentistry less painful, our listening more enjoyable—there is no reason to believe it will not make administration more effective and more understandable. As a profession, we must accord it a stellar role.

6. *Get primary assistance from the staff.* No one can do really well in an administrative position who does not have the respect and confidence of his staff. Integral to this belief is the understanding on the part of the administrator that he can't know everything. An administrator gains strength only by admitting his weaknesses.

What does a staff have to offer? In addition to loyalty, understanding, and support, they have knowledge. Knowledge of the community because some of them were born there and many of them play important parts in community life. Knowledge of children because they teach them, encourage them, test them, and see them every day. Knowledge of parents—which ones are indifferent, overindulgent, dependable. Knowledge of best practice, in the school they are in, in schools elsewhere. Teachers know. They can see problems in the making, and can work to head them off. They can sense an unsatisfactory condition and work to improve it. They can do these things if they are encouraged in that direction by the administration.

7. *Get involved in professional activity.* Opportunities exist, or can be made to exist, for school administrators to *do* things that enchance their efficiency. It's a truism that one learns more in teaching a subject than in taking it. The recommendation here is obvious: Administrators should occasionally teach, give seriously prepared addresses, participate in forums, meet in deliberation with colleagues. Of special significance is activity in cultural areas. After all, an educator's in-service growth should not be restricted to the tasks he performs—not if he assumes with seriousness his role as community educational leader.

The Board of Education

Superintendents forget, on occasion, that they are employed to do a job for someone else. Caught in the detail that demands immediate attention, they lose sight of the fact that the board of education is charged with the responsibility of operating the schools, and that the superintendent is employed by them to do a job *for them.* Boards are composed of men and women in whom public trust has been vested. These are people with a primary interest in the welfare of the schools. They are the ones who must understand what the schools are trying to do at all times in order that they may assist in its implementation.

State associations of boards of education are becoming a major force in many states, making determined efforts to improve the educational program through promoting beneficial legislation, instructing and informing their constituents, and providing an opportunity for local boards to work together on problems of mutual interest. School board associations can not only influence the continuing growth of board members but can persuade boards of the importance of in-service education for the school staff.

Boards can aid an administrator's in-service growth by approving adequate budgets for professional meetings, in-school consultants, and current books and journals. From board members, too, the alert administrator gets cues for new ideas, experimentation, and even new areas for his own study. The complete role of boards in the area of in-service education has yet to be spelled out as fully as it should be, but the recent acceleration of board association activity predicts better days ahead.

Higher Education Institutions

American business has conclusively proved the value of trade names and brands. The public appreciates knowing the producer of what it consumes and has come to identify certain labels with quality. Further, the consumer can retaliate when he discovers a fault in a well-known product he has purchased in good faith. Our manufacturers have long since learned that some of their best advertising comes from the satisfactory adjustment of claims for reimbursement. The national movement that places the responsibility for establishing the eligibility of an individual for a teaching or administrative certificate on the preparing institution is a step in the same direction.

Colleges and universities that prepare school administrators should not place their label on a poor product, nor should they allow their product to fail if they can help it. With respect to the latter case, in all too many instances, the university is not aware any difficulty has arisen and learns of it only when a public announcement of resignation is made. It is probable that the fault for this lack of utilization of the institution's service lies more with the administrator than it does with the school. A man may believe, particularly if he is beset with problems that seem overwhelming, that any request for assistance would be interpreted as an indication of basic weakness, with a resultant decline in the esteem in which he is held. This could be particularly unnerving if he intends in the future to return to that school for yet another degree. Thus, he fails to call on Alma Mater for help in time.

Colleges and universities are places of great resources for learning. These are the agencies that prepare our administrators in the first place, and they can be of great assistance throughout a man's professional life.

Once these institutions have accomplished a preparation program of worth, there is no reason why in-service education of a high degree of value cannot continue to be offered practicing administrators. Providing for these men to participate in the institution's activities will bring about mutual benefits. Some of these benefits are identified as follows:

1. The administrator will be involved in intellectual pursuits not always possible in the town where he is employed. Being asked to help develop the institution's program for school administrators will provide a rewarding experience for the practitioner. Involvement of this type benefits both the institution, which will receive ideas from the individual, and the administrator, who profits from helping think through policy in an important area of collegiate concern.

2. The administrator will often gain much more than he can give when he accepts in his system an intern, or participates in a survey, or serves on a university committee screening applicants for admission to a program in administration. Interns, consumed with a desire to learn, can often see elements in a situation new to them that have escaped the administrator's attention (some superintendents report they learn almost as much from the intern as vice versa). A survey can reveal weaknesses not formerly recognized. Serving on a university committee can bring identification with a high standards approach.

The institution that really wishes to assist in the in-service education of school administrators in its area will do such things as the following:

1. Provide competent field services which will assist in the introduction and evaluation of new practices in the schools;

2. Operate or participate in a regional research center, study council, or demonstration and "tryout" program;

3. Invite superintendents and principals to be "scholars of the house," making facilities and consultative service available to them on a noncredit basis;

4. Provide institutes and workshops that are not just more of the same, but which will utilize the most promising techniques and approaches for instruction—the use of case studies, "in-basket" materials, and research findings, the participation of behavioral scientists, brainstorming;

5. Maintain, with the assistance of practicing administrators, a list of promising candidates for school administration;

6. Involve administrators in research programs in depth. Rather than leaving practitioners to "stew in their own juice," arrange 10-day periods with practicing social scientists, economists, behavioral scientists—carrying out investigations of agreed-upon worth;

7. Provide a "core" program that is based on interdepartmental understanding and cooperation;

8. Accept foundation funds as "risk capital" in order to demonstrate new concepts, making certain that proper safeguards are established.

The future in-service role of the collegiate institution is bound to change. The bulk of in-service offering today is a hybrid of degree pursuit and in-service assistance. As the day comes, however, when beginning administrators are the products of *adequate* preparation programs, the in-service role will become much clearer. For the administrator, credit toward further prescribed courses will be less important than a genuine keeping-up-to-date with current experiments and concepts. Thus tomorrow's role of the collegiate institution as it serves on-the-job school administrators will be *to share and interpret the findings of research.*

United States Office of Education

There has always been some timidity on the part of local and state school authorities with respect to ascribing functions to the U.S. Office of Education. Taught from the first day of their preparation that "education is a state function" but "carried out on the local level by a duly constituted board of education," it takes little to raise the spectre of FEDERAL CONTROL. While few persons question the validity of the position that our schools should not be operated by a federal agency, any reluctance to admit some appropriate role to the U.S. Office of Education would be ridiculous. Although the government has not seen fit to establish education under a separate Secretary, it does accord it an important position in the Department of Health, Education, and Welfare where it performs these major functions:

1. The dissemination of grants, including the funds made

available by the National Defense Education Act and other federal legislation.

2. The collection and dissemination of information relative to the operation of schools.

3. The conduct and encouragement of research studies.

It is with respect to this latter point that the Office has a particular role to play as far as the in-service education of school administrators is concerned.

There is no validity to the statement that "too much research" is being done in educational administration. There is considerable validity in the statement that quality is lacking in what is being produced. Griffiths[1] found in 1956, 1957, and 1958 that there was an annual average of 594 researches in educational administration, 7705 in psychology, and 114,000 in chemistry. Surely this belies the concept of a "flood" of researches in the field. His criticism of research procedures[2] is merciless. He describes how feasibility is a sole criterion, research is sublimated to policy development, "action" research is action only and not research. Failures of research in administration are many: neglect to utilize previous research, lack of summaries, research done by the wrong people, lack of sequential research, failure to publish, failure to use. If all of these things are wrong, what then must be done to improve the situation?

Perhaps the first thing would be for the people connected with in-service agencies to agree that no action should be taken that is not based on the best information available. This might be called *action based on knowledge.* Knowledge can come from many sources—from education, from experience, from observation, from research. But is there any real excuse for not keeping up to date on research findings? Something useful is found, and years later we find responsible educators totally unaware of its existence and acting in violation of what is known to be "best practice." Would this be tolerated in other professions? Could an engineer survive who failed to keep abreast of new techniques of construction? An architect unaware of new materials? A physician uninformed on new developments? These professions recognize the need to keep current and they let the world know

---

[1] Griffiths, Daniel E. *Research in Educational Administration: An Appraisal and a Plan.* New York: Teachers College, Columbia University, 1959. p. 24.

[2] *Ibid.*, Chapter 2, "An Appraisal of Research in Educational Administration," p. 6-38.

it, and they run some severe risks if they remain uninformed on new developments.

Basic to whatever is done in education is the fact that a teacher and a classroom of children constitute the center of the whole enterprise. Whatever an administrator does should be done to assist in that undertaking. The college that prepares the teacher and the one that prepares the administrator exist for the same purpose. The state department of education has little other reason for existence. Recognizing such singleness of purpose, is there any reason why all of those concerned could not join together in furthering the concept of *action based on knowledge?*

We know a great deal more about children and how they learn than we did a hundred, or even a dozen, years ago. We have used this knowledge in improving our instructional practices. But are we using it consistently as an integral part of our considerations at all levels of educational enterprise? When the superintendent adds to his staff, is he motivated by squeaking wheels or is he employing a person whose abilities will permit capitalizing on additional avenues of learning? When the state department of education recommends special legislation, does it do so to appease some special-centered group, or to make possible the realization of yet another method of educating children? No one should permit himself to become so engrossed in his particular work that he allows his decisions to be made outside the expanding body of knowledge concerned with the learning process.

What can be done? We can move educational administration toward professional status by publicly adopting a premise that knowledge is basic to the learning process and its improvement; that we are united on every level in the furtherance of knowledge; that our actions are based on knowledge. We must become research-minded. By so doing, we will improve what we are doing and strengthen public confidence in our acts.

The U.S. Office of Education is in a position to provide valuable research leadership in school administration:

1. A "clearinghouse" listing of all educational research, giving careful attention to proper classification.[3]

---

[3] In the manner of *REPORTER, Clearinghouse of Studies on Higher Education.* U. S. Department of Health, Education, and Welfare, Office of Education. Washington, D. C.: Superintendent of Documents, Government Printing Office, 1959.

2. Reproduction of the findings of particularly significant studies in administration.[4]

3. A series of meetings to stimulate interest in research.

Through careful allocation of grants, as well as these actions, the U.S. Office of Education can take the lead in encouraging both research and research-mindedness. Our progress as a profession hinges on these outcomes, and the Office can assume a stellar role in promoting them.

State Departments of Education

While state departments of education were identified in Chapter IV as "one of the most fruitful possibilities for systematic in-service growth for superintendents," it was also indicated that the services available vary greatly from state to state. This variation is understandable when it is realized that these departments owe their support to state legislatures and that the financial resources and attitudes toward progress cover a wide span. No agency should be more concerned with the improvement of administration than a state department of education, whatever its resources, because this agency is the one that is called upon to help in the solution of many of the problems that arise. What can these departments do to improve in-service education of administrators? Many of the suggestions which follow are already accomplished facts in some states:

1. *State departments of education can dedicate themselves to service.* The law in most states gives a state department of education three functions—a police function which enforces the statutes; an operating function, ranging from overseeing education in unorganized territories to the job of offering television programs; and a service function which provides assistance to school districts. Of these three, the last must be paramount if a department is to be of any real worth. A decreasing number of districts attempt to break the law; hence, a reduced police function. Operations that were undertaken because no one else was available can be passed into proper hands and careful

---

[4] In the manner of *SPECIAL REPORTS, Clearinghouse of Studies on Higher Education.* U. S. Department of Health, Education, and Welfare, Office of Education. Washington, D. C.: Superintendent of Documents, Government Printing Office, 1959.

thought taken before others are added. Assistance, however, is increasingly sought as schools face up to new conditions—more children, programs for the retarded, emphasis on foreign language, tracking, staff utilization, testing and guidance, experimentation, the veneration of science and mathematics, "throw out the nonproducers"— the list is endless. Service is being sought and it must be provided, on this level, if we are serious about improving our schools. State departments are not associations manned by volunteers but publicly supported organizations charged with enhancing existing programs.

2. *Staffing must be improved.* This takes money. In some states, in past years, every opening in the state department of education was eagerly sought by the top practitioners in the public schools because of the prestige and higher salary involved. Today, public school salaries in these states, particularly among administrators, have far outstripped those paid by the state. Recruitment, under these conditions, is most difficult. Unless staff members can be found who have a genuine interest in some facet of state department of education work, the temptation is to fill positions with tired oldsters who are looking for a home, or young people with little experience who use the position as a first steppingstone career-wise. State legislatures should have dinned into their ears, through the concerted efforts of the entire education profession, that the improvement of state departments of education is both important and necessary. The best possible people need to be obtained and salaries provided commensurate with their contribution.

3. *The research function must be stressed.* Research in school administration needs a great deal more attention than it has been getting—a point carefully made earlier in this chapter. Priority should be given to studies of supply and demand for administrators, the quality of existing programs, the value of current in-service programs for the development of school superintendents. State departments of education should conduct research concerning instruction—methods, class size, environment. State departments of education, armed currently with Title X of the National

Defense Education Act, should be able to encourage research not previously possible.

4. *Freedom to allocate funds must be granted.* The support of public education is a shared enterprise, with part of the funds being provided locally and part by the state (with a dribble from federal sources). In most states, the amount provided for state subsidies to education runs into millions of dollars. These subsidies are strictly regulated to ensure fairness and equity in their distribution. This is proper. The plea that is made here is to permit state departments of education, working under policies established by the state board of education, to dispense limited grants for special promising and experimental activities. These funds might be granted for such things as:

a. An experimental in-service program for training administrators.

b. An exchange of prospective administrators between school districts. Small communities, interested in securing training for a prospective administrator, could secure this from a larger community, with the state participating in the cost.

c. Grants for special study.

Grants such as these, judiciously awarded, could add yeast to the "dough" we already have.

5. *In-service activities for administrators must be stepped-up and improved.* There are workshops and workshops. There are field services of all types. Not all of these are successful and very few have real depth of content. If state departments of education really want to do something for administration in their state, these are the things to consider:

a. Standards for approval of preparing programs must be raised.

b. Certification standards must be more appropriate to the importance of educational administration. They must be made with the active participation of the entire profession.

c. A state council on school administration must be

established.[5] The state department should take the lead in bringing together representatives of all of the institutions that prepare school administrators, representatives from the state educational associations, the superintendents association, the principals association, the school boards association, the state board of education, and the state department of education. Some of the functions to be performed would be:

(1) Making recommendations concerning the initial and continuing approval of preparation programs;

(2) Formulating policies for selection, preparation, and in-service development of school administrators;

(3) Eliminating overlap in services to administrators;

(4) Providing a sounding board for institutional and administrative problems.

The Professional Association

Voluntary professional associations can perform a unique function in the improvement of the practice of any profession. Their funds are not dependent on legislative action; they are free to be critical; they rule with the consent of the governed. Professional associations can be catalysts when others must be cautious.

In the improvement of in-service education for school administrators, no one has a greater interest or greater stake in the results than the American Association of School Administrators. What must this organization do to enhance its role in this respect?

1. It must continue in close working relationships with the National Education Association and with regional, state, and local associations.

2. Having placed a requirement on membership based on initial preparation that involves the quality of the pre-

---

[5] This is suggested by the Colorado State Committee for the Cooperative Program in Educational Administration. See Nolte, M. Chester. *Selection, Preparation, and In-Service Development of School Superintendents.* Colorado: State Committee for the CPEA, May 1959.

paring institution, the Association should be prepared to enforce and improve these standards. The Association's Committee for the Advancement of School Administration should be encouraged to continue its pioneer efforts in this area.

3. Having made plain who shall enter, there is an equal obligation to clarify who will be separated and for what cause. Once adopted, ethics should be rigorously upheld.

4. Every assistance shoud be given in promoting the research programs so necessary to improvement of in-service education.

5. Careful study should be given the national convention. Great care has been taken to make it as valuable as possible *in its present form.* Does the need still exist to cover all bases each year or should we concentrate attention on one major issue at a time? Would meetings in one, two, or three state regions be more helpful and less costly? Should some funds be diverted for small in-state groups? Could the mountains come to Mohammed?

6. More of the "Hogs, Ax Handles, and Woodpeckers" type of policy statement should be forthcoming. Nothing is more appreciated by the school administrator than a clear, thoughtful, and usable problem analysis. Associations can help when they publish a "this is important"—"look into this"—"watch out for that" type of quick assistance on a crucial issue.

COORDINATED CONTINUING EDUCATION

Nothing makes one quite so lonely as being out on a limb; and the farther out, the lonelier. Some comfort comes as a result of knowing there are those who watch with concern for one's welfare, but this is tempered somewhat by the sober realization that there are others who watch with the same motives as the first-row Romans awaiting the entrance of the day's number one Christian in the ancient arena. Why should the pseudo-Romans seem so much more numerous and so much better organized? we sometimes ask. Is there any reason why the interest of five strong groups cannot be welded together and a

206

serious, formal effort made to offer not protection, but the assistance and support that will make protection unnecessary?

The five, of course, are—the university, which has its label on the administrator and its continuing reputation in his hands; the board of education, whose judgment will be in question if he fails, and which is aware of the cost of failure to the school program and the school district; the U.S. Office of Education and the state department of education, both charged under the law with providing assistance and anxious to avoid the problems attendant upon an administrator's falling short; and the professional organizations of which he is a member.

The university must develop a climate of assistance, offering personal counseling, holding clinics, inviting the participation of practicing administrators in program planning, and having someone available for field studies. The board of education must encourage its superintendent to seek assistance when he has problems that surpass his ability, provide funds when this is necessary, keep informed of what services the university or the state department of education has to offer, help find assistance when the need becomes apparent. The state department of education must realize that the typical superintendent is in a small system, that he does not have the staff assistance that others have in larger places, that he does not have the answers to many questions and not too much chance of finding them in the resources at hand. The department must offer more service, more in the office and more in the field. Careful instruction as to how to best use consultant service should also be given. Little results from such service if it is asked for too late, the wrong type of consultant invited, or no preparation made before he arrives.[6] The U.S. Office of Education must take the lead in making research findings available, emphasizing and reporting those that have the most obvious worth. The professional associations must increasingly take assistance to their members in the field. Conventions are not the answer. Conventions, as now carried on, are not included among the most valuable means

---

[6] An excellent treatment of this topic can be found in the following copies of the Midwest Administration Center's *Administrator's Notebook*, University of Chicago:
Vol. I, No. 3—Oct. 1952—"Making the Most of the Consultant"
Vol. II, No. 8—Apr. 1954—"Which Consultant?"
Vol. IV, No. 2—Oct. 1955—"Local School Systems and Their Consultants"
Vol. IV, No. 3—Nov. 1955—"The Value of State Consultative Service."

of in-service growth.[7] It would be surprising if these five agencies, working together, could not offer more assistance than is often the case when they work separately. By "following-up" and not leaving everything to the operating administrator, great assistance can be rendered and more effective operation should result.

The best insurance of good initial performance and of improved later performance lies in the upgrading of standards. If there is any virtue in the idea that education is effective and useful, or that experience is of benefit, there is promise in the "high standards" approach.

The state department of education, charged with developing and administering certification laws, can work with the organized profession in raising requirements over a period of time. Equally, they can encourage boards of education to set up standards for positions that will require applicants to have superior preparation. Professional organizations have consistently sought higher standards, and their continued pursuit of this objective will be necessary.

There is no guarantee of satisfactory performance in school administration. Recognition on the part of everyone in the educational enterprise, however, that leadership is important, that it requires cooperation to be effective, that action should be based on knowledge, that assistance is sometimes necessary— these are the concepts that will make it possible to improve administrative performance. The schools of this country need strong and effective leadership. Lifelong continuing education for administrators of the schools will be necessary to insure such strength and effectiveness.

---

[7] Moore, Hollis A., Jr. "How Superintendents Grow Through In-Service Opportunities." *Nation's Schools* 51:56-59; May 1953. *See also* Chapters II and IV of this yearbook.

chapter IX

How To Pay
for What We Need

In projecting the kinds of programs that are essential to the effective pre-service and in-service preparation of school administrators, this Yearbook Commission has presented some bold, far-reaching, and imaginative proposals. It is quite apparent that a quality of excellence is envisioned in these proposals far greater than has been seen to date in the development of educational leadership in the United States.

But it all costs money. Such adequate financial support must include provisions for the *students* who are preparing for careers in school administration as well as for the *institutions* that offer the preparation programs. A wholly new concept of adequate financing arrangements must prevail in both instances—for students and institutions. An examination of this concept and attendant problems is the concern of Chapter IX.

ESTIMATING THE COSTS

It is probably safe to assume that there are few if any preparation programs currently in operation anywhere in the country that measure up completely to the professional standards and requirements proposed in this yearbook. For this reason the evidence available to serve as a guide for the accurate and precise determination of the financial resources required to support defensible preparation programs is limited. Nevertheless, this Commission felt an obligation to make some estimates on cost. Failure to do so would open the way to criticism that proposals were made with our heads in the clouds—without regard for cost. The facts of financing, terrestrial as ever, follow.

Comparisons with Other Professions

A doctoral dissertation at Stanford provides one of the few studies of the cost of professional preparation of school administrators. In 1954 Boortz[1] compared the costs of educating school superintendents, lawyers, dentists, and physicians. The purpose of the study was to determine the relative cost to educational institutions and to students for professional education preparatory to careers in the four professions. It covered educational programs in the following western universities: University of Arizona, University of California (both at Berkeley and at Los Angeles), University of Southern California, and Stanford University.

The results suggest quite clearly that programs for the preparation of school administrators are receiving considerably less financial support than is expended on programs in law, dentistry, and medicine. Worse, there is evidence to show that payments by school administration students indirectly subsidize other professional students.

Boortz defined "professional education" as that period of formal instruction between the bachelor's and doctor's degrees in the field of education; and between admittance to the professional schools and the completion of the LL.B. degree in law, the D.D.S. degree in dentistry, and the M.D. degree in medicine.

Costs to institutions were limited to "basic operating costs": administration, instruction, operation and maintenance, and library. The "full-time equivalent student" concept was used as the unit for comparison.

Basic nonliving and living costs were determined for both married and single students enrolled in the professional schools which are maintained by the five universities. All costs were computed for the year 1952-53 and were extended over a three-year period and compared with national costs of studies for dental

---

[1] Boortz, Nathan Harold. *Costs of Educating School Superintendents, Lawyers, Dentists, and Physicians.* Doctor's thesis. Stanford, California: Stanford University, 1954.

schools (1949-50) and for medical schools (1947-48 and 1950-51) extended over a four-year period.

In simplified form the results of the study are shown in Table 1.

1 AVERAGE COSTS TO SOCIETY (EDUCATIONAL INSTITUTIONS) AND TO THE INDIVIDUAL FOR PROFESSIONAL EDUCATION IN FOUR AREAS

	EDUCATIONAL ADMINISTRATION 3-Yr. PROGRAMS	LAW 3-Yr. PROGRAMS	DENTISTRY 4-Yr. PROGRAMS	MEDICINE 4-Yr. PROGRAMS
Institutional Expense	$ 1,628	$ 2,884	$ 5,264	$10,064
Personal Expense				
Married Students	11,111	10,995	17,588	17,111
Single Students	4,962	4,882	8,667	8,332

The results of the study reveal that in each of the five universities expenditures for educating school administrators were lower than for any of the other professions studied and far below the institutional costs for training dentists and physicians. When the costs of programs in educational administration are compared with the costs of the other professional programs, the relative institutional investment was approximately 6 to 1 for physicians, 3 to 1 for dentists, and 2 to 1 for attorneys. Granted that preparation programs in medicine and dentistry will always require somewhat larger expenditures because of the special high costs involved. It is extremely questionable, however, to assume that the present ratios of expenditures in law, dentistry, medicine, and educational administration could (or should) be maintained when the need for improved professional programs in school administration becomes more widely recognized and accepted. Our evidence of present practices in Chapters II and III underscores the absence of essential—but costly—instructional aids such as laboratories, field internships, and seminars with teaching teams.

The results of the study as they relate to the costs for individual students reveal that for those students who were married, law students made the smallest average personal investment of the group ($10,995), followed by administration students ($11,111). Medical student costs averaged $17,111 while dental student costs, the highest of the four, averaged $17,588. Although costs for single students were appreciably lower, the order of rank was the same.

Competition in the Talent Market

The profession is vitally interested in improving American education by augmenting the supply of able candidates for top administrative positions. This is based on the assumption that, since the quality of education is affected by the competence of its leaders, it is extremely important to the future of educational systems to do a better job of selecting and training future administrators.

As a prerequisite to training administrative candidates of executive potential, a concentrated entry into the "talent market" for candidates must be made with all the resources available. In terms of selection, retention, and training programs, this can only mean a greater expenditure of funds. In one sense, such money is necessary just to keep up with similar inducements from other professions and business interests.

As an initial step in this direction, the University Council for Educational Administration, which has been studying the recruitment problem for some time, has worked to develop a set of selection criteria to be used in identifying persons with potential top-quality executive ability.* A complementary step has been the approximation of student costs for a 12-month period of advanced graduate study (projected for the 1960's). These approximations, originally drawn up as part of a prospectus to induce foundation support for student selection, are shown in Table 2.

Personal Cost to the Student

The data from the foregoing studies suggest two things that must be given major consideration in the development of more adequate support of preparation programs in educational administration. Educational institutions require increased finan-

---

* The DCS project described in Chapter VI, p. 157.

2 APPROXIMATION OF STUDENT COSTS FOR
12-MONTH PERIOD OF GRADUATE STUDY

	RANGE	
	LOW *	HIGH
1. Living costs. (Vary according to number of children in recipient's household, section of country where university is located, extent to which an automobile is needed, etc.)	$3,000	$5,000
2. Tuition charges and related expenses. Vary by university	500	1,000
Probable range of fellowships	3,500	6,000
3. Institutional supporting payments. (Based upon estimates that a full doctoral year costs a minimum of $1,000 over tuition per candidate)	1,000	
4. Administrative costs in searching for and identifying candidates	Probably best put at 5% - 10% of total amount handled, decreasing in percentage as total increases.	

* Based on **current** living costs and **present minimum** tuition charges.

cial support to enable them to provide facilities and services on a scale closer to what is being expended currently in the preparation of lawyers, doctors, and dentists. The costs of improved and extended graduate study will involve personal expenditures that will eliminate many potentially promising candidates unless more adequate provisions are made for fellowships, scholarships, and other forms of student aid.

In the survey of current preparation programs reported in Chapter III, institutions were asked to report the number of students who were receiving financial aid in the form of scholarships, fellowships, and part-time work. Of the 1306 who completed programs of preparation in 1957-58, 420 received a scholarship or fellowship. This is slightly under one-third of the

213

number graduating. The attempt to ascertain how much money was received by students was not very successful. Of the 86 who did report, the range was from under $100 to $5564, with a median of $900.

The survey reported in Chapter III asked preparing institutions: "Given the funds, facilities, and staff, what would you do to improve your program in educational administration?" Forty-six different improvements were suggested. An analysis of the suggested improvements as they appear in Table 12 of Chapter III indicates clearly that most of them are costly—internships, surveys, smaller seminars.

In Chapter II data are reported dealing with student costs. Superintendents were asked what it cost them to complete their programs of preparation. They were requested to report only net costs, which meant that they were to subtract scholarships, fellowships, government aid to veterans, and other nonloan subsidies. They were also asked not to include wages they could have earned had they not been in school. The results indicate that the median *net* cost of a doctorate was $4438; of a 60-hour program, $2356; and of a master's degree, $1490. The range for the doctorate was from no net cost to over $10,000; for the 60-hour program, from less than $500 to over $10,000; and for the master's, from no net cost to $8000.

When the superintendents were asked to report on the amount of financial aid they received as they did their graduate work, over three-fourths reported that they received no aid at all. Practically all of the aid was received by 19 percent of the respondents, with 1.2 percent (nine superintendents) receiving $5000 or more.

PRICE TAG ON PROGRAM CHANGES

The proposals presented in this yearbook for the development of improved professional programs include a variety of activities ranging from initial identification and selection of candidates through placement and follow-up on the job. The quality of the total program of pre-service and in-service education depends upon the effectiveness with which each of these activities is planned and administered. An analysis of the activities suggests both the need for more adequate financial support and for additional sources of income.

The Preparation Program

In Chapter VII a comprehensive preparation program in school administration is proposed for State University. Although State University is a fictitious institution, the personnel, facilities, and services proposed are in no sense fictitious. Neither are the financial needs.

A strong faculty with demonstrated competence in scholarly pursuits, in teaching, and in the practice of educational administration is essential to the development of a professional program in school administration. The great importance of a strong faculty is emphasized in Chapter II. Practicing superintendents, when requested to indicate the major strength of the program of preparation in which they had been involved, ranked "faculty's ability, practical experience, and interest in students" highest. If the school administrator of the future is to be a broadly educated, highly competent, and resourceful individual, it is imperative that his preparation be in the hands of faculty personnel who themselves possess the personal and professional qualifications they are expected to develop with their students.

The problem of attracting a competent faculty is a difficult one. Individuals who can meet high standards of professional competency are now and will continue to be in short supply. Adequate salaries will be an essential condition for attracting able faculty members.

To staff adequately an institution preparing administrators, it is anticipated that the following faculty and supplementary personnel will be needed in the area of educational administration if the average annual number of full-time students is 60:

3 senior faculty members at a salary of $20,000 each

5 associate faculty members at a salary of $15,000 each

2 assistant faculty members at a salary of $12,000 each

10 assistants at a salary of $3500 each

7 secretaries at an average salary of $3500 each.

Additional fixed expenditures of $183,125 would mean that provision for a total budget of $401,625 would be needed. It is further expected that in 10 to 15 years, salaries of senior faculty members may well be $30,000; associate faculty members, $22,500; assistant faculty members, $18,000; with assistants receiving a salary of $5000. Additional increases in salary to non-faculty personnel and in fixed costs would mean an approximate annual budget of $629,250. A 60-student program would include participation in several areas of administration, not alone the superintendency.

If the concept of administrator preparation presented in this yearbook is to become a reality, financial provisions for its development must be forthcoming.

Throughout the yearbook the fact has been emphasized that a relatively few educational institutions, which are strategically located and adequately supported, can prepare the limited number of educational administrators that are needed annually to fill the vacancies that occur. It is hoped that leaders of educational institutions will accept the wisdom of this recommendation not only from the standpoint of supply/demand figures, but also in view of the necessarily high costs. It would not be sound stewardship of public or private funds to continue more high-cost programs than the demonstrated need for new administrators calls for.

Identification and Selection

The need for improved programs in the identification and selection of candidates for school administration is considered extensively in Chapter VI. The proposals made in the chapter interpret the responsibility for improved practices as one to be shared jointly by school systems and educational institutions. Candidates for graduate study of educational administration will come mainly from public school systems. In Chapter II, two major career patterns are identified. In cities of over 100,000 population, the most common pattern reported by superintendents is teacher—principal—central office administrator—superintendent. In smaller communities the central office step is bypassed.

A joint enterprise. Indeed, it must be recognized that if any significant advance is to be forthcoming in the identification, selection, and training of school administrators, this must be a shared responsibility—shared between college and school district. Certainly, the school districts are in the most advantageous position for the initial identification of potentially outstanding young administrators. Second, they are in a key position for evaluating the products of the university training program as these trained personnel re-enter the field. Although it is the primary responsibility of the university to train potential top administrators for key administrative positions, there are few schools of education which have the complete resources financial and otherwise to provide this training without entering into a cooperative agreement with the school districts from whence these candidates come. Inasmuch as the school district is the final beneficiary of the training program, it must assume a larger share of responsibility for financial support of the program. This can be done through developmental leave, in-service seminars, testing programs, and other selecting or training operations.

Some school administrators argue that to send a promising young man off to further training is to see him never again. This is not a defensible position for a school district to take. It is quite possible that the potential administrator, once trained, may not return to their district. But some other promising young man, financially aided to further his training by another prudent school district, will come to serve them. No school district in its wisdom would argue for keeping a potential top-quality candidate in a less well-trained category in order to keep him in service "at home." Rather, it should expect and get from the university well-qualified individuals who have been well trained to fill the personnel needs of the school system.

Financially, this means that school systems must be prepared to liberalize their positions for providing leaves of absence to promising potential administrators to secure advanced work in universities and colleges that have outstanding administrator preparation programs. Involved in this financial assistance are not only the payments to the candidate but some assistance to the university which prepares these candidates. It is just not possible for the university, which has traditionally been in a less sound economic position than the public school system, to identify, select, and prepare outstanding candidates only to turn them over to the public school system. Proper responsibility for the financing of this training must be assumed by those who benefit from it. To this end, it is suggested that universities and school districts form local and/or regional agreements for this purpose—agreements which in turn will bring the university preparation program closer to the realities of the educational practitioner. How much should a school system devote to this purpose? A figure of 1 percent of total annual operating budget is suggested.

Promising practices. Significant beginnings have already been made in this regard in some forward-looking school systems. They argue well for the future. As potentially promising teachers and principals have been identified in local school systems, boards of education and superintendents have provided developmental leaves with full or partial salary payments, thus permitting and encouraging these individuals to engage in graduate preparation for educational administration. In many places throughout the country, school systems have cooperated with collegiate institutions in the development of internship and apprenticeship programs and have assumed considerable responsibility for the financial support of the programs; however, direct grants to trainees are still rare.

Reference has been made in Chapter VI to the use of the project known as "Discovery of the Criteria of Success" and its attempts to employ new techniques for screening potential educational administrators. Several school systems have participated in the experimental use of this technique and have willingly assumed responsibility for the costs involved. As educational institutions continue to develop more refined techniques for the identification and selection of candidates, it can be expected that more and more school systems will accept their responsibility for cooperation and financial support.

The yearbook has emphasized the importance of community studies, surveys, and school improvement projects as a desirable means of pre-service preparation for educational administration. School systems profit immeasurably from these cooperative projects and can justify generous financial support of the programs in terms of the services received by the community.

Boards of education have a vested interest in any efforts that are made to improve practices in the identification and selection of future educational administrators. To the extent that they provide substantial financial support for these efforts they will serve not only their own self-interest but will contribute enormously to the professionalization of school administration throughout the country.

The concept of selection and preparation as a joint enterprise has been promoted at one university. It is shown in the diagram, Figure I, as seven steps toward leadership development. Steps B, E, and F call for financial sharing by district and college at a considerably higher level than is currently the case.

FIG. I THE STANFORD PROGRAM FOR LEADERSHIP DEVELOPMENT IN PUBLIC SCHOOL ADMINISTRATION

1 PREPARATORY AND INDUCTION PROGRAM:	Concentration in one of the following specialized fields for INITIAL SERVICE:	1. Elementary, or 2. Secondary, or 3. Pupil Personnel and Guidance

A	SUCCESSFUL TEACHING	A minimum of two years is generally expected. From among successful teachers, those with outstanding personality characteristics, interest in education as a life-long career, and greatest apparent promise for success in administration will be selected by local school systems.	2 YRS.
B	ADMINISTRATIVE TRAINEE PROGRAM	Selected trainees undertake important typical administrative assignments on a released-time basis from their classrooms, under the joint supervision of local system administrators and Stanford School of Education staff members.	1 or 2 YRS.
C	PROBATIONARY ADMINISTRATIVE POSITIONS Vice-Principals Deans Administrative Assistants Principals	This first experience as assigned administrator is regarded by all to be fundamentally a training period. A program of continuing induction is arranged, to be carried on jointly by local school system personnel and training institution staff members.	2 YRS.

2 ADVANCED AND CAREER-LONG PROGRAM:	Concentration in one of the following specializations for CAREER SERVICE:	

1. Elementary school administration
2. Secondary school administration
3. Pupil personnel and guidance administration
4. School finance and business administration
5. School plant administration
6. Staff personnel administration
7. Chief administrator role
8. Public school administrative research

D ONE OR MORE YEARS OF OUTSTANDING SERVICE AS A "PERMANENT" ADMINISTRATOR		1 YR.

E	DEVELOPMENTAL LEAVE	The outstanding young administrator has one year of carefully planned advanced training. Partial or full salary is paid during this leave period, provided two years subsequent service is pledged.	1 YR.
F	INTERNSHIP OR FELLOWSHIP	A few of the most promising young administrators who emerge from the preceding stages of the program are given substantial grants, either internship or University fellowship, to spend an additional period of concentrated study in their respective areas of specialization.	1 YR.
G	CONTINUING IN-SERVICE EDUCATION PROGRAM	A career-long in-service educational program for the eight specializations will be maintained.	CAREER SERVICE AS ADMIN.

Guidance and Follow-Up

An effective preparation program will include a wide range of learning experiences and will employ a variety of instructional methods and techniques. Provision will need to be made in the program for extensive instruction in such disciplines as philosophy, political science, economics, sociology, and anthropology. It is quite apparent that internships, apprenticeships, and field service programs will increasingly become important parts of good preparation programs. These programs, if they are to relate administrative theory to practice successfully, will require continuing supervision by competent faculty members and by administrators in the field. As a means of adapting theory into operational terms, considerable use will be made of the group analysis of educational problems through case studies and seminars.

All students preparing for school administration will not be expected to engage in all of the learning experiences that are provided. Continuing emphasis will need, therefore, to be focused upon the adjustment of both content and methods of instruction to the individual needs of students. The extent to which the variety of learning experiences is geared effectively to the needs of students will depend greatly upon the number of faculty members available and the amount of time at their disposal for individual guidance and counseling and the guidance that can be given by local administrators. It is estimated by competent observers that a ratio of one faculty member to six students is highly desirable.

It is true that the provision of adequate guidance and counseling services in the preparation program will be expensive to support. One must recognize that the proposals made in this yearbook seek to achieve an extended program of preparation for school administration at a level of excellence that has never before been attempted. Today there exists everywhere throughout the country great public interest in the achievement of excellence in educational policies and programs. It seems appropriate to assume that this public interest does encompass the preparation of school administrators.

The responsibility for the preparation of school administrators does not end when the candidate has completed the formal requirements for the administrative certificate or the doctoral degree. Educational institutions in cooperation with local school systems should be greatly concerned with the proper placement of the individual on the job and with appropriate follow-up services as a means of insuring continued professional growth and development. The problems that arise when a board of education is confronted with the employment of a new school administrator are presented in Chapter I and suggest quite clearly the need for improved placement and follow-up services. The financial support of improved practices in these areas will be, quite properly, a joint responsibility of educational institutions and local school systems.

Continuing Education

In Chapter IV the need for extended and improved programs of in-service education is presented. Many of the current methods of providing in-service education opportunities for school administrators have value and should probably be continued. It is evident, however, that there is urgent need for the development of new in-service programs that will provide practicing school administrators with more effective opportunities to deal with some of the critical issues with which educational leadership is now and will continue to be confronted. Programs that provide only opportunities for an exchange of experiences with problems of finance, personnel, buildings, and the like will not be adequate for school administrators who are responsible for developing educational programs in an age of nuclear energy and space travel.

If the in-service educational needs of school administrators are to be served effectively in the future, educational institutions will need to make available the total resources of the institution in programs that are highly structured and focused on problems of critical public concern. To be specific, the institution must enlist scholars in economics, anthropology, sociology, and other fields to help with the in-service development of school administrators. Boards of education will need to recognize more than they have in the past the urgent need for in-service education of their administrators and allocate substantial funds for these purposes.

221

Physical Facilities

In the Boortz study reported earlier in the chapter it was recognized that certain courses of study in the preparation of dentists and doctors might justify somewhat higher costs than are involved in the preparation of school administrators. It is extremely doubtful that the considerable differential in costs that now exists can be maintained if preparation programs in school administration are to be supported with appropriate physical facilities, equipment, and supplies.

The tremendous changes that are taking place constantly in the development of new instructional equipment and supplies suggest the need for laboratories and materials centers in which these new developments may be demonstrated and observed. With the continuing demand for new school buildings it is desirable that many educational institutions be equipped to maintain school plant planning laboratories. The effective administration of field services and research activities makes it imperative that there be adequate facilities equipped with modern computing and accounting machines.

All educational institutions have long recognized the need for adequate and extensive library facilities for the professions of law, medicine, dentistry, and the like. It is evident that the professional preparation of school administrators will require equal consideration for library facilities and services. To this will be added case development, in-basket and other simulated situation materials, films, recordings, and TV in observing administrative problems in motion. There is quite general agreement that instructional practices in the public schools have not kept pace with what is known concerning the learning process. There is great need for carefully controlled experimentation as a means of developing more effective techniques of teaching and learning. It is to be hoped that educational institutions will, in the future, include plans for campus laboratory and experimental schools as integral parts of their professional programs of preparation for school administrators.

Financial Aids to Students

Any consideration of the problem of securing adequate financial support of professional programs in school administration must, of necessity, include the problem of financial aid for students. The proposals made in this yearbook for the preparation of school administrators assume discriminating selection of candidates. Only those individuals endowed with superior intelligence, scholarly interests, and marked capacities for leadership should be considered as prospects. In the years that lie ahead business, industry, and government will engage in keen competition with education for potentially promising individuals. If education is to receive a reasonable share of competent candidates, incentives for enrolling in preparation programs in school administration will need to be equally as attractive as they are among the competitors.

Age as a factor. In Chapter II the replies of practicing superintendents indicate that too much time is being spent in the completion of graduate programs in school administration. The median length of time is five years and seven months, but the range is from one year to 20 years or more. It is quite apparent from these data that preparation for school administration has been done, in the past, largely on a part-time basis. The members of the Yearbook Commission are in essential agreement that effective preparation for school administration cannot be done on a part-time basis and urge that students be required to spend at least a full year in residence beyond the completion of the master's degree. Full-time participation in graduate programs will require greater costs over a concentrated period of time to the student than are required when graduate work is done on a part-time basis.

The age at which the student engages in graduate preparation is still another factor that implies need for financial assistance. In Chapter II the replies of superintendents reveal that the median age at which graduate study was begun was 28 years and six months. Although there is evidence that superintendents are now beginning their graduate study at a somewhat earlier age, it is doubtful whether the age at which graduate study is begun will ever be much below 25 years. Candidates who are 25 years of age or older will have been earning salaries; many will be married men with families; and some will have assumed substantial financial obligations. Unless provisions are made for financial aid to students, it is evident that the recruitment and selection of candidates will be severely limited to relatively inexperienced, affluent young men or to those who are less-than-promising prospects.

Changing viewpoint toward student assistance. There is abundant evidence that the need for financial assistance to students as a means of developing more effectively the nation's human resources is gaining widespread public interest and acceptance. Over a span of seven years following World War II the federal government spent $14 billion for the education of 8 million soldiers under the Veterans Bill of Rights. The Ford Foundation has set aside $500 million to establish national competitive scholarships for American colleges and universities and offers to match contributions from industry for the same purpose. The recently passed National Defense Education Act provides for $290 million in student loans, as well as a substantial fellowship program. The National Science Foundation offers annually 2000 awards for graduate study in the various sciences and has recently made available substantial contributions for high school science teachers who attend the year-long Academic Year Institutes.

Possibilities for the development of financial aid programs for students in school administration are suggested in a recent report of the Harvard Graduate School of Education.[2] In the report Young lists the following forms of student aid and the estimated amounts of each that were made available to students in the Graduate School of Education for the year 1959-60.

1. School of Education scholarships and fellowships
   a. For degree programs $205,000
   b. Academic Year Institute 247,000
2. General University scholarships 15,000
3. Scholarships and fellowships from outside agencies 12,000
4. Summer school scholarships 900
5. Teaching fellowships 40,000
6. Research assistantships 60,000
7. Internships 192,500
8. School of Education loans 60,000
9. Loans from outside agencies 10,000
10. Part-time administrative work in the University 45,000

   TOTAL $887,400

---

[2] Young, Joseph J. *Financial Aid to Students at the Graduate School of Education.* Cambridge, Mass.: Harvard Graduate School of Education, March 1959.

SOME PLANS ... SOME PROPOSALS

It is apparent from the foregoing list that there are many different types of financial aid that can be developed for graduate students in educational administration. The nature and amount of aid will need to be determined on an individual basis and will involve consideration of many factors. In general, married students with families who have become financially indebted will require greater assistance than single candidates. Parental income should undoubtedly be taken into account. The abilities of the candidates and the time at their disposal will determine to what extent teaching fellowships, research assistantships, and part-time work will be included in the financial aid program. Careful assessment of individual needs will result in patterns of financial aid that will combine several forms of assistance with varying amounts of aid provided.

The College's Responsibility

During the summer of 1959 Stanford University invited a group of 25 educational leaders to participate in a conference for the purpose of evaluating their program in school administration. A committee, of which Dean Francis Keppel of Harvard University served as chairman, submitted a report on the financing of preparation programs in school administration. The report included an analysis of the amounts and the sources of financial aid to students currently provided in the Stanford program. The present candidate group was being supported with total funds of roughly $106,000. The following list shows the types and the sources of candidate support in 1959.

From local school districts—	
internships and sabbatical leaves	36%
University or private contracts	33
Foundation and U.S. government research	28
Fellowships and scholarships	3
	100%

In commenting upon the Stanford program of financial aid to students, the committee made the following pertinent observa-

225

tion. "The figure for fellowships and scholarships seemed to the group much too low for a permanent program of recruitment. Clinical experience is valuable and should be a source of candidate support, but a student supported by scholarships and fellowships can probably get a wider variety of experiences than it is possible for him to receive by participation in a clinical experience in which he has some kind of particular, necessarily limited responsibility from which he derives financial support."

In addition to its analysis of the current program of financial aid to students, the committee was requested to develop a more desirable program and to project estimated costs of the program for a period of from 10 to 15 years.

In presenting its proposed program the committee assumed that the goal would be 40 full-time students entering annually and that 20 to 30 of this number would stay on for a second year. It was assumed that ultimately 75 percent of all entering candidates would earn degrees. It was further assumed that the typical candidate group would have the following experience and age characteristics:

NUMBER	AGE RANGE	EXPERIENCE
10 candidates	25-30 years	No experience
20 candidates	30-35 years	Junior experience
10 candidates	35-45 years	Senior experience

It was finally assumed that financial support for the three groups should be of this order:

AGE	PRESENT SUPPORT SHOULD BE	SUPPORT IN 1970
25-30 years	$3,000	$4,000
30-35 years	4,000	5,300
35-45 years	5,000	6,700

Based upon the foregoing proposals the committee recommended that Stanford University should seek to provide an amount of $240,000 annually as a means of recruiting and supporting 40 able candidates a year with 20 needing support for a second year.

Additional committee recommendations included the following:

1. That support should be drawn from the following sources in approximately these amounts:

   Fellowships, local and others _____$ 50,000

   Research _____ 40,000

   Contracts _____ 50,000

   School systems _____ 100,000

2. That the figures suggest there will be heavy demands on the faculty in school administration to recruit and to work with school districts and other income sources to develop these sources of support.

3. That the university take the initiative in arriving at national and regional agreements with other universities to create a pool of fellowship funds from which some three to four hundred young administrators annually could draw funds to finance graduate study. It is possible that this fellowship pool could be at least partially supported by the federal government.

Local District Contract Agreements

A further aspect of candidate and program support is university contact with school districts. Long-term working arrangements with school districts in neighboring counties are formalized through continuing contracts between the districts and the university and are handled through the offices of the county superintendents and the associations of district superintendents. The superintendents associations set the fees and through committees screen requests for services. Survey and consultant services to the districts on their educational problems are furnished at district request. The continuing contracts make it possible to build up comprehensive files, knowledge of the districts, and good working relationships with the administrators; and make budgeting of time and money much easier for the survey staff.

These relationships serve four objectives:

1. Service to the field,
2. Training of graduate students in a practical situation,
3. Raising money for assistantships to attract and hold superior students,
4. Feedback of thoughts and problems of administrators to faculty.

The field activities are under the direction of a faculty member who can call on other faculty members in the university as need arises. Three or four graduate assistants also serve on the staff. In addition, as opportunity arises, other graduate students are involved in the projects so that each student in administration takes part in field work during his graduate training.

These examples are taken from the recommendations given to a single university. They apply widely, however, and a collegiate institution interested in maintaining a top-quality professional program for school administration can adapt these cost figures to its own program projections for the future.

National Fellowship Proposal

In a report prepared by the University Council for Educational Administration in 1957, the estimated costs of fellowships and institutional supporting payments were projected to provide for an ultimate number of 400 students preparing for careers in educational administration. See Table 3.

3 PROJECTED COST SUMMARY

	20 STUDENTS		50 STUDENTS		400 STUDENTS	
	LOW*	HIGH	LOW*	HIGH	LOW*	HIGH
1	2	3	4	5	6	7
Fellowship funds needed	$70,000	$120,000	$185,000	$300,000	$1,400,000	$2,400,000
Institutional supporting funds needed	20,000	20,000	50,000	50,000	400,000	400,000
Administrative costs	9,000[1]	14,000[1]	11,750[2]	17,500[2]	45,000[3]	70,000[3]
Total 1-year program	99,000	154,000	246,750	367,500	1,845,000	2,870,000
Total 2-year program	198,000	308,000	512,000	734,000	3,690,000	5,740,000

* Based on **current** living costs and **present minimum** tuition charges.
[1] 10% [2] 5% [3] 2½%

CONCLUSION

Basic to the entire program of upgrading educational administration is financial assistance to administrator preparation programs. Yet there is hope for considerable improvement in financial support of adequate programs, since the number of institutions needed to prepare well-qualified educational leaders is considerably smaller than the current number of colleges offering study in this field. A concentration of resources, human and physical, can only be accomplished by making available greater monetary resources than are now found at any institution preparing school administrators. If the profession of school administration is to attract outstanding quality candidates, it must be able to compete successfully with other professions such as law, business, medicine, and dentistry.

As part of the cost of the preparation program, top priority must be given to improving faculty salaries in order to attract top-quality professional educators. Further, professors must not be lured to an institution by the promise that much of their income can be gained by consulting fees and other distracting operations which seriously cut into contacts with students. A second need is provision of financial assistance to the candidates selected. Men of outstanding ability who have assumed financial and family obligations are not apt to give up their positions of employment to seek advanced training without first being given some degree of assurance that they will have the financial resources necessary to complete the program. We need no more disappointed "all but the dissertation" men in administration.

Although the primary responsibility remains with the universities and colleges, it must be increasingly recognized that school districts, professional associations, and other agencies must become involved and concerned with the selection, training, and placement of individuals selected for the advanced graduate program. It is not outside the realm of possibility that major institutions in the near future will realize the necessity of cooperating in establishing a national scholarship pool from which well-qualified candidates may secure financial assistance.

The need for greatly increased budgets is evident. The recommendations found in Chapters VI, VII, and VIII cannot possibly be realized at present levels of support. Few improvements are cheap, and progress is rarely a bargain in terms of initial outlay of money. New sources must be tapped, and present supporting agencies and institutions must enlarge their contributions. Sources include local district funds, foundations, government contracts and individual subsidies, loans, and institutional scholarships. All elements of the profession must bend strong efforts toward solution of the financial problems in preparation of school administrators.

chapter X

Getting Around
the Obstacles

To improve an educational enterprise is not merely to change it. Improvement is, rather, *planned* change based on understanding of the past, keen appreciation of present realities, and clear perception of future possibilities and alternatives. Such a process of improvement (closing gaps between what is currently seen to exist and what is perceived to be better) underlies the proposals of Chapters VI through IX. Yet, countless obstacles lie along the road to betterment. The problem of overcoming these obstacles constitutes the subject matter of this chapter.

THE PROBLEM OF IMPROVEMENT

It is abundantly evident from the content of this yearbook that what is visualized for the profession of educational administration vastly exceeds current practice. We presently use only a small fraction of the techniques at our disposal for the identification, recruitment, and selection of potential educational leaders. Only a few universities, widely scattered across the country, approach the level of preparation program described in Chapter VII. Many activities for the in-service education of administrators are conducted in such fashion that the administrators consider them to be unrewarding.

At first glance, the discovery of a gap between what is envisioned and what is being done is no cause for surprise. Perceptual psychology tells us that perceptions of alternative possibilities precede deliberate change. But *who* perceives is of utmost importance to the process of change. For somebody to perceive a desirable change for someone else is of secondary importance. The essential element is that the individual in whom change is desired perceive the desirability of changing himself.

But still other conditions are necessary if change is to occur. The steps along the road to be taken must be clearly marked and the individual must feel confident of his ability to take these steps. If an individual is unhappy with present circumstances but the alternatives suggested appear to be far beyond him, he may settle for much less than his ideal, or he may decide to do exactly nothing, since reaching the announced goal is an obvious impossibility. Help from outside his own resources may therefore be required.

From the above general analysis, it may be concluded that there are two major focal points of attack in advancing the profession of educational administration. First, the *perceptions* of those persons encompassed within the field of educational administration must be changed so that they see clearly alternatives to present circumstances. Furthermore, these persons must become motivated to improve present practices. Second, the *structures* within which the practice of educational administration and the preparation of school administrators are conducted must be reordered so as to support and encourage individuals in their efforts to improve.

Perception as a Factor

We know very little about present perceptions of persons in the field of educational administration regarding the conduct of various phases of this field. How widespread, for example, are the views of inadequacy expressed by this Yearbook Commission? To what extent do certain groups of persons perceive possibilities for changing preparation programs? To what degree and for what reasons are these persons motivated to move toward selected alternatives? What is their degree of confidence in being able to move forward, and what are the reasons for this confidence or lack of it?

It is immediately apparent that the kinds and quantities of data needed for analyzing questions of this kind are not in this yearbook in optimum amount. However, the data reported in

Chapters II and III, if read as a unit and judiciously interpreted, have certain oblique significance. Superintendents report considerable satisfaction with their own preparation programs. These reactions could be very misleading, however, if interpreted to mean that superintendents know *present* conditions with respect to preparation programs and are satisfied with what they see. Actually, their self-reported perceptions may very well represent little more than a halo-effect. Superintendents are generally perceived by themselves and others to be members of a successful group. Their own preparation programs are, then, a part of the success picture. Their responses should not be interpreted to mean that superintendents are either aware of or concerned about preparation programs as they currently exist.

Let us suppose, for a moment, that the faculty members of an institution preparing educational administrators did misinterpret the reactions reported in Chapter II. That is, they interpreted favorable reactions of superintendents to their own preparation programs to mean satisfaction with preparation programs as they currently exist. These faculty members might easily lull themselves into a lotus land of inertia regarding improvement, not realizing that most superintendents probably know very little about the conduct and content of a preparation program today, and if they do, they have no other approach with which to make comparisons.

But let us suppose that superintendents were made generally aware of the current status of programs as described in Chapter III. And let us assume that they came to agree on the wisdom of the proposals in Chapter VII. Suppose, too, that their resulting dissatisfaction came to match the size of the gap between what is and what might be. The previous feeling of warm self-satisfaction probably would shift to one of discomfort with what exists coupled with motivation to move toward other alternatives. We then would have a potentially powerful force to join with other forces in implementing improvement.

The data of this yearbook become, then, a source for changing perceptions of practicing administrators. These changed perceptions, in turn, become a force for overcoming obstacles to change. These data, therefore, must be widely disseminated. It is the responsibility of the reader to ponder them, to see that others become aware of them, and to see that proposals for

233

improvement are vigorously discussed in formal and informal groups.

It was stated earlier in this chapter that desirable changes must be perceived by those to be most directly involved in making them. Therefore, it would seem that it is more important for professors of educational administration than for practicing school administrators to perceive the need and direction for change in preparation programs. The data of Chapter III suggest that, in large measure, the university and college group does see the need for a variety of promising improvements. The problem is that they have seen the need for a long time but move discouragingly slowly to bring practices into line with recognized needs. The obstacle to improvement here, then, lies not so much with present perceptions of this group as with inertia. Present circumstances must, somehow, be made less comfortable or alternatives more motivating, or—ideally—both. Changing the perceptions of school administrators regarding present conditions and other possibilities is thus viewed as a powerful lever in motivating college and university personnel to change. This lever constitutes part of the reordered framework considered as necessary to broad-scale improvement.

A Framework for Improvement

The energies of any one group or, for that matter, several groups focused quite separately are not likely to produce significant change. All of these energies must be focused in a structure that expedites effective, cooperative action. Machinery must be established for examining, revising, and clarifying goals for preparation programs. This machinery must assure the public and the profession alike that those conducting preparation programs for educational administration will be guided by more than personal needs and interests. For those responsible to be effective, the actions satisfying their own needs and the actions appropriate to program goals must closely coincide.

Many groups are responsible in one way or another for the conduct of educational administration and, therefore, for the quality of preparation programs. These groups include practicing superintendents, professors of educational administration, college administrators, school board members, state and national educational officials, and others. Each of these groups is responsible to a variety of other groups: elected officials, the electorate itself, donors of funds, and so on. Each of them, then, in varying degrees, must deal with its special assortment of forces in carrying out its business. The nature, variety, and influence of these forces create formidable obstacles to the improvement of preparation programs. In effect, the unique problems of any one group in the total complex increase the difficulty of bringing all groups into common focus for the attainment of mutually advantageous goals.

For example, state departments of education are woefully handicapped by the pressure of political forces. As a result, they are often impotent in enforcing standards and in expediting the abandonment of weak institutional programs. The movement to appoint rather than elect chief state school officers is a step forward (see Chapter IV), but even when all states move to this policy, we will have only a partial answer to the central problem.

Required, then, is a professional structure of such strength that it cannot be sabotaged by any of the forces impinging upon the component parts. Such structure provides unity of purpose and defines the function of pertinent segments of contributing groups. But it leaves each group relatively free to be creative in making its unique contribution. The bases, function, and operation of the professional controls required are described in Chapter XI. There must be clear-cut requisites for admission to the profession—enforced at both the state and national level—that go beyond the immediate interests of any single group. These requisites, enforced by the profession itself, thus become prerequisite to the certification action of state bodies. They become, also, criteria to be used in appraising the qualifications of any college faculty to develop or continue a preparation program. Only through the protective strength of such a professional structure will any single group be able to free itself adequately from often shortsighted local pressures.

COLLEGE AND UNIVERSITY RESPONSIBILITIES

Four sets of obstacles are considered here. First, the development of weak preparation programs in some colleges and universities. Second, inadequate and inappropriate curricula. Third, blocks to full application of faculty resources. Fourth, recognition and promotion policies which divert faculty members from their central tasks.

The Institutional Commitment

A substantial proportion of the colleges and universities now conducting preparation programs are ready in neither seriousness of intent nor resources. Some of these have been seduced by short-term motives that run counter to the best interests of American society. The problems and difficulties of getting these institutions out of the business of preparing administrators are discussed in Chapter XI.

Self-limitation. Occasionally — very occasionally — a college decides to face up to its verbal commitments regarding a limited, quality job in teacher education and drops its program for preparing educational administrators. This laudable step should be loudly proclaimed in the educational world. Unfortunately, the decision usually is made quietly and few people realize the institution's contribution to educational progress. By contrast, there are colleges and universities across the land now contemplating going into the business that cannot conceivably do a quality job, at least not without seriously crippling other programs in the college. Ironically, their action will be loudly lauded, if not by others, at least by themselves. Unfortunately, too, there are many institutions that do not claim a program but offer enough courses to permit a student to sneak under the certification wire.

Some people—alumni, college administrators, and professors of education, for example—genuinely believe that for their institution to create a new program constitutes the meeting of responsibility in a time of educational crisis. The opposite is generally the case. It is necessary for the AASA and other responsible groups to point out again and again the shortsightedness of such action. Perhaps the application of professional controls proposed in Chapter XI will provide the necessary dissuading influence to a college about to launch an ill-advised preparation program in school administration.

The regional approach. There have been some notable attempts at state or regional cooperation designed to reduce duplication of effort and poorly supported programs. The Southern Regional

Education Board with headquarters in Atlanta, Georgia, has been effective in reducing duplication of effort in fields such as oceanography, veterinary medicine, and nursing education through negotiations designed to support strong regional centers. State university systems, such as North Carolina and Oregon, make some attempt, usually, to establish high-cost professional work in only a few designated institutions.

Cooperative efforts to establish regional centers are of limited effectiveness, however, in the drastic reduction of inadequate programs considered necessary. These processes do not even keep pace with the rate of adding newcomers.

Perhaps states, at least, will move toward the establishment of cooperative centers for the preparation of educational administrators when they come to perceive that high-cost programs are required to do the job properly. But the failure of colleges to so perceive in the past provides little hope for a better future.

Minimum essentials. The ultimate answer is that colleges and universities be selected, in a sense, rather than self-appointed to prepare administrators. That is, they must first meet the minimum essentials laid down within the structure of professional controls proposed in Chapter XI. The following factors, for example (based upon the program proposed in Chapter VII), constitute minimal resources for maintaining or implementing a program preparing educational administrators: (a) a full complement of graduate work in academic fields, with special strength in the behavioral sciences; (b) an education faculty qualified by reason of advanced degrees and experience for membership on the graduate faculty; (c) a sufficient number of persons on this education faculty prepared to conduct, without the necessity of assistance from outside personnel, a year-round program in educational administration; (d) accessibility to public schools of various sizes and types for laboratory experiences ranging from short-term observation to long-term internship.

The essential point here is that strong, cooperatively established professional controls constitute a block to self-appointment and a spur to the elimination of weak institutions in the preparation of school administrators. Such institutions need not be weak, however, in other aspects of their operation. Energies conserved through abandoning inadequate programs can then be turned to more vigorous fulfillment of central goals of liberal, general education, the kind of education that must undergird professional schools or of teacher education, which may require less graduate work than school administration.

Curriculum Problems Unique
to Professional Education

Elementary and secondary school teachers spend a prodigious amount of time in determining goals of the educative enterprise and in selecting and arranging learning opportunities. Comparable activities are woefully lacking in the conduct of higher education. Those institutions that have carried through a creative effort to develop a curriculum within a conceptual framework are so few as to be conspicuous case studies recounted again and again in the literature of higher education. Most professors of education receive some formal education in the processes of educational planning for which the faculty presumably is responsible. But they show no great disposition to apply whatever they may have learned. Even to the professor of curriculum, the principles of curriculum construction which he teaches frequently are presumed by him to be for somebody else.

In recent years, campus seminars for faculty members in educational administration such as those sponsored by the University Council for Educational Administration have dealt with questions of theory fundamental to the development of preparation curricula. It will be interesting to see the extent to which outcomes are expressed in curriculum revision.

Curriculum revision. There is some doubt, however, that college and university professors are generally aware of the questions to be answered in developing a curriculum and of the data sources appropriate to answering these questions. Very often, when faculties do manage to get around to considering curriculum revision, their concerns are peripheral. Thus the curriculum gets tampered with periodically, but there is no inner consistency to assure increasingly precise decision making on curriculum matters.

A major obstacle to curriculum improvement, then, appears to be lack of understanding of what is involved. The most obvious answer to overcoming this obstacle is to provide institutional in-service education in curriculum planning. The questions to be answered in curriculum planning at all levels and in all types of education are essentially the same. The data sources to be sought in answering these questions likewise are approximately the same, although the significance to be placed upon each source frequently varies according to the type of program. The specific data to be drawn from each source vary markedly from level to level and type to type of education. Both planners of nursery school programs and planners of professional education must consult learners as a data source in determining educational objectives.

As a long-term recommendation, this Commission proposes that institutions of higher learning develop their own centers for curriculum study, a primary purpose of which would be the continued study of curriculum problems within the institutions themselves. It is not proposed that each center take responsibility for actually developing the curriculum of each department and professional school. Rather, each institutional center would be available to help various groups clarify their curriculum problems. They might also assist in the collection of data pertinent to appropriate decision making.[1] Meanwhile, they would give central attention to questions of curriculum theory and research common to the whole spectrum of institutional curriculum-building processes under way.

Defining professional content. One of the issues leading curriculum planners in educational administration (as in other fields) far astray arises out of misinterpreting the significance of "needs." A professional program is very much concerned with needs in the sense of closing gaps between where the learner is and where he must be if he is to be considered adequately prepared. It is concerned, too, with helping the learner to perceive his own needs and to cope with them successfully. This is simply sound pedagogical procedure. But if closing these gaps is essential to adequate performance, then the program cannot permit each student to identify a quite different set of gaps and elect courses accordingly. All too often, the curriculum of many preparation programs is simply what the

---

[1] A treatment of the technical problems involved in curriculum construction is beyond the scope of this yearbook. Many groups, however, have used with profit a handbook prepared by Ralph W. Tyler. It poses the key questions to be answered and steps for dealing with these questions in a systematic fashion. Tyler, Ralph W. *Basic Principles of Curriculum and Instruction.* Chicago: University of Chicago Press, 1950.

student chooses to elect. His choices may be motivated, not by his needs in line with a set goal, but almost entirely by the time of the course, its rigor or lack of it, or even the location of the classroom. No theory of curriculum proposes these as valid bases for curriculum decision making.

If a profession has "a body of knowledge" which is known and applied by the members and not generally by others (see Chapter XI), then a professional preparation program must assure the possession of such knowledge by its graduates. It must assure, also, the graduates' ability to apply this knowledge in the activities called for in the conduct of the profession. No institution can put a label "complete" on professional study until performance in the job situation is observed—in as real a situation as possible.

There are two necessary steps to these ends. First, the kinds of behaviors required by the learner must be specifically defined. Unless they are clear, the major criterion for selecting learning activities is missing. Second, the central concepts, principles, and ideas around which the curriculum is to be organized must be identified. These are to be viewed as longitudinal threads underlying each learning activity and providing a framework for determining sequence. Thus one thinks of what threads are to be developed rather than of what courses are to be offered. It then becomes possible to conduct instruction by means of a number of cases, problems, or administrative situations (the in-basket technique, for example) in which the developing insight, skill, and point of view of the student may be observed and guided.

It is not necessary to start from scratch in these processes. Some useful general analyses are available. For example, a group of university examiners already has analyzed and classified the major types of human behavior involved in educational goals and subclassified the behaviors in the first of three types.[2] It is necessary, however, that these be related to the specific and unique learnings of educational administration. The identification of a set of essential curricular threads (not courses!) is an appropriate activity for the University Council for Educational Administration. While there may be disagreements over some areas, a common set representing general agreement should not

---

[2] See Bloom, Benjamin S., editor. *Taxonomy of Educational Objectives.* New York: Longmans, Green, 1956. 207 p.

defy human perception. After all, the concepts of educational administration examined in New York should not be essentially different from the basic concepts examined in Texas any more than the principles of physics dealt with in these two states need be different.

It must be remembered that identification and classification of the subject-field, educational administration, does not yet constitute a curriculum. From subject classification can come only one of several components to be synthesized in curriculum development. There are other essential curricular ingredients.[3] But these acts do represent appropriate activities to be conducted at the national level under the sponsorship of a group such as the UCEA. Continued refinement of the subject-field at the national level would do much to overcome inertia at the institutional level.

Using Faculty Resources

One of the observations of this yearbook is that a body of theory pertinent to administrative decision making is emerging. Some of this theory is derived from the behavioral sciences. A major obstacle to program improvement is that the academic talent necessary to infuse this knowledge into programs is not readily accessible. The ever-present challenge to an institution, then, is to muster the faculty resources to work on problems that cut across departmental lines.

Borrowing behavioral scientists. Some schools and departments of education have inched ahead in finding ways to gain the needed manpower. First, of course, it is necessary to have someone (normally the chairman or dean) perceive the need for including behavioral and leadership theory in the preparation program.

From this perception, departments and schools of education have proceeded in one or both of two directions. First, they have brought sociologists, anthropologists, psychologists, and political scientists into their unit of the institution on a permanent or semipermanent basis. A common criticism of this practice is that the professors involved lose touch with their own disciplines and become neither fish nor fowl. No doubt this

---

[3] Goodlad, John I. "Three Dimensions in Organizing the Curriculum for Learning and Teaching." *Frontiers of Elementary Education III.* (Edited by Vincent J. Glennon.) Syracuse, N. Y.: Syracuse University Press, 1956.

sometimes occurs. However, the subject matter of the behavioral scientist is people and their problems. Educational administrators and their problems are fruitful sources of research data. There is no need for a scholar to desert his discipline because he applies it to the analysis of the educational field. The main advantage to the school or department of education in engaging behavioral scientists as staff members is that this procedure assures a more certain claim to the resources offered by such people than is otherwise possible.

A second approach is much less formal. On the assumption that the rightful place for sociologists is in the sociology department, schools of education have resorted to various temporary and persuasive approaches. Frequently, they are able to offer attractive research opportunities. From time to time, specialists from other departments are invited to participate in conferences, classes, and seminars for school administrators. Sometimes, short-term appointments are negotiated for the duration of a given project. These arrangements have the advantage of avoiding complicated budgetary allowances and ambiguous promotion responsibilities. They have the disadvantage of being precarious: they may not appear to offer necessary stability. There is a reluctance, often, to launch new ventures until the availability of resources is assured. Good will provides little bargaining power in the competition for high-level competence if the specialist comes to see requests as no longer pertinent to his own interests and advancement.

University-wide cooperation. The long-standing strife between schools of education and the rest of the university has tended to hold up progress in the interdisciplinary approach and to deprive the school administrator of the breadth and depth of preparation he should have. In only a handful of institutions across the land is he exposed to graduate courses and instructors in fields other than education. (Although the data in Chapter II show that his undergraduate study is typically liberal arts.)

However, the old saw about the rest of the university being disinterested in the problems of the school or department of education grows increasingly rusty. Admittedly, any attempt to discuss educational issues or philosophies in general is likely to˙bring forth harsh words of mutual condemnation. It is futile to begin negotiations at the philosophical level. At those institutions where cooperative work is proceeding smoothly, one finds that the focus always is upon a specific problem. The faculty in law cannot resist the invitation to explore the legal aspects of education; the faculty in economics, an invitation to explore a problem of school finance; and so on. Out of such explorations come, first, respect for the complexity of the problems in education, and second, respect for the people dedicating their lives to day-to-day attack upon them.

The burden of responsibility for taking the initiative lies with the school or department of education. A major challenge for the dean or chairman is to find techniques appropriate to his institution for bringing all needed human resources behind the best possible preparation programs for school administrators.

Professorial Perceptions and Institutional Support

One of the problems that plague almost all efforts to commit personnel resources grows out of certain academic traditions. These traditions are characteristic of institutions of higher learning in general, but they vary in strength and influence from university to university.

The kind of curriculum planning proposed here demands dedicated, time-consuming commitment of many persons from a variety of backgrounds. It is a team activity, requiring regular work sessions, the compilation of data essential to curriculum decision making, and the management of routine. Many universities and the professors in them are committed to the idea, however, that the search for truth is an individual matter and that the curriculum is largely the vehicle through which the scholar-teacher teaches his view of truth in whatever way his perceptions guide him.

The problem, in essence, is how to assure program development without destroying the virtues obviously inherent in the free pursuit of knowledge. Or, conversely, how to preserve the free pursuit of knowledge in the face of time-consuming departmental "chores." The dilemma is compounded to the extent that a departmental chairman and his faculty come to hold differing perceptions. Resolution of the dilemma may be virtually impossible if the chairman's role is perceived by him to be curriculum development and the faculty role is seen by the members to be basic research.

Is it lethargy? Let us analyze the problem from the percep-

243

tion of the professors of educational administration in relation to the program building tasks herein recommended. Earlier in this chapter, it was suggested that a comfortable lethargy might well settle over the professors of educational administration familiar with superintendents' favorable reactions to their preparation programs but unfamiliar with the halo-effect hypothesis posed to explain these reactions (see Chapter II).

A strong argument that this lethargy hypothesis is at least only a partial explanation for the gap between what is envisioned and what is done derives from the observation that these professors, for the most part, are not lethargic people. Many of them maintain grueling, and sometimes phrenetic, schedules of teaching, directing student research, conducting workshops and institutes, writing, speaking, consulting, and occasionally, conducting research of their own. Whether or not they are busy doing what they should be doing is another matter.

Certainly there is motivation for doing these things. The data of Chapter IV show that superintendents rate reading of professional literature high among in-service helps. For there to be reading there must be writing. Universities look not unkindly at a man's bibliography in deciding to promote him and, in the volume of decision making conducted, frequently pay less attention to quality than to quantity. Honorariums sometimes are linked with consulting and speaking.

The motivations suggested above appear to be getting close to the nature of *Homo sapiens* as a species. Man craves success and recognition. He tends to do the things he perceives to be associated with success in his environment. Professors, like others, strive to do the things they perceive to be important and potentially satisfying.

Publish or perish. Universities generally do not advance a man rapidly for participating in planning the curricula of that institution. In fact, a man who engages heavily in this activity is likely to be passed by in the competition for promotion. And many deans and departmental chairmen will testify to the difficulties of enlisting faculty members for the arduous tasks of program development when promotions follow publication. Tenured men have a freedom that surpasses their imagination in employing it. Nontenured men are busily following in the well-worn grooves of their academic forefathers. It's as though they already had graduated *magna cum laude* from the school for little locomotives wherein the most important lesson was Staying on the Rails No Matter What.

These words should not be construed simply as an attack upon college and university personnel. Rather, the circumstances outlined above are descriptive of the *milieu* in which certain roles are to be fulfilled. Those to fill them direct their behavior accordingly. At the same time, however, colleges and universities are made up of people who contribute to the establishment and maintenance of these roles and who derive some satisfaction from filling them successfully.

Rewarding program improvement. We began this discussion in an attempt to analyze professorial perceptions. The analysis brought us around inevitably to institutional structure. Both are basic to obstacles in improving preparation programs. The two are inseparably interwoven.[4]

The way out of the dilemma of professorial perceptions appears to have two branches. First, the program development role must be materially elevated in its ranking among institutional expectations. This does not mean that all professors must in like proportion raise program development in their perceptions of what is important for them. For some professors to involve themselves greatly with the activities of curriculum planning would be damaging to their research activities and disastrous to the program! For other professors, participation in curriculum planning should have high priority. Frequently, an academic person will be employed for the chief purpose of developing and conducting a given program.

Second, the institution must reward performance in all the roles it approves and maintains. Otherwise, certain tasks will come to be recognized as leading only to dead ends, and they will be assiduously avoided. In many universities, some of the important pre-service and in-service activities related to the preparation of school administrators are conducted by peripheral staff members and graduate assistants. Key faculty members are more likely to become involved only when success and satisfaction are perceived to be derived from roles that differ somewhat from those they have played in the past.

---

[4] Getzels and his associates have developed a model for carrying out research on the interplay of these dimensions. See, for example: Getzels, J. W., and Guba, E. G. "Social Behavior and the Administrative Process." *School Review* 65: 423-41; Winter 1957.

The University of Pittsburgh is seeking to provide these mutually supporting conditions through unique administrative arrangements. The faculty in the academic disciplines is responsible for serving the various divisions of the entire university that depend upon these disciplines for their best execution. The chairman of the department of psychology, for example, must staff with the needs of the professional schools as well as with the traditional interests of psychologists in mind. He has no real choice over whether or not to participate in university-wide interests that might profit through the involvement of psychologists. The university, then, in making its commitments, automatically commits the appropriate resources for the roles thus defined.

Institutional support must be consistent up and down the hierarchy of administrative authority. One department of education engaged constructively over a period of years in the complete, systematic overhaul of its curriculum. Meanwhile, the chairman pleaded with higher administrative authority for the easing of teaching loads for some personnel who perceived their best contribution to lie in the realm of research. In effect, he was pushing in two directions simultaneously to fulfill two important university functions. Both efforts received a cruel blow when a dean suggested that a request for more teaching time on one hand and the expenditure of several valuable hours of valuable faculty time in program development on the other seemed to him to be incompatible!

We come around full cycle. University administrators and professors must come to hold comparable perceptions of institutional role if institutional commitments are to be met efficiently. These commitments must include effective means for the development of best possible preparatory programs for educational administrators.

INSTITUTIONAL RELATIONSHIPS

Public schools and institutions of higher learning have certain interdependent responsibilities for preparation programs. The obstacles in establishing and maintaining appropriate relationships grow largely out of failure to separate certain areas of independence from these areas of joint responsibility.

Preparation Versus In-Service Education

Universities must develop curricula designed to provide a minimum pre-service preparation floor. Increasingly, this floor must be seen as prerequisite to practice. The future superintendent graduates with his basic credentials. From here on, presumably, the pressure to study is to keep up to date, to improve in service.

School systems are staffed preponderantly with practicing superintendents who have not yet reached this minimum floor in the formal sense. But to assume that they must now abstain from practice in order to prepare to practice is to compound confusion. Still, there is much to be learned. To cease to study is to cease to develop.

Out of the juxtaposition of these two complexes, one pre-service and the other in-service, comes a threat to the integrity of both. The superintendent wants help, as the analysis of Chapter IV suggests, but he wants university credit to accompany that help. In the search for an appropriate credit course, his in-service needs are distorted and abandoned. He comes to settle for what is close at hand and conveniently scheduled. Meanwhile, however, he frequently lets his displeasure be known to university officials who may yield to pressure, sometimes against their better judgment, sometimes without full realization of what they do.

There are several ways around the apparent impasse. First, pre-service preparation must come to be perceived largely as resident study. A sequential, correlated program involving blocks of time and uninterrupted periods of internship can then be planned for a specified corps of students. There is no place for the in-service practitioner in such a scheme except as a contributing member of a team of instructors.

Second, in-service education must come to be perceived as meeting the needs of the practitioner. It may be organized by informal groups who choose to invite university personnel for specific contributing roles. Or, the activity may be organized by a university after careful exploration of superintendent needs not necessarily expressed by the superintendents themselves. Some universities, for example, feel responsibility for disseminating research through sponsoring informal seminars. Credit has no place in such a conception of in-service education.

There are, however, two positions lying midway between the two described above, necessitated in part by the developmental status of the profession itself. The first of these is represented, for example, in the intent of the ruling of the AASA to require members to complete at least six years of formal study beyond their secondary schooling. Strong institutions with first-rate doctoral programs already established, it is assumed, will plan programs for a special group of practicing superintendents who wish to bring themselves up to the AASA standard. While these programs are to be organized with the current problems of these practitioners in mind, the central purpose is one of filling in gaps—providing those components of a core of essential studies found to be lacking in the preparation programs of the participants. Such a program might well be taken in a series of summer sessions, but a planned sequence would be required.

A second alternative is well expressed by organizations such as the Atlanta Teacher Education Service sponsored jointly by Emory University, the University of Georgia, and cooperating school systems. The Service was organized expressly for the purpose of bringing in-service assistance to teachers and administrators in the Greater Atlanta area. Several staff members are appointed to the faculties of the two supporting institutions and assigned full time to the Service. Others are recruited for specific purposes from departments of the two institutions and serve on a limited basis. Such participation provides in-service education to these instructors and consultants who might not otherwise have more than incidental contact with ongoing educational practice in the public schools. An advisory council representing the school systems recommends areas for in-service development. An executive committee representing the two universities determines institutional commitments on the basis of the appropriateness of the suggestions and the availability of personnel. The planning of at least part of a six-year program falls within the jurisdiction and structure of the Service. The specific role of the Service is prescribed by the respective faculties of the two institutions and approved by their graduate deans.

Cooperation with Local Districts

It has been pointed out above that pre-service and in-service education must be sharply differentiated if the best interests of both are to be served. At the same time, however, the closest cooperation between preparing institutions, primarily responsible for pre-service programs, and school systems, wherein in-service education is conducted, is essential. Colleges cannot provide the internship proposed in Chapter VII if cooperating school systems are not available. Likewise, school systems are handicapped in providing growth opportunities for personnel if resources in higher education are lacking.

Colleges and universities frequently report difficulty in finding school systems willing to accept administrative interns. School boards sometimes question the advisability of paying stipends to "assistants" who are not assuming clear-cut administrative responsibility. Conscientious superintendents and principals are aware of the additional demands placed upon their energies if they properly supervise the interns. Some administrators expect interns to be self-propelling; in fact, to be ready to take over major responsibilities from the beginning. These problems are not new to professional education. Hospital superintendents and deans of schools of nursing have a history rich in debate over the desired balance between service to the hospital and educational return to the student nurse.

To expect cooperation from school boards and administrators "for the good of the cause" is a fine ideal that has been harmoniously achieved in some sections of the country. However, exhorting others elsewhere to do likewise is not likely to produce spectacular results.

Perhaps there *is* a telling argument, however. School administrators are eager for the unique contributions to in-service growth that can be provided by colleges and universities. Increasingly school administrators are coming to recognize that they need most the research findings and theoretical formulations of established professors, usually senior men. They must come to perceive that these are the very men likely to be most interested in establishing cooperative arrangements for administrative internships. It follows, then, that the establishment of an internship program is likely to bring into the schools the very academic personnel most sought after for in-service education. It should not be difficult to elicit the help of these professors or, for that matter, to establish specific agreements for using their services.

Professors of school administration seeking to develop internship programs are anxious to find the most promising permissive settings. Likewise, they value opportunities to mold these settings, to have a part in shaping forward-looking practices. This they can very well do through participation in the ongoing in-service program.

The ultimate solution, then, to the problem of cooperation lies in each half of the proposed bargain recognizing the potential contribution of the other. Mutually advantageous arrangements become gains in advancing the profession of educational administration.

RESPONSIBILITIES OF AGENCIES

Problems of professional improvement in the field of education are compounded by the multiplicity of organizations. It is necessary to separate rather sharply those agencies that are fundamentally professional from those that are governmental in nature in considering matters of authority and responsibility. Because of the comprehensive treatment of professional controls in Chapter XI, only a few observations regarding professional agencies are included here.

Professional Organizations

Agencies such as the NEA and the AASA always face a dilemma in determining who shall be eligible to join. On one hand, they must set some professional criteria for membership. On the other hand, they feel obliged to stimulate professional growth for all who hold educational positions. The latter consideration tends to predominate. As a result, some organizations have requested little more than a ten-dollar bill and the ability to sign one's name. The recently enacted provision of the AASA requiring the completion of two years of advanced study for membership is a step in the right direction.

The new AASA membership requirement has elicited, in addition to certain irresponsible resistance to anything upsetting the status quo, genuine fear that study requirements will become restrictive. There is fear, too, that weak institutions unable to provide doctoral programs will stretch a little and establish sixth-year programs. It would be most unfortunate if, in meeting the AASA membership requirement, the focus were to be placed upon quantity rather than quality. A heavy responsibility will fall upon accrediting procedures to assure quality preparation programs.

But it is not only institutions which need to be measured against a quality yardstick; we need to evaluate, as well, the quality of the individuals prepared. This kind of evaluation is now made almost entirely, and with great difficulty, by local boards of education composed of laymen. These laymen, as indicated earlier in this yearbook, need help in evaluating the competence of candidates for the superintendency. In some other professions, such as medicine, procedures have been established for representatives of the profession to testify to the competence of individuals seeking to practice in the various specialties of that profession. "Passing the boards" has come to be expected procedure for several professions. Such professional boards may be useful, also, to appraise the competence of specialists in the various branches of educational practice, including school administration. The establishment of boards and standards on a national basis would reduce the possibility of undue personal influences which might hamper objectivity of evaluation in a local community.

Such procedures for professional approval of the competence of educators would remove a considerable burden from professional organizations which have spent much time and energy worrying about and working on means of establishing and enforcing professional standards. They could then devote more energy to the educative processes of upgrading the profession. Over a period of time, local, state, and national conferences would more and more turn to reporting research, securing funds for research, demonstrating experimentation, and encouraging tryout. They would, of course, continue to exercise (and, hopefully, to perfect) controls designed to protect public and profession alike.

State and Federal Government

State and federal governmental agencies must be viewed in a somewhat different light. In a sense, they stand between the profession and the public but are directly responsible to the electorate or to elected officials. One of their major functions is to see that educational opportunities are made available to all, irrespective of locale, ability to pay, and other variables. The very fulfillment of this function, coupled with an essentially political structure of authority and responsibility, creates obstacles to professional advancement of fields such as educational administration.

For example, weak school systems are obviously needy recipients of services from state departments of education. Thus, viewed in short-term perspective, it is justifiable to deploy services from the state office to maintain minimal conditions in an undernourished setting. It is possible, however, for a lethargic community (especially one with strong lobbies at the state capitol) to come to enjoy lethargy together with outside assistance. The strong political lobby provides considerable assurance that such assistance will not easily be withdrawn. Weak personnel who cannot readily find employment elsewhere tend to gravitate to weak school systems.

Given, however, minimum professional standards established by the profession itself, state departments of education would escape considerable political pressure by insisting that no services be provided school systems failing to employ certified superintendents. Similarly, assistance would be withheld from colleges and universities failing to meet accreditation standards.

In brief, then, state departments of education should not be required to determine *minimum* standards for certification and accreditation. Rather, they should be free to require whatever *additional* standards appear to be appropriate for each state's unique problems. Florida, for example, has set up special requirements to protect the state from the immigration of physicians seeking relief from rigorous winters. In so doing, they actually protect physicians already practicing in the state through controlling supply and demand, and other states through forcing thousands of doctors to stay where they are. They also protect the standards considered essential by the profession itself.

The principle being developed and applied here is that the profession of educational administration should be recognized as the logical determinant of minimum professional standards to be developed nationwide and applied at local, state, and regional levels. Governmental agencies support professional controls, protect the public to which they are responsible, and protect themselves from political interference by recognizing these minimums and using them as criteria in directing the deployment of resources. It becomes difficult for a legislator to lobby unreasonably for a constituency that has not exerted sufficient effort to attract professionally recognized personnel.

Application of this principle at the federal level would expedite difficult decisions of the Department of Health, Education, and Welfare. Increasingly, that office is assuming significant responsibility for coordinating federal funds designed to recruit and educate leadership personnel and to promote research needed for the nation's welfare. These funds must be distributed with a view to accomplishing the most good with the least money.

Federal offices of education should not set accreditation-type criteria for determining which institutions of higher learning will receive grants. This would be the very interference that opponents of any federal aid to education most fear. Furthermore, to do so would be to recognize pathetic failure on the part of professional organizations and the whole structure of institutional accreditation. And yet, officials in the federal offices soon come to know that many institutions preparing educational administrators do a sorry job. It would be in the best interests of the public and the profession if the federal funds necessary to the survival of sickly programs were withheld. Then again, it is difficult to justify such policy to a determined state representative anxious to please the people back home. Without the presence of a vigorous system of professional controls such as that proposed in Chapter XI, the federal office is in a weak position to defend its judgments. It simply must have recourse to meaningful accreditation as a minimum basis for allocating funds in such a way that they will have cumulative effect.

THE PERSONAL COMMITMENT

This chapter has emphasized structural devices for overcoming blocks to advancing educational administration as a profession. The emphasis was deliberately designed in an attempt to balance what might be termed "exhortation to be professional." Educators appear to be overimbued with the fuzzy notion that to be professional and to be respected as such simply mean to be fine, dedicated people engaging in a sort of missionary activity involving the welfare of young people. There tends to be zealous exhortation to join the appropriate association and "be professional," which often leads to the conclusion that professionalism is synonymous with joining.

In recognizing that exhortation is relatively fruitless in promoting true professionalism, one must be realistic in recognizing that no framework, however rigorous, guarantees professional behavior. Such a framework merely provides a sort of minimum tolerance point as well as a lever for exerting pressure where all the good will in the world would serve little purpose. Ultimately, then, the focus narrows to the dedicated, competent, ever-growing individual. Without thousands of such individuals, the proposals intended here to overcome obstacles to professional advancement have a hollow ring. And the professional framework, so strongly urged, is but a fragile shell. For professionally minded people, these proposals constitute an assist. In a sense they run interference for the dedicated individual who is blocked, abused, and bruised in seeking to run the course alone.

This discussion of personal commitment to constructive change brings us back full cycle to the beginning of this chapter. Perhaps it will be sufficient to remind the reader that there appear to be two major approaches to closing the gap. First, individuals must come to perceive increasingly more appropriate ways of performing the functions they have assumed. Second, existing structures must be reordered so as to support the efforts of creative institutions and individuals and so as to eliminate the lethargic. Surely this yearbook suggests alternatives enough to keep the profession constructively busy for years to come.

chapter XI

Effective
Professional Controls

A profession was once defined by Roscoe Pound as "an organized group pursuing a learned art in the public service." To Frank Lloyd Wright, however, a profession was "legalized gangsterism." Although the lawyer and the architect were obviously miles apart in their feelings on the matter, both nonetheless implied that *controls* are basic to the operation of a profession.

Preceding chapters of this yearbook have recommended solutions for many of the problems faced by the profession of school administration. A preparation program has been recommended, policies of student identification and evaluation have been proposed, and machinery to keep administration up to date on research has been described. Even if the necessary initial steps are taken by appropriate agencies, the staying power of the changes depends on the strength and determination with which the profession will back them up.

All professions exercise controls. As Dean Pound has said, a profession is "an organized group"— organized not for fraternal purposes, but as the means of enforcing standards, ethics, and quality of service in the public welfare.

Effective machinery for the preservation and control of improvements becomes necessary. Just as important—and often overlooked in the zealous rush to establish minimum controls—is the guarantee of institutional freedom to experiment, change, and emerge with better programs than are required of all institutions.

255

Some observers see this as the basic dilemma of professional controls: the police function and the improvement function. Whether the dilemma can be resolved is still an open question in educational administration. Experience in other professions indicates, however, that inflexibility, rigid uniformity, and strict control by a small group with police power and authority are possible hazards but by no means certain dangers. Neither is it a demonstration of weakness and indecision to stress the improvement function and to permit wide latitude of freedom for experimentation and unique curricular characteristics. This Yearbook Commission takes the position that cooperation of all essential elements of the educational administration profession can build procedures which could lead to support as well as to sanctions.

The term "professional control" implies some common agreement on the elements of quality in a preparation program and maintenance of these standards through enforcement procedures endorsed by the members of the profession. Such controls can and probably must occur at several levels: the state, a several-state region, and the nation.

In general, the history of professional control in education has seen the states assume responsibility for awarding licenses to persons who are approved for the practice of a profession. Such certificates to individuals are issued by the legally constituted state agency. In addition, some states develop lists of approved colleges within the state boundaries. (In essence, all states "accredit" by recognizing for credential purposes the completion of courses in certain colleges and not in others.)

It is at the regional level that much control of educational institutions has taken place. Regional accrediting associations have typically been the source of profession-wide appraisal of professional programs of preparation in teacher education; until recently only the undergraduate phase of teacher education was under the purview of the regional associations. The national accreditation movement is a relatively recent development.

Basic to the exercise of effective professional controls are two basic assumptions. First is the implication that when we refer to school administration we are dealing with a *profession* in the true sense of the word. Second is the assumption that the practitioners of a profession should exercise influence on the preparation and selection of professional novitiates.

PROFESSION DEFINED

What do we mean when we say "profession"? The term obviously cannot be used accurately to designate all of the vocational activities in our society. A profession may be said to differ from the great mass of occupations by having a body of knowledge which is known and practiced by the members and not generally by others. This body of knowledge is largely intellectual in character (although in some professions, such as dentistry, a marked degree of manual skill is also required) and is based upon, even though it does not end with, formal learning. Such a body of knowledge, then, depends initially on organized study in a college or university. During the time such training proceeds, it differs from general education in the college in that the student in professional training has a specific and clearly defined professional job in mind and the emphasis of his training is on developing acceptable behavior in the job.

A profession is characterized also by a strong, voluntary association of its members. Such an association typically erects barriers for entry into its ranks in such a way that entrance into the profession and membership in the association are virtually synonymous.

A profession also has an enforceable code of ethics with recognized procedures for applying sanctions to carry out its provisions without regard to risk of suit by disfranchised members and without succumbing to unreasonable protection of its members through tenure laws and traditions.

A profession has a literature of its own, even though it may draw heavily on many academic disciplines for the content. A profession promotes the value of research and provides for ways in which new knowledge and new skills in the performance of professional tasks may be pursued.

A profession is further distinguished by being "in the public service." Members must be motivated primarily by ideals of service which transcend purely selfish aims. The professional man is a dedicated man, devoted to his art and convinced his profession renders valuable service to society at large.

The final criterion is sometimes the most difficult to achieve. Not only must the group *be* professional; the public must so perceive its professional character. Prestige in the public eye is due partly to demonstrated ability to control one's own members and to set standards they must, without exception, meet. As controls change, professional prestige does, too.

SCHOOL ADMINISTRATION AS A PROFESSION

How well does school administration measure up against the criteria for a profession?

A Definitive Body of Knowledge

Evidence in Chapter III shows little agreement as to content of our preparation programs. Various groups interested in educational administration—state legal authorities, university graduate schools, school boards—all have had influence on the content of training programs; yet, a great deal of progress will have to be made before the body of knowledge for school administration is clearly defined. The individual student is the creator of the professional curriculum by his selection of courses, as our data reveal in Chapter III. Enormous gaps occur side by side with redundancy of content as long as the definition of professional curriculum is left to the individual student. A self-determined "needs" curriculum does not agree with the definition of a professional body of content.

A Strong, Voluntary Association

We have a "strong, voluntary association." Yet, outside the ranks of the American Association of School Administrators are many school administrators. The 1960 membership figures show approximately 10,000 active members, at least 2000 of whom do not administer school systems. The impact of the AASA must be measured against these facts: there are more than 40,000 school districts in the United States; there are 16,000 superintendencies where more than one-half of the superintendent's time is given to administration rather than to teaching (there are still several thousand teaching principalships which constitute the "chief local administration"); there are separate organizations for specialties in school administration, and the trend appears to be toward proliferation rather than unification. Elementary school principals, secondary school principals, and supervisors have their associations within the over-all, loosely knit National Education Association structure. Even the county superintendents have their separate organizations (a group by no means justifiable by virtue of common problems, since they vary from rural counties, which are basic units, to metropolitan suburban districts, which are a kind of sub-state department of education, rendering service and consultation only). School business officers are organized apart from any connection with NEA.

School administration gets a score that's both plus and minus on the "voluntary association" measurement. There is today a strong, voluntary association which has recently awakened to its obligations to help build a strong profession. But it is not nearly strong enough. On the minus side, entry into the profession and on the membership rolls of the association are today not by any means "virtually synonymous." Too, the profession of school administration is so poorly defined that many associations serve it—with overlap as to constituency and needless duplication.

Some Rules for Entry

As Robert Cunningham has written: ". . . the portal of entry to teaching is formalized and clearly marked and everyone in school administration has crossed its threshold. But the portal of entry from teaching into school administration itself is rather dimly lighted in some instances, and one gets the impression that ticket takers at the side doors and back doors are doing a lively business."[1] Data presented in Chapter II bear this out. As long as some states have no certificate for a school administrator and others have requirements so minimal as to be meaningless, we must conclude that school administration does not, by this measure, qualify as a profession.

Recommendations in Chapter VI will largely overcome our present failure to regulate entry into the profession. Early identification of able students who appear to have administrative talent and interest can be followed by careful screening and selection—a joint responsibility of college and local district. State licensing authorities must protect the colleges which impose selection qualifications and require completion of a rigorous training program. In the final analysis, of course, school boards must stick to a policy of employing only well-trained persons for the local administration positions.

---

[1] Cunningham, Robert M., Jr. "Is School Administration a Real Profession?" *Nation's Schools* 62: 49-53; November 1958.

A Code of Ethics

There is none, nationally, at least. Some state associations of administrators have adopted codes, but few of them have followed through with clear provisions for enforcing sanctions. To be sure, school administrators have tacit agreement as to ethical behavior. But a true profession will formalize, codify, and create enforcement mechanisms so that the few school administrators who are plainly unethical may be disqualified from further practice of the profession. This we have yet to do.

Professional Literature

Judging from volume alone, school administration makes the passing grade on this one. However, as pointed out in Chapter IV, "disciplined professional reading" is lacking.

A fortunate outcome of the Cooperative Program in Educational Administration has been the attraction of social scientists to study issues surrounding school administration. In promoting the value of research, leaders in the field of school administration are turning to sources which contribute to the solution of administrative problems whether or not schools were at the center of the researcher's thoughts. In a recent book on role analysis, we are reminded: "There is a great need for concepts in social science that can be played 'across the board,' that is, concepts whose utility is not limited to a single discipline but which can be used by students of the several social science disciplines in conceptual formulations of certain of their strategic problems."[2]

In brief, the problem is one of improving our research sources, establishing an authoritative research journal in our field, and moving beyond the present preoccupation with "promising practices" and "how-we-did-its" in our articles, speeches, and investigations.

Service and Dedication to the Job

On this criterion, school administrators are clearly professional. Yet this measure alone does not, in absence of the others—the body of knowledge, united professional voice, code of ethics, and professional literature—establish school administration as a profession.

---

[2] Gross, Neal; Mason, Ward S.; and McEachern, Alexander W. *Explorations in Role Analysis.* New York: John Wiley & Sons, 1958. p. 325.

Recognition by the Public

This is a difficult measure to take. Since the school superintendency is largely a product of the present century, one could argue that acceptance has come rapidly.

Public recognition is a changeable thing, and if education becomes the key concern of Americans during the 1960's as events in the 50's suggest may be true, school administration may well join medicine, law, engineering, and the clergy as an "acknowledged profession."

The universally acknowledged professions of today have not always been in such repute. Nancy Wilson Ross in one of her stories about the missionary explorer, Marcus Whitman, says it was considered a misfortune that Dr. Whitman was a "doctor not of divinity but of medicine, a status considerably lower in the prevailing social scale of the period. . . . He had . . . been unable to finance the seven years required for earning a minister's degree, though he had fulfilled more than the usual period of training then expected of doctors."[3]

Without question, the public will withhold full professional stature for school administrators until a vastly different pattern becomes common—fewer colleges, higher standards of student achievement, more rigorous application of selection requirements, longer minimum preparation periods, and closer national agreement on the curriculum in educational administration. In addition, school administration will assume new dimensions in the public eye when professional self-governing is brought into the picture and when research becomes the solid background for the whole enterprise.

IMPACT OF PRACTITIONERS

Professional controls substantiate the belief that both the means of admission into the profession and the process by which members of the profession are trained are matters of concern to the practitioner himself, not alone to the institution of higher learning. The person who practices the profession must continue, through his professional association and in other ways,

---

[3] Ross, Nancy Wilson. "Murder at the Place of Rye Grass." *American Heritage* X: 42-44, 85-91; August 1959.

to keep in contact with and to have an impact on what is done in the colleges, universities, and special professional schools. We must assume, then, that school administrators will have a role to play in the inspection of colleges, in the approval of such colleges, and in the enforcement of standards dealing with the excellence of the college preparation programs.

Other professional groups maintain professional controls by the practitioner on the training institutions in various ways. An examination of such undertakings may be helpful in suggesting alternative courses which may be followed for school administration.

Dentistry

Almost all of the impact on preparation programs in dentistry comes from the local, state, and regional dental societies as they work closely with the appropriate dental schools. At the national level, the American Dental Association has little, if any, direct impact on training standards. Instead, the local and state societies exercise discretionary authority with the 47 independent dental training schools in the United States. Each dental school is autonomous within this informal framework of cooperation.

The nature of the cooperation on in-service education procedures has, however, resulted in influencing preparation programs; the nature of dentistry requires a constant "keeping up" that is a strong institutional and individual motivating force. Research is reported at the national level and tends to standardize its effect in application at the training institutions. Local societies are perhaps the chief instrument for action and influence with programs and professional activities of nearby dental schools.

Medicine

The field of medicine is the one most often cited as an example of close control by practitioners on the preparation program. Dating as far back as the Flexner report in 1910, the movement to enforce standards of excellence has grown to the point where approval by the American Medical Association is considered to be a "must" for recognition of a preparatory or postgraduate school of medicine.

262

Accreditation of medical education is performed jointly by the Council on Medical Education of the American Medical Association and the Association of American Medical Colleges. Inspection of medical schools is conducted jointly by representatives of both organizations. Important action pertaining to medical education is taken by either organization only after discussion and concurrence with the other.[4]

The AMA established a Council on Medical Education in 1904 (in 1920 the name was expanded to include hospitals) as a means of improving the education of physicians. The next year the Council published its first list of approved schools based on an ideal standard promoted by the five-member council. Following the Flexner survey in 1910 the Council adopted specific standards for medical education and four years later published the first list of hospitals approved for internships. Later (1923) standards for specialty training were established, and in 1927 the list of hospitals approved for residencies was published.

Medical education is undergoing careful reappraisal today, and the impact of practitioners has much to do with it. In announcing a revised program of medical education at Johns Hopkins University, officials stated:

. . . some undesirable features have emerged in the American system of educating physicians. First, the number of years required for students of medicine to reach a productive stage in practice or research has gradually increased to the point where it is beginning to discourage able candidates from entering the field of medicine. Secondly, the need to concentrate on science, necessitated by the rapid advance of knowledge, has made it increasingly difficult for prospective physicians to acquire an adequate understanding of the cultural and historical forces which have molded modern civilization—an understanding essential for the most productive service to society. And thirdly, for a variety of reasons a relative decrease in faculty strength has occurred in the basic science departments of American medical schools, particularly during the last two decades.[5]

It is evident from this statement that curriculum and student recruitment remain sensitive to changing times and new societal

---

[4] Blauch, Lloyd E., editor. *Education for the Professions*. U.S. Department of Health, Education, and Welfare, Office of Education. Washington, D. C.: Superintendent of Documents, Government Printing Office, 1955. 317 p.

[5] The Johns Hopkins University School of Medicine. *Forward, 1959-60 Catalogue*. Baltimore, Md.: the University, 1959. p. 6-7.

conditions. The practitioner is indispensable as the reflector of needs for changes in college policy.

The Council on Medical Education and Hospitals (now a 10-member body) has been an extremely important force in the upgrading of medical education. Today its annual budget is about $400,000, and it employs a sizable professional staff. It is clearly the unit of the practitioner's association which is charged with exercising controls on the preparation programs. The AMA cooperates with other organizations such as the American College of Surgeons and the American Hospital Association in evaluating educational facilities which are available for interns and residents. For a hospital to be removed from the approved list of internship and residency hospitals is an effective penalty. There is a joint commission on the accreditation of hospitals which includes representatives of the American Medical Association, the American Hospital Association, and the American College of Surgeons.

In summary, preparatory programs in medicine are influenced by: (a) standards continuously applied to training institutions, (b) evaluation of facilities and personnel in the intern and resident program, and (c) the accreditation of hospitals. There are today 82 accredited medical schools in the United States which graduate approximately 7000 medical doctors per year. The number of medical schools had reached a total of 160 prior to the Flexner report 50 years ago.

Law

Bar associations, largely social and fraternal in character, were in existence during the nineteenth century, but only within the last 30 years has the legal profession concerned itself actively with improvement of the profession. When the American Bar Association was founded in 1878, law office training was the common route into the legal profession. The ABA awakened to a concern about legal education in the 1890's and was strengthened by the establishment in 1900 of the Association of American Law Schools.

The American Bar Association has since 1923 maintained a list of approved law schools based upon inspection and appraisal by a committee of practicing attorneys. This recognition is accorded even though only about 40 percent (in 1957) of the practicing lawyers in the United States are members of the ABA.

Prior to action by the Association in the early 1920's, the situation in legal education was similar to the state of medicine before the issuance of the Flexner report: lawyers were trained either through apprenticeship or in so-called profit schools, some of which were outright diploma mills. While the ABA has never had legal powers to set standards, its recommendations have been written into law by most states. Thirty years ago the Association began a campaign to have two years of college and three years of law school adopted as minimum standards. Beginning in 1952 the official ABA recommendation was raised to a standard of three years of college work. All law schools approved by the Association meet these standards; in some instances, states have officially adopted the recommendations, also. The American Bar Association maintains its list of approved law schools in the United States through means of an arm of the Association known as the section on Legal Education and Admissions to the Bar. This section supervises the approval of new schools and the revisitation of other schools which offer legal education.

There is also an Association of American Law Schools which represents the leading institutions in the country. Membership in that association is not identical with the list of schools on the ABA approved list, although it is largely so. In 1957 there were 167 law schools in operation, with 130 on the approved ABA list and 108 members of the Association of American Law Schools. Committees of the American Bar Association announce publicly their decision to accept or reject the institution after they appraise the facilities at the law schools.

In spite of the rigorous appraisal of colleges through the accreditation procedure, there appears to be relatively little sentiment to abolish the bar examination and depend solely on approval of institutions. The American Bar Association, instead, insists on both tests—accreditation of the school itself and examination by state-controlled exams of the candidates who are graduates of those schools.

City Management

The job of city manager is similar to school administration in that it has aspects both public and professional. It is a newer profession than school administration, and it has had many of the same problems in getting started. As late as 1958 only two universities in the United States offered a program of preparation specifically designed to produce city managers: the University of Pennsylvania and the University of Kansas. There are almost 100 colleges and universities, however, which offer some work labeled "public administration." This includes not only work for the city managership but also for administration at the state, federal, and international level of government. Like school administration, which began as a course or two in the field of education, professional preparation for the city manager began only as a course in political science or government.

The International City Managers' Association, which enlists approximately 75 percent of the city managers in the United States as members, does not as yet have plans for bringing direct impact to bear on the preparation programs in city management. There is a possibility the Association will in time award citations signifying successful completion of training and/or experience which would bear the stamp of approval of the Association but which would have no legal status. At the present time, The International City Managers' Association does not plan to engage in a system of appraisal or accreditation of the special colleges.

What can be learned from these programs of other professions? The illustrations show clearly that controls on quality of professional training are in the hands of organizations of practitioners. The controls are operative at several levels: a list of approved college training programs is maintained; licenses are based on completion of approved programs; membership in the practitioners' organization is limited to those who are graduates of approved programs. Action of the established professions is often tantamount to law.

Attorneys, dentists, and physicians approve strict screening devices for new practitioners. The general public awards status to the professions which appear to be in control of their own affairs. The public may occasionally cry "closed shop," but respect is given the profession nonetheless.

ACCREDITATION OF COLLEGES AND UNIVERSITIES

Accreditation has been defined as ". . . recognition accorded to an educational institution . . . by means of inclusion in a list of institutions issued by some agency or organization which sets up standards . . . that must be complied with in order to secure approval."[6] Accreditation apparently began in 1872 at the University of Michigan with the development of approved lists of high schools. The first list of approved institutions of higher education was published in 1913 by the North Central Association.

Accreditation of higher education is a practice unique to the United States. It has no counterpart in other nations where ministries of education of the central government generally exercise direct control over units in the educational system, including universities and colleges.

Purposes of Accreditation

The president of Western Reserve University, John S. Millis, has called higher education's stewardship of public trust one of the most significant objectives of accreditation. Accreditation gives the college an opportunity to report to the American public how well it is discharging the staggering responsibilities and the deep hopes laid upon it by modern society. In addition, accreditation is the "pure food and drug act" of higher education, protecting the public from malpractice and establishing some standardization of nomenclature.[7]

A recent review of accreditation of higher education published by the United States Department of Health, Education, and Welfare lists several purposes for accrediting institutions of higher education.

1. To encourage institutions to improve their programs by providing them with standards of criteria established by competent bodies.

2. To facilitate the transfer of students from one institution to another.

3. To inform those who employ graduates of an institution about the quality of training the graduates have received.

4. To raise the standards of education for the practice of a profession.

5. To serve as a support to administrative officers or faculty who want to maintain high standards but face considerable local difficulty in bringing about improvements.

---

6 Zook, G. F., and Haggerty, M. E. *The Evaluation of Higher Institutions: Principles of Accrediting.* Chicago: University of Chicago Press, 1936. p. 18.

7 National Commission on Accrediting. *Report of Workshop Conference on Accrediting.* June 25-26, 1957. Washington, D. C.: the Commission, 1957. p. 5-7.

6. To serve the general public by supplying to the layman some information about the institutions he may wish to patronize.[8]

It should be pointed out that accrediting is largely carried on by voluntary organizations which have no legal power to control institutions of higher education. They have come, however, to exercise a considerable influence over them; were an institution to ignore standards set up by the accrediting organizations, they would quickly fall into disrepute.

Accrediting by legal state agencies is on a limited basis. Such control usually comes about by the setting of policy which governs the issuance of licenses or certificates to persons who complete specified courses in approved institutions. The New York State Board of Regents is one of the most active of the state agencies in maintaining a program of accreditation. Its sphere extends to institutions outside the state as well as to those within. (In New York the term "register" is used instead of the term "accredit," but it is generally recognized as an accrediting agency.)

From 1953 to 1956 the Cooperative Development of Public School Administration was an active project in New York State. One of the aspects of the project was to involve college professors, representatives of the state education department, and administrators from the field in a consideration of programs of preparation. The state education department at that time indicated that it would register new programs in school administration only if they were first reviewed by the professors of school administration from the various colleges and universities in the state. Following the demise of the CDPSA, a group was formed known as the Collegiate Association for the Development of Educational Administration (CADEA). CADEA holds three meetings a year. Any college or university that wishes to have a new program in school administration registered by the state education department must present its program at one of these meetings. The program is presented in considerable detail, a procedure normally taking a full afternoon; then the various professors raise questions about aspects of the program. In summary, then, the so-called accreditation is a review—first by

___

[8] Blauch, Lloyd E., editor. *Accreditation in Higher Education.* U.S. Department of Health, Education, and Welfare, Office of Education. Washington, D. C.: Superintendent of Documents, Government Printing Office, 1959. p. 4.

the professors in the CADEA organization. If it meets their approval the program is then sent to the state education department to be reviewed again. Usually this is accompanied by a visit from the Bureau of Teacher Education to the campus of the university requesting the program registration. Finally the program is registered, which means that a graduate of the program is eligible for state certification.

Early Development

Henry Barnard, first United States Commissioner of Education, recognized the confusion among colleges in such matters as entrance requirements, curricula, and resources. In his first statement after becoming Commissioner in 1867, he made it clear that he intended to apply a fairly comprehensive and searching analysis of the work offered by colleges before including them on an official list from the United States Department of Education. Barnard stated quite boldly that he intended not only to ascertain the number of colleges in each state but the "circumstances of their origin, the conditions of admission, courses of study, equipment of libraries and material aids of instruction, their students, professorships, graduates, and endowments—what they profess and what they really accomplish as well as their relation to . . . professional and special schools of the country."[9]

There was one time in the history of the United States Bureau of Education when a classified list of colleges was drawn up with colleges grouped in classes I to IV depending on the records made by their graduate schools. It occurred during the tenure of Philander P. Claxton as United States Commissioner, while the nation at large was engaged in the famous muckraking era of the Theodore Roosevelt and Taft Administrations; strict evaluation of colleges seemed in tune with the times.

The list was to be official when issued by the Division of Higher Education of the United States Bureau of Education. Just prior to the publication of the list, President Taft was pressured into requesting the Commissioner of Education to withhold publication. A few months later Woodrow Wilson became President,

---

[9] As quoted in Sanders, Jennings B. "Evolution of Accreditation." *Accreditation in Higher Education.* (Edited by Lloyd E. Blauch.) Chapter 2, p. 16.

and he also refused to allow the list to be published. In spite of this official action by two Presidents, copies of the list were distributed generally. Educational historians of the period report considerable influence was stimulated by the document which became known as Babcock's College Classification List. (Kendric C. Babcock was the first specialist in higher education in the Bureau.)

In subsequent years the Office of Education has continued to resist any pressure to become a rating, standardizing, or prescriptive agency for education. Such pressure occurred in the 1920's and again in the late 1930's, the second time after some urging by the National Council of Chief State School Officers. In short, effective professional controls do not, and apparently should not, emanate from the United States Office of Education.

Accreditation by the Professions

Early accreditation was based on over-all quality of the college or university and did not attempt to disclose strengths and weaknesses of units within the institution. In fact, weak programs within the institution in many cases were allowed to continue because they were offset by strong and effective elements. This "all or nothing" policy permitted serious deficiencies to continue. Representatives of the profession soon demanded the right to pass on the merits of preparation programs in their respective occupational fields.

Accreditation of the total resources and program of the colleges remains a function of the regional accrediting agencies. Professional accreditation bodies do not attempt to duplicate the same coverage of facts although they refer to the regional reports when appropriate. Some differences in approach and purpose are evident between professional accrediting agencies and the regionals. The major emphasis of the regional associations, which are composed of institutional members, is on improvement of institutions. A major emphasis of some of the professional agencies, in which the practitioners exert a strong influence, appears to be on minimum qualifications for the protection of society, as well as for the protection of the profession.

Accreditation by groups representing the professions dates back to 1905 with the first publication of an approved list of medical schools. This was followed by a list of accredited schools in dental education in 1918, legal education in 1923, engineering education in 1936, pharmaceutical education in 1940. At present, some form of accreditation is found in almost every field of professional education.

There is no single pattern for accreditation by the professions. Some accrediting is done by an association of practitioners; some, by an association of the preparing schools. In recent years the trend has been toward a joint council of practitioners and preparing schools and—in those instances where state licenses prevail—a combination of practitioners, institutions, and the state licensing officials. This last form of organization is true, for example, in education, dentistry, law, architecture, and pharmacy.

Experience shows that accreditation by professional organizations tends to be more rigorous than accreditation by organizations representing solely the schools which give professional training. Presumably practitioners are more directly affected by inadequately trained colleagues than anyone else. Professional schools need income from higher enrollments, and consequently they sometimes resist the strict application of high standards. If an association of professional schools includes relatively weak institutions from its inception (and this is unquestionably the situation with the National Council for Accreditation of Teacher Education), then a vigorous policy of accreditation would mean putting some of its own members out of business (which, of course, might be a blessing to all).

Establishing high standards is not easy. Accrediting bodies are usually made up of representatives from member institutions of all sizes and qualities. The representatives are rarely interested in establishing criteria for approval that their own institutions could not meet. Yet, standards enforced by an accreditation body can give strong support to efforts of deans and department chairmen who struggle within the institution for adequate resources in administration preparation. The NCATE wisely includes practitioners on its governing body. It has representation from school boards and local school systems, as well as from the colleges. Unless practitioners are alert, standards which are adopted may be characteristic of the weak, marginal institutions.

Teacher Education

From 1927 until 1954 accreditation of teacher education was carried on by the American Association of Teacher Colleges and later by the American Association of Colleges for Teacher Education. Some institutions, however, chose not to invite accreditation by the AACTE; thus the annual lists of approved colleges were only partially complete.

In 1954 the National Council for the Accreditation of Teacher Education was established on a base more broadly representative than that of the AACTE. It represented an effort to form an accreditation body which would meet with universal approval and acceptance. In time the NCATE annual lists will be comprehensive for approved colleges offering teacher education.

The Council as now constituted has 19 members: three collegiate representatives appointed by an ad hoc committee constitutive of the National Commission on Accrediting, seven collegiate members appointed by the American Association of Colleges for Teacher Education, one chief state school officer appointed by the Council of Chief State School Officers, one state director of teacher education and certification, six persons representing the profession at large appointed by the NEA's National Commission on Teacher Education and Professional Standards, and one school board member appointed by the National School Boards Association.

Administrator Preparation

In the field of school administration, approval of preparation programs is a recent development. A guide for the accreditation of institutions preparing school administrators first became a reality in June of 1957. Prepared by the Committee for the Advancement of School Administration, the document, "A Guide for the Accreditation of Institutions Preparing Administrators," became part of the accreditation materials of the NCATE. During the school year 1957-58, the first accreditation visits were made. As in any movement of this magnitude, the first efforts were weak and ineffective. However, it was a beginning; a way had been made for school administrators to exercise some control on professional preparation programs. A companion—and more significant document—was under production in the fall of 1959: an approved set of standards for preparation programs in educational administration.

There are several possible routes which the accreditation movement in school administration can take in the future.

1. The AASA could in time form its own accrediting agency, following the lead of the American Bar Association.

2. The AASA in cooperation with colleges for teacher education, the NEA's Commission on Teacher Education and Professional Standards, and other groups could continue to recognize jointly a body representing several groups of the educational profession which could perform the accreditation function. Presumably, such body would be the National Council for the Accreditation of Teacher Education. This route would be more in keeping with the procedures employed in medicine and supported jointly by the AMA, the AHA, and the American College of Surgeons. (The AASA is not officially represented on the Council, although a school administrator is usually one of the appointees from the NEA Commission on Teacher Education and Professional Standards.)

3. The AASA could gradually step back from the direct control of the colleges once an initial approved list was devised and could leave quality control solely to self-improvement by the individual graduate schools themselves. This would mean that the only remaining means of control would be at the state level through certification. This would place school administration in a position similar to some of the occupational trades for which there is state licensing as a means of protecting the public against quacks and incompetents but no authoritative voice by the total profession as to quality of the curriculum and admission policies.

The second alternative is probably the wisest one. The first policy (AASA accreditation) would divide the single accrediting body in the field of professional education (agreement on *one* such agency was the result of a hard-fought battle); the third choice would open the way for proliferation of graduate schools in educational administration.

Speed in anticipated accreditation of programs in school administration is tremendously important. The profession has an obligation to protect young people who aspire to be school administrators from unwittingly choosing improperly oriented, poorly conceived collegiate programs of study.

Other problems face professional accreditation, also. How do we maintain standards without standardizing the colleges? How can we get a corps of accreditors who will be reasonably consistent and who will have high standards? How can a brief accreditation visit give adequate insights about the educational institution so that judgments may be made about the quality of its offerings? How can we assess the relative importance of staff, curriculum, and facilities? How can supporting departments (cognate fields) be assessed in terms of contribution to professional preparation? Should an institution with high potential strength be held to higher standards than one which is inherently weak? How can we account for the allowable variations of off-campus work, internships, and other deviations from typical college procedure?

Certification

Roman Empire rulers more than 1500 years ago issued edicts making penal the opening of schools by persons unauthorized by the government. In this country state acceptance of the obligation for the licensing of teachers moved slowly at first, but by 1955 all states issued certificates for teachers.

Certificates for administrators of schools developed much later and more slowly. The first administrative certificate was established for superintendents in 1854 in Pennsylvania, but the practice did not spread to any extent until after about 1910. By 1958 all states except Michigan and Wisconsin issued certificates covering some administrative position.

There are wide differences among the states today in the kinds and number of certificates issued as well as the administrative positions covered. Some states have general administrative certificates; others have special certificates that apply to certain positions, such as the superintendency. As recently as 1957 a survey of practices and contemplated changes revealed no clear-cut trends among the states toward one approach or the other.[10]

---

[10] Howsam, Robert B., and Morphet, Edgar L. "Certification of Education Administrators." *Journal of Teacher Education* 9: 75-96, March; 187-203, June 1958.

All of the issues concerning the wisdom of various methods of certification will not be discussed here. The principle of certification itself has been at various times during the history of American education a point of controversy and debate. In spite of opinion differences which still exist, there is an unmistakable trend toward increased centralization of the administration and control of licenses to practice a profession. Standardization of requirements is an obvious goal of this process. Fifty years ago 3000 local authorities certified teachers on the basis of examinations given in each community. Seldom were college credits evaluated or required. Today, however, the authority is centralized in state departments of education and rarely is reliance placed on the examination procedure.

Administrator certification requirements in most states followed a clear sequence of steps:

1. A certificate to administer schools based on number of years of teaching experience.
2. A given number of course credits "in administration and supervision."
3. Increased number of credits, with certain areas specified such as finance and personnel.
4. Master's degree with highly specialized course titles listed.
5. Certificate based on approval of the institution and subsequent endorsement of its graduates by the institution.

As of 1960, there are some states on each of the five steps. Most recommendations in recent years have called for accreditation of the institution rather than a list of credits in courses whose titles are specifically required by the state certification laws. It is almost certain that endorsement of the institution must accompany completion of certification requirements if the control on certification is to bring about the promotion of high-quality preparation programs.

An example of recommendations for changes in present certification provisions which tend to fall in line with contemporary recommendations are those which were developed by a special committee of Missouri's Association of School Administrators and released in the summer of 1958. These recommendations were formed after careful consideration of the various groups interested in the promotion of high-quality preparation programs. They are as follows:

1. The applicant for the Superintendent's Certificate should hold a valid teaching certificate.

2. The applicant for the Superintendent's Certificate should have a minimum of three years of administration and/or teaching experience which should have been acquired during the five years immediately preceding certification.

3. The applicant for the Superintendent's Certificate should have a minimum of two years of graduate professional training.

4. The applicant for the Superintendent's Certificate should be recommended for certification by the training institution in which the major portion of his graduate work was taken.

5. The graduate training program of the applicant for the Superintendent's Certificate should be of such quality and scope as to indicate a satisfactory competency in each of the following areas:

   (a) School Administration

   (b) Curriculum and Instruction

   (c) Research and Measurement

   (d) Socio-Cultural Foundations

   (e) Behavioral Sciences

6. Missouri institutions engaged in the training of superintendents of schools should seek, at the earliest possible date, accreditation of their Administrator Education Programs by the National Council for the Accreditation of Teacher Education by using the Guide developed by the Committee for the Advancement of School Administration.

7. As soon as practicable, the Missouri State Department of Education should require that only institutions whose Administrator Education Programs have been approved by the National Council for the Accreditation of Teacher Education may recommend applicants for the Superintendent's Certificate. Until such time as this is feasible, the Missouri State Department of Education should satisfy itself that applicants for the Superintendent's Certificate who are recommended by institutions outside the state of Missouri have received training comparable in quality and scope to that given by Missouri institutions.

8. An internship in the superintendency served under the supervision of a training institution whose Administrator Education Program has been approved by the National Council for the Accreditation of Teacher Education is strongly recommended and should be required for the Superintendent's Certificate as soon as deemed possible.

9. The Superintendent's Certificate, when issued, should be valid during acceptable service.

10. The Missouri State Department of Education should make provision for periodic cooperative examination and study of certification standards of the superintendent of schools.

MEMBERSHIP QUALIFICATIONS FOR PROFESSIONAL ASSOCIATIONS

On February 18, 1959, the American Association of School Administrators became the first national professional organization in education to attach a graduate study qualification for membership. Called "the next big step" in the title of a publication issued by the Committee for the Advancement of School Administration (the group which originated the membership proposal), the action was similarly hailed in the press the following day as "the most significant step in the Association's 94-year history." Actually it was a logical extension of the professional controls discussed in this chapter—accreditation, certification, and common agreement on standards of performance. The Committee for the Advancement of School Administration urged adoption of the proposal as the best way practitioners themselves could give their support to high standards:

> As a committee we have urged colleges and universities to experiment with new techniques in the training of school administrators. At the same time we have urged changes to be made in state certification regulations for administrators. We drafted a guide for the accreditation of colleges which prepare school administrators, and this guide was adopted by the National Council for the Accreditation of Teacher Education. We have urged school boards to adopt policies limiting the selection of local administrators to graduates of approved institutions only.
>
> This proposal for membership criteria based on completion of graduate study represents our hope that AASA members will endorse and promote in the most logical way possible the same devotion to higher standards for school administrators we are asking other people to support. . . .

No other proposal dealing with standards of preparation has at any time stirred up interest comparable to that engendered when this amendment was proposed. While some professional journals editorialized on the apathy of many members at the convention, the amendment was nevertheless adopted. The vote was 946 to 387.

The official proposal was worded as follows:

> Beginning on January 1, 1964, all new members of the American Association of School Administrators shall submit evidence of successful completion of two (2) years of graduate study in university programs designed to prepare school administrators and approved by an accreditation body endorsed by the Executive Committee of AASA.

In statements by officials of the AASA before and after the passage of the amendment, the "accreditation body" referred to in the amendment was said to be the NCATE. Close cooperation between the NCATE and the AASA had been evident almost since the beginning of the establishment of the AASA "advancement committee."

Following the passage of the amendment, the AASA agreed to support the activities of the NCATE with personnel and financial resources if the Council would agree in turn to speed up its procedures for accrediting the collegiate institutions which prepare school administrators, particularly those which give two or more years of work at the graduate level. Action followed closely. A committee was appointed to develop standards for the accreditation of collegiate institutions which offer work in this field. The procedures of the Council with respect to visits and appraisal were reorganized to permit more rapid response to requests from institutions for accreditation visits. In addition, extra staff for the Council were employed.

From this proposal came the encouragement state associations of school administrators needed to develop programs at the state level for investigating and improving the work of the collegiate institutions and for reviewing state certification processes.

The biggest risk inherent in the action was the danger that it would cause an epidemic of new two-year graduate programs in school administration. The AASA and the NCATE moved quickly to ward off this eventuality. Jointly the two groups announced in the summer of 1959 that all institutions, including those currently on the approved list, must submit descriptions of their preparation programs for approval by a special panel appointed by the NCATE. Visits will subsequently be made to institutions where any part of the program appears doubtful.

We have stated earlier in this chapter that one characteristic of a profession is a strong, voluntary association managed by the members themselves—an organization which is concerned with competent performance of their jobs and standards for admission into their professional rank. To fulfill this definition, it is inevitable that professions take steps similar to the amendment adopted by the AASA.

SUPPORTS FOR PROFESSIONAL STANDARDS

One characteristic distinguishing school administration as a profession from such other groups as doctors, lawyers, and dentists is that in the case of the other professions one is a member by virtue of the completion of training and the satisfaction of whatever professional controls exist. In other words, once he meets the special training and examination qualifications that have been set up, he is a member of his profession if he says he is. On the other hand, with school administrators, all the preparation programs in the world won't create a school administrator unless some school board somewhere first recognizes him as such. This combination of the professional and the political aspect of the job is one of the points on which many discussions of control by the profession have bogged down. True it is that any attempt to enforce quality controls on the preparation of school administrators must be supported by members of local school boards.

Policy of Local School Boards

The first recommendation in *Something to Steer By* [11] is: "School boards [must] agree to employ as superintendents only persons who have completed bona fide programs of preparation for administration in colleges approved through the profession's accrediting process." It was evident from the descriptions in Chapter I of this yearbook that boards of education typically have little if any definitive information about the kinds of preparation programs which candidates have completed. Indeed, it is doubtful if boards could ever be expected to make a careful and complete analysis of the preparatory training of men they are considering for administrative positions at all levels of the school system. And still, a major responsibility for effective professional controls lies with boards of education and their employment policies. What, then, is the answer?

School boards must rely on the recommendations of the professional groups especially charged with the responsibility of evaluating the quality of professional training programs. To be specific, we should waste no more time before a list of approved colleges is printed and made available to every school board in the country. Regional and state school board associations (en-

[11] American Association of School Administrators, Committee for the Advancement of School Administration. *Something to Steer By.* Washington, D. C.: the Association, a department of the National Education Association, 1958.

couraged at all times by policies of the National School Boards Association which is, in effect, an association of state organizations) can be the instrument by which these lists are distributed and promotion made of their use.

The procedures outlined in Chapter VI can contribute to this recommendation when local school systems accept the responsibility for the identification and, in part, the training of local personnel for prospective administrative positions. They can exercise greater discretion in the selection of universities which their employees attend and, also, can exercise some direct influence on the curriculum itself. Such local plans for recruitment, training, and selection will have the added impact of making school boards sensitive to the need for an evaluation of the kind as well as the amount of training administrators have received.

Placement officers in universities across the country have obligations to assist board members in analyzing training programs. They must supply the school boards with records of applicants which are sufficiently detailed to facilitate the difficult task of selection.

Action at the State Level

It became evident to this Yearbook Commission as it studied carefully the preparation of school administrators that specific action by legal and professional groups is necessary in order to establish sanctions and professional controls which will guarantee progress. Most of such action must take place at the state level. The state license for school administrators is a crucial problem in at least two-thirds of the states at the present time. Accreditation, while it is a professional function at the national level, must receive its stimulation and certainly must be carried out in institutions, many of which have a student clientele largely within the confines of a single state. Leadership of state departments of education must be improved not only in service to local and intermediate districts but as a strong, clear voice of professional interest within each state. Policies of school boards must be clear with respect to employment of administrators only from high-quality programs. State school board associations can be effective in influencing such policies on the part of local boards.

Following up the conviction that controls must be instituted at the state level, the AASA appointed regional committees in the winter of 1959 and urged them to take the lead in bringing together in each state the many persons who have responsibility for making decisions about educational administration, its preparation and its performance. Such committees were assisted by the Committee for the Advancement of School Administration, and support for them was made possible by a grant from the W. K. Kellogg Foundation. In essence the committees were made responsible for bringing action on professional controls.

RECOMMENDATIONS FOR THE FUTURE

There is potential danger in professional controls. There is danger in the possible superficiality of accreditation visits and inflexibility of regulatory provisions. Perhaps another danger is even more basic—our zest for controls may easily be motivated and determined by the need for a feeling of status or a pampering of our professional vanity. We will lose the public service aspect of the profession if we should ever rely on controls as status builders or as means to obtain prestige. Prestige must be earned rather than learned.

The primary reason for prestige, status, and insistence on high-quality standards for the profession is, at all times, to assist effective performance on the job and ultimately the impact of such performance on the education of boys and girls. No other purpose for professional controls is justified. The application of standards may appear at first glance merely to be the protection of the trained against the ill-trained applicants for professional positions. In a deeper sense, however, it is protection of the public against the possibility of incompetent management of the schools.

This Yearbook Commission was appointed in 1958 for the sole purpose of recommending policies for the future which would insure true professional character of educational administration. Our rationale was this: The duties faced today by the school administrator are not only changing rapidly but are essential to the ultimate development of the democratic system in this country at the community level. Chapter V described the wide range of responsibilities and the importance of educational administration in the total scheme of things. When we reviewed the data available to us about the identification, selection, initial, and on-the-job training for administrators, we came to the inevitable conclusion that the way things happen now is rapidly becoming obsolete and will, if continued, seriously lower the effectiveness of local school administration and, in turn, the contribution of the public schools.

We have recommended, then, a planned program of preparation in a graduate/professional school—given only in institutions of unusually high quality. In fact, we insist on a clear statement of purpose by the collegiate institution that the training of educational administrators is so crucial for the days ahead that it must be a central, and not an incidental, function of the institution.

Our problem of identifying and selecting persons of strong leadership ability and scholarly interests is aggravated by what is unquestionably the manpower situation in the years ahead. In a society influenced at every turn by automation, the demands for people with executive, professional, and managerial talents will become increasingly severe year by year. A proportion of our total population—much larger than we have known before—will be engaged in pursuits which give strong competition to educational administration. Our Commission argues for a preparation program of real depth, one which requires broad understanding. We do so not only because of the impact of such a program on the individual but because the evidence is clear that only such a program will be attractive to the best minds from among the college students who anticipate a professional career.

An ideal preparation program is described in Chapter VII at our fictional State U. It is a program which has a clear sequence of experiences and which reflects *careful attention to the development of the professional content*. It recommends that at least one full year of the two graduate years which we accept as minimal preparation must be done in full-time residence on campus. The curriculum that is outlined here is more than task-oriented. It includes material which is designed to develop a philosophy and the basic approach to the problems of education in a community. Heavy reliance is placed on the social and behavioral sciences.

We have sketched here a preparation program which we believe is professional because it focuses not only on knowledge but on the behavior of the individual in the job for which he is being trained. For this reason we have said quite clearly that professional education is not a spectator sport—it must get the student out of the grandstand and onto the playing field under close and careful supervision. For this reason we anticipate an internship or apprenticeship and participation in a community school survey as essential elements in a preparation program.

In Chapter IV we expressed with real feeling our dissatisfaction with current in-service offerings for school administrators. In Chapter VIII we examined the contributions which can be made to the in-service growth of school administrators by the various resources which are most directly concerned in this field. We have described in-service education primarily as the function of bringing new research findings to the man or woman who occupies administrative positions in our public schools. This we see removed from the basic preparation program and, as such, we see it also removed from college credit. We have applauded those few in-service activities which probe in depth the crucial issues of the day, and we have insisted that in-service workshops and conferences that deal only with the minutiae of the job of administration are unworthy of the tremendous contribution which in-service resources can make.

In-service education should help the school administrator solve problems, not merely resolve situations. Educational policy, then, can result from attention to the full and complete intellectual growth of the administrator himself. Tasks which our school administrators will face tomorrow are of a magnitude which can be dealt with successfully only by men with big minds. Since no man can ever congratulate himself that he possesses all the understanding and the insight he needs, he should accept personal responsibility for continuous study throughout his career.

Like all our educational problems, the improvement of professional preparation for administrators is related in part to money. We must finance the institutional programs adequately, and we must recognize our responsibility to the oncoming generation of school administrators who will need help with their personal expenses if they are to engage in the preparation program at the most fruitful time of their lives. This Yearbook

Commission has outlined some of the need for funds. Making the case for such funds is about as far as we can go. The profession itself must now turn with imagination and vigor to the job of paying for the high-quality preparation of administrators we must have. Much of our financial contribution must also go to more adequate research in the problems of administering schools. We cannot continue to rely on theses and dissertations by graduate students as the primary source of new ideas. Both collegiate and governmental units must accept responsibility for vastly increased research undertakings.

Through all of these recommendations we have tried to build a case for educational administration as a profession of stature in the years ahead. America has entrusted its future to education, and the educational enterprise will fulfill its expected role only with thoroughly enlightened leadership.

APPENDIX

APPENDIX

DEFINITION OF CONCEPTS

Concepts Listed in Part Four of Questionnaire Regarding Superintendents' Concerns About Administrative Theory (Chapter IV). Prepared by Steven P. Hencley, Midwest Administration Center, University of Chicago.

1. *The "Hawthorne Effect":* The Harvard Group's Western Electric studies at the Hawthorne plant revealed the effect that interest in and attention to a worker and his duties resulted in better on-the-job performance and higher morale.

2. *Span of Control:* This concept is concerned with the number of positions reporting directly to a single executive. The limits of adequate coordination, communication, and supervision define the optimum span for a given situation.

3. *Zone of Acceptance:* Used by Chester I. Barnard in referring to the limits within which exercise of authority by a superior will be accepted without question by a subordinate.

4. *POSDCORB:* Gulick's famous administrative process formulation—planning, organizing, staffing, directing, coordinating, reporting, budgeting.

5. *Informal Organization:* Refers to the network of personal and social relationships which is not defined by the formal organization, i. e., when the aggregate of interpersonal relationships are without conscious joint purpose, even though common or joint results may come from them. Cliques and friendship groups are illustrations of informal organization.

6. *Charismatic Leadership:* The type of leadership in which staff organization consists of personal servants, authority is exercised directly with no delegation, and the staff is obedient to the idealized person of the leader. This is Max Weber's definition.

7. *Line and Staff Functions:* (a) Line positions form a vertical chain of authority and responsibility in the administrative organization extending through the various levels from the chief executive to the operating personnel; (b) staff positions are based primarily upon specialized functions and/or knowledge. Staff positions are advisory and auxiliary to the line and possess neither operating responsibility nor authority in the line.

8. *Initiating-Structure-in-Interaction:* Refers to the leader's behavior in delineating the relationship between himself and the members of his group, and in endeavoring to establish well-defined patterns of organization, channels of communication, and ways of getting the job done.

9. *Alter-Group Expectations:* Refers to the expectations held for administrator behavior by the administrator's various alter or reference groups. Since these expectations are often at variance among alter groups, they introduce various elements of conflict in the administrator's role.

10. *Scientific Management Movement:* Refers to the movement pioneered by Frederick Taylor in the early 1900's. This movement was characterized by emphases upon time and motion studies, functional foremanship, and the fitting of men to jobs on the basis of careful and minute testing of aptitudes and capacities.

11. *Nomothetic and Idiographic Considerations:* Concepts enunciated by Jacob W. Getzels concerning two of the administrator's major functions: goal achievement and group maintenance.

NOMOTHETIC DIMENSION

Institution . . . Role . . . Expectations

Social System

Behavior

Individual . . . Personality . . . Need disposition

IDIOGRAPHIC DIMENSION

12. *Situationist Theory of Administration:* Situationist theorists advance the idea that leadership is the product of the situation in which the leader finds himself. Moreover, it is contended that leaders in different kinds of situations show different characteristics.

13. *Vertical and Horizontal Organization:* (a) Vertical organization is the embodiment of the scalar chain which functions to channel authority and responsibility within the administrative organization, binding together the various levels as parts and subparts of an integrated work unit; (b) horizontal organization refers to levels in the administrative organization which result from grouping positions horizontally in terms of approximately equal status.

14. *The Rabble Hypothesis:* An early concept which denied the importance of human motivations in other than economic terms. It overlooked human motivation and sentiment growing out of the human desire for acceptance and recognition by friends and work associates.

15. *Organizational Effectiveness and Efficiency:* Chester I. Barnard defined these terms as follows: (a) Effectiveness refers to the accomplishment of organizational purposes or goals. This is nonpersonal in character.

287

(b) Efficiency refers to the satisfaction of individual motives while achieving organizational goals. The test of efficiency is the eliciting of sufficient wills to cooperate in achieving organizational purposes.

16. *Rational Authority:* Refers to the type of authority evident in an organization which is characterized by bureaucratic organization, in which authority is exercised through rational delegation, and in which the staff is obedient to the legally established impersonal order.

17. *Parsons' Input and Output:* These two terms are parallel to Getzels' nomothetic and idiographic dimensions and also to Barnard's effectiveness and efficiency. Parsons states that input and output operate at three levels: community, managerial, technical.

18. *Role Theory:* A role represents the dynamic aspect of a status. The individual is socially assigned to a status and occupies it with relation to other statuses. When he puts the rights and duties which constitute the status into effect, he is performing a role. Every individual has a series of roles deriving from the various patterns in which he participates and at the same time a role, general, which represents the sum total of these roles and determines what he does for his society and what he can expect from it. The Theory of Social Role indicates that the conflicts between the Traits theory of leadership and the Situationist theory can be resolved by viewing groups as not entirely unique—that they have some common needs and some unique needs. Leaders, then, must have first those characteristics common to all leaders which are required to fulfill the common needs of all groups and second, those unique characteristics which are required to fulfill the special needs of their particular group. There is need for both goal achievement and group maintenance.

19. *"Degrees of Freedom" in Organizational Therapy:* Refers to the extent to which an administrator is free to make changes in the organization without encountering serious resistance from personnel who do not wish to see changes made. The administrator may be "boxed in" by various organizational factors which will permit or handicap his efforts to move the organization in directions which he may see as desirable.

20. *Unity of Command:* This concept suggests that one position in the administrative organization has the authority and responsibility for the administration of the entire organization. The delegation of all authority is from one executive to a subordinate and no position is subject to definite orders from more than one source at a given time, or in relation to a given task.

21. *Group Maintenance and Group (Goal) Achievement:* This concept, as enunciated by Cartwright and Zander is very similar to Getzels' nomothetic and idiographic dimensions, Parsons' input and output, and Barnard's effectiveness and efficiency.

22. *Social Mobility:* Social changes associated with urbanism have been manifest in various forms of occupational mobility. If such movements

involve a measurable change in socioeconomic status, whether upward or downward, it is vertical mobility; if there is no significant change in status, it may be referred to as horizontal mobility.

23. *Invasion and Succession:* When population moves into an area for residential purposes, the phenomenon is termed ecological invasion. If the original occupants are completely displaced by the invaders, the term succession is commonly applied to describe what has occurred.

24. *Urban Fringe:* Refers to urbanized areas surrounding a central city. The 1940 U. S. Census listed an "urbanized areas" category which was designed to include in the urban population those persons living under distinctly urban conditions on the fringe of the larger cities.

25. *Power Structure:* Supplanting the formal power structure of municipal government and business or industrial bureaucracies is a power system which tends to be somewhat amorphously structured and which makes decisions outside of any bureaucratic framework. Such decisions are often made informally by men of prestige and transmitted informally to government bureaucrats for official action. In some cities major decision-making procedures of this type are monopolized by men of corporate wealth and power.

RECENT AASA YEARBOOKS

OFFICERS 1959-60
AMERICAN ASSOCIATION OF SCHOOL ADMINISTRATORS

President

MARTIN ESSEX, Superintendent of Schools, Akron, Ohio

President-Elect

FORREST E. CONNER, Superintendent of Schools, St. Paul, Minnesota

Vice-President

EVART W. ARDIS, Director, Bureau of Appointments, University of Michigan, Ann Arbor, Michigan

Executive Committee

NATT B. BURBANK, Superintendent of Schools, Boulder, Colorado

JOHN S. CARTWRIGHT, Superintendent of Schools, Allentown, Pennsylvania

WENDELL GODWIN, Superintendent of Schools, Topeka, Kansas

J. WIN PAYNE, Superintendent of Schools, Ponca City, Oklahoma

THE PRESIDENT, PRESIDENT-ELECT, and VICE-PRESIDENT, ex officio

Executive Secretary, FINIS E. ENGLEMAN

Secretary Emeritus, WORTH MCCLURE

Associate Secretary, SHIRLEY COOPER

Assistant Secretary, WILLIAM J. ELLENA

Committee for the Advancement of School Administration

Executive Secretary, HOLLIS A. MOORE, JR.

Executive Assistant, RODERICK F. MCPHEE

INDEX